Taste of Home
Sides, Salads
& more

TASTE OF HOME BOOKS • RDA ENTHUSIAST BRANDS, LLC • MILWAUKEE, WI

Taste *of* Home

Sides, Salads

& more

Page 165

©2022 RDA Enthusiast Brands, LLC.
1610 N. 2nd St., Suite 102
Milwaukee, WI 53212-3906
All rights reserved. Taste of Home is a registered
trademark of RDA Enthusiast Brands, LLC.

Visit us at tasteofhome.com for other
Taste of Home books and products.

ISBN: 978-1-62145-786-2

Executive Editor: Mark Hagen
Senior Art Director: Raeann Thompson
Senior Designer: Jazmin Delgado
Designer: Carrie Peterson
Deputy Editor, Copy Desk: Dulcie Shoener
Copy Editor: Kara Dennison

COVER
Photographer: Mark Derse
Food Stylist: Josh Rink
Set Stylist: Stacey Genaw

Pictured on front cover:
Tra Vigne Green Beans, p. 55
Speedy Stuffed Potatoes, p. 148
Veggie Spiral Salad, p. 8

Pictured on spine:
Mixed Fruit with Lemon-Basil Dressing, p. 262

Pictured on back cover:
Acorn Squash Slices, p. 36
Grilled Chicken Ramen Salad, p. 111
Confetti Cornbread, p. 276

Printed in China

1 3 5 7 9 10 8 6 4 2

INSTANT POT® is a trademark of Double Insight Inc.
This publication has not been authorized,
sponsored or otherwise approved by
Double Insight Inc.

Page 98

345 Easy Sides Dishes Ideal for Any Occasion

Planning weeknight meals, creating memory-making holiday menus and rounding out Sunday dinners has never been easier or tastier! Just turn to the sensational recipes inside **Sides, Salads & More** from the experts at *Taste of Home*!

Page through this delightful collection and you'll discover enticing add-ons that complete meal plans, finish up workweek suppers and make your holiday lineups shine. You'll find salads and slaws as well as the veggie, pasta, bean and grain dishes that have family and friends asking for more.

You'll even enjoy a section of breads that includes stuffings and dressings perfect for Thanksgiving, Christmas and other special gatherings. A chapter featuring no-fuss breakfast sides is sure to make brunches special, and an area of crowd-pleasing favorites offers dishes to pass at larger get-togethers such as potlucks, block parties, barbecues and church suppers.

Best of all, three icons make it a snap to locate the dishes you need most...

FIVE INGREDIENTS Recipes that come together with five items or fewer (not including water, salt, pepper, oils or optional ingredients)

HEALTHY COOKING Sides that cut calories, fat, sodium, carbohydrates and/or sugar

SLOW COOKER Dishes made conveniently in a slow cooker

Never worry about what to serve on the side again! No matter what dinner accompaniment you're looking for, you'll find the perfect option in this all-new kitchen helper, *Taste of Home Sides, Salads & More.*

Page 285

Contents

MORE WAYS TO CONNECT WITH US:

Garden Pesto
Pasta Salad, page 19

Page 11

Page 16

All-Time Classic Side Dishes

Numerous sides come to mind when planning a menu. From simple hash browns and no-fuss buttered noodles to traditional green bean casserole and colorful Spanish rice, these are the dishes memorable meals are made of.

Page 26

Page 31

Creamed Spinach & Pearl Onions

VEGGIE SPIRAL SALAD

My husband and son detested pasta salad before I came up with this one. Filled with fresh, crunchy radishes and celery, juicy tomatoes and cucumbers, this nutritious recipe is one to try on your salad skeptics.
—Melody Loyd, Parowan, UT

TAKES: 20 min. • **MAKES:** 5 servings

- 1 cup uncooked tricolor spiral pasta
- ½ cup chopped seeded cucumber
- ½ cup thinly sliced celery
- ½ cup chopped red onion
- ½ cup sliced radishes
- ½ cup chopped tomatoes
- ½ cup sliced ripe olives, drained
- ½ cup shredded Swiss cheese
- ⅛ tsp. garlic powder
- ⅛ tsp. pepper
- 1 Tbsp. Italian salad dressing mix
- 2 Tbsp. plus 1½ tsp. cider vinegar
- 2 Tbsp. olive oil

1. Cook pasta according to package directions. Meanwhile, in a large bowl, combine the cucumber, celery, onion, radishes, tomatoes, olives, cheese, garlic powder and pepper. Drain pasta and rinse in cold water; stir into vegetable mixture.
2. In a bowl, whisk dressing mix, vinegar and oil. Drizzle over salad and toss to coat. Serve immediately or refrigerate.
¾ cup: 186 cal., 10g fat (3g sat. fat), 10mg chol., 356mg sod., 18g carb. (4g sugars, 2g fiber), 6g pro.

Test Kitchen Tip
Have fun with this colorful pasta salad. Add chopped red or green peppers, sliced carrots or even diced zucchini. Make it an entree salad with some strips of grilled chicken or pork. Toss in a few cooked shrimp for a light summer dinner.

CREAMED SPINACH & PEARL ONIONS

When I was a culinary student, this creamy dish wowed me, and I don't even like spinach. This side is a keeper!
—Chelsea Puchel, Pickens, SC

TAKES: 25 min. • **MAKES:** 8 servings

- ¼ cup butter, cubed
- 1 pkg. (14.4 oz.) frozen pearl onions, thawed and drained
- 2 cups heavy whipping cream
- ½ cup grated Parmesan cheese
- ½ tsp. salt
- ¼ tsp. pepper
- 10 oz. fresh baby spinach (about 13 cups)

1. In a large cast-iron or other heavy skillet, heat butter over medium heat. Add pearl onions; cook and stir until tender, 6-8 minutes. Stir in cream. Bring to a boil; cook until liquid is reduced by half, 6-8 minutes.
2. Stir in cheese, salt and pepper. Add spinach; cook, covered, until spinach is wilted, 3-5 minutes, stirring occasionally.
½ cup: 307 cal., 30g fat (18g sat. fat), 102mg chol., 328mg sod., 8g carb. (4g sugars, 1g fiber), 5g pro.

Veggie
Spiral Salad

SPANISH RICE

You'll find my Spanish rice is so much better than any boxed variety in grocery stores. Best of all, it can be prepared in about the same time as those so-called convenience foods, using items in your pantry.
—Anne Yaeger, Washington DC

TAKES: 25 min. • **MAKES:** 6 servings

- ¼ cup butter, cubed
- 2 cups uncooked instant rice
- 1 can (14½ oz.) diced tomatoes, undrained
- 1 cup boiling water
- 2 beef bouillon cubes
- 1 medium onion, chopped
- 1 garlic clove, minced
- 1 bay leaf
- 1 tsp. sugar
- 1 tsp. salt
- ¼ tsp. pepper

In a saucepan, melt butter over medium heat. Add rice; cook and stir until lightly browned. Add remaining ingredients; bring to a boil. Reduce heat; cover and simmer until the liquid is absorbed and rice is tender, 10-15 minutes. Remove bay leaf before serving.

¾ cup: 217 cal., 8g fat (5g sat. fat), 20mg chol., 886mg sod., 33g carb. (4g sugars, 2g fiber), 4g pro.

WHY YOU'LL LOVE IT...

"This recipe was easy to make with ingredients that I had on hand. I will definitely make it again!"

—AMSM, TASTEOFHOME.COM

Spanish Rice

5i
MAPLE-GLAZED ACORN SQUASH

With a maple syrup and brown sugar glaze, this squash becomes pleasantly sweet. This is comfort food—easy to prepare and a tasty pairing with nearly any entree.
—Nancy Mueller, Menomonee Falls, WI

PREP: 10 min. • **BAKE:** 55 min.
MAKES: 2 servings

- 1 medium acorn squash, halved
- ¾ cup water
- ¼ cup maple syrup
- 2 Tbsp. brown sugar
- ½ tsp. ground cinnamon
- ¼ tsp. ground ginger
- ¼ tsp. salt

1. Preheat oven to 350°. Scoop out and discard seeds from squash. Place cut side down in a 13x9-in. baking dish; add water. Bake, uncovered, for 45 minutes.
2. If necessary, drain water from pan; turn squash cut side up. Combine maple syrup, brown sugar, cinnamon, ginger and salt; pour into squash halves. Bake, uncovered, 10 minutes or until glaze is heated through.
½ each: 251 cal., 0 fat (0 sat. fat), 0 chol., 311mg sod., 65g carb. (43g sugars, 4g fiber), 2g pro.

Easy Grilled Corn with Chipotle-Lime Butter

5i
EASY GRILLED CORN WITH CHIPOTLE-LIME BUTTER

Grilling corn in the husks is so easy. There's no need to remove the silk and tie the husk closed before grilling. Just soak, grill and add your favorite flavored butter.
—Taste of Home *Test Kitchen*

PREP: 5 min. + soaking • **GRILL:** 25 min.
MAKES: 8 servings

- 8 large ears sweet corn in husks
- ½ cup butter, softened
- 1½ tsp. grated lime zest
- 1 tsp. minced fresh cilantro
- ½ tsp. salt
- ½ tsp. ground chipotle pepper
  Coarse sea salt, optional

1. In a large stockpot, cover corn with cold water. Soak 30 minutes; drain. Grill the corn, covered, over medium heat until tender, turning occasionally, 25-30 minutes.
2. Meanwhile, combine the remaining ingredients. Carefully peel back husks; discard silk. Spread the butter mixture over corn.
1 ear of corn with 2 Tbsp. butter: 225 cal., 13g fat (8g sat. fat), 31mg chol., 265mg sod., 27g carb. (9g sugars, 3g fiber), 5g pro.

TUSCAN-STYLE ROASTED ASPARAGUS

This is especially wonderful when locally grown asparagus is in season and so easy for celebrations because you can serve it either hot or cold.
—Jannine Fisk, Malden, MA

PREP: 20 min. • **BAKE:** 15 min.
MAKES: 8 servings

    1½ lbs. fresh asparagus, trimmed
    1½ cups grape tomatoes, halved
     3 Tbsp. pine nuts
     3 Tbsp. olive oil, divided
     2 garlic cloves, minced
     1 tsp. kosher salt
     ½ tsp. pepper
     1 Tbsp. lemon juice
     ⅓ cup grated Parmesan cheese
     1 tsp. grated lemon zest

1. Preheat oven to 400°. Place the asparagus, tomatoes and pine nuts on a foil-lined 15x10x1-in. baking pan. Mix 2 Tbsp. oil, garlic, salt and pepper; add to asparagus and toss to coat.
2. Bake 15-20 minutes or just until asparagus is tender. Drizzle with remaining oil and the lemon juice; sprinkle with cheese and lemon zest. Toss to combine.
1 serving: 95 cal., 8g fat (2g sat. fat), 3mg chol., 294mg sod., 4g carb. (2g sugars, 1g fiber), 3g pro. **Diabetic exchanges:** 1½ fat, 1 vegetable.

Tuscan-Style Roasted Asparagus

German Potato
Dumplings

GERMAN POTATO DUMPLINGS

Potato dumplings (called Kartoffel Kloesse in Germany) are a delightful addition to any German feast. The browned butter sauce is simply delectable.
—Arline Hofland, Deer Lodge, MT

PREP: 40 min. • **COOK:** 10 min.
MAKES: 8 servings

- 3 lbs. medium potatoes (about 10), peeled and quartered
- 1 cup all-purpose flour
- 3 large eggs, lightly beaten
- ⅔ cup dry bread crumbs
- 1 tsp. salt
- ½ tsp. ground nutmeg
- 12 cups water

BROWNED BUTTER SAUCE
- ½ cup butter, cubed
- 1 Tbsp. chopped onion
- ¼ cup dry bread crumbs

1. Place potatoes in a Dutch oven; add water to cover. Bring to a boil. Reduce heat; cook, uncovered, 15-20 minutes or until tender. Drain; transfer to a large bowl.

2. Mash potatoes. Stir in flour, eggs, bread crumbs, salt and nutmeg. Shape into 16 (2-in.) balls.

3. In a Dutch oven, bring 12 cups water to a boil. Carefully add the dumplings. Reduce the heat; simmer, uncovered, 7-9 minutes or until a toothpick inserted in center of dumplings comes out clean.

4. Meanwhile, in a heavy saucepan, heat butter and onion over medium heat. Heat 5-7 minutes or until butter is golden brown, stirring constantly. Remove from heat; stir in bread crumbs. Serve with dumplings.

2 dumplings with 2 Tbsp. sauce: 367 cal., 14g fat (8g sat. fat), 100mg chol., 524mg sod., 51g carb. (2g sugars, 5g fiber), 9g pro.

Simple
Waldorf Salad

MEXICAN STREET CORN BAKE

We discovered Mexican street corn at a festival. This easy one-pan version saves on prep and cleanup. Every August, I freeze a lot of our own fresh sweet corn, and I use that in this recipe, but store-bought corn works just as well.
—Erin Wright, Wallace, KS

PREP: 10 min. • **BAKE:** 35 min.
MAKES: 6 servings

6   cups frozen corn (about 30 oz.),
    thawed and drained
1   cup mayonnaise
1   tsp. ground chipotle pepper
¼   tsp. salt
¼   tsp. pepper
6   Tbsp. chopped green onions, divided
½   cup grated Parmesan cheese
    Lime wedges, optional

1. Preheat oven to 350°. Mix the first 5 ingredients and 4 Tbsp. green onions; transfer to a greased 1½-qt. baking dish. Sprinkle with cheese.
2. Bake, covered, 20 minutes. Uncover; bake until bubbly and lightly browned, 15-20 minutes longer. Sprinkle with remaining green onions. If desired, serve with lime wedges.
⅔ cup: 391 cal., 30g fat (5g sat. fat), 8mg chol., 423mg sod., 30g carb. (4g sugars, 3g fiber), 6g pro.

Did You Know?
Frozen vegetables usually offer all of the same nutrients as fresh. Frozen veggies are flash frozen at their peak, making them a perfectly healthy (and convenient) alternative to fresh produce.

SIMPLE WALDORF SALAD

This is my go-to salad when I need a quick little something for a meal. When I want a sweeter taste I use whipped cream instead of yogurt.
—Wendy Masters, East Garafraxa, ON

TAKES: 10 min. • **MAKES:** 6 servings

2   large Gala or Honeycrisp apples,
    unpeeled and chopped (about 3 cups)
2   cups chopped celery
¼   cup raisins
¼   cup chopped walnuts, toasted
⅓   cup reduced-fat mayonnaise
⅓   cup plain yogurt

Combine apples, celery, raisins and walnuts. Add the mayonnaise and yogurt; toss to coat. Refrigerate, covered, until serving.
Note: To toast nuts, bake in a shallow pan in a 350°; oven for 5-10 minutes or cook in a skillet over low heat until lightly browned, stirring occasionally.
¾ cup: 140 cal., 8g fat (1g sat. fat), 6mg chol., 119mg sod., 17g carb. (12g sugars, 3g fiber), 2g pro. **Diabetic exchanges:** 1½ fat, 1 fruit.

Mexican Street
Corn Bake

EASY SLOW-COOKER MAC & CHEESE

My sons always cheer, "You're the best mom in the world," whenever I make this creamy mac and cheese perfection. You can't beat a response like that.
—Heidi Fleek, Hamburg, PA

PREP: 25 min. • **COOK:** 1 hour
MAKES: 8 servings

- 2 cups uncooked elbow macaroni
- 1 can (10¾ oz.) condensed cheddar cheese soup, undiluted
- 1 cup 2% milk
- ½ cup sour cream
- ¼ cup butter, cubed
- ½ tsp. onion powder
- ¼ tsp. white pepper
- ⅛ tsp. salt
- 1 cup shredded cheddar cheese
- 1 cup shredded fontina cheese
- 1 cup shredded provolone cheese

1. Cook the macaroni according to package directions for al dente. Meanwhile, in a large saucepan, combine the soup, milk, sour cream, butter and seasonings; cook and stir over medium-low heat until blended. Stir in cheeses until melted.

2. Drain macaroni; transfer to a greased 3-qt. slow cooker. Stir in cheese mixture. Cook mixture, covered, on low until heated through, 1-2 hours.

¾ cup: 346 cal., 23g fat (14g sat. fat), 71mg chol., 712mg sod., 20g carb. (4g sugars, 1g fiber), 15g pro.

Easy Slow-Cooker
Mac & Cheese

PORTOBELLO RISOTTO WITH MASCARPONE

Portobello mushrooms add a beefy flavor to this creamy classic. Each serving is topped with soft, buttery mascarpone cheese, which makes it extra special.
—Carmella Ryan, Rockville Centre, NY

PREP: 20 min. • **COOK:** 25 min.
MAKES: 6 servings

- 1½ cups water
- 1 can (14 oz.) reduced-sodium beef broth
- ½ cup chopped shallots
- 2 garlic cloves, minced
- 1 Tbsp. canola oil
- 1 cup uncooked arborio rice
- 1 Tbsp. minced fresh thyme or 1 tsp. dried thyme
- ½ tsp. salt
- ½ tsp. pepper
- ½ cup white wine or additional reduced-sodium beef broth
- 1 cup sliced baby portobello mushrooms, chopped
- ¼ cup grated Parmesan cheese
- ½ cup mascarpone cheese

1. In a large saucepan, heat water and broth and keep warm. In a large saucepan, saute shallots and garlic in oil 2-3 minutes or until shallots are tender. Add the rice, thyme, salt and pepper; cook and stir for 2-3 minutes. Reduce heat; stir in wine. Cook and stir until all liquid is absorbed.
2. Add heated broth, ½ cup at a time, stirring constantly. Allow the liquid to absorb between additions. Cook just until the risotto is creamy and rice is almost tender. (Cooking time is about 20 minutes.)
3. Add mushrooms and Parmesan cheese; stir gently until cheese is melted. Garnish each serving with a heaping Tbsp. of mascarpone. Serve risotto immediately.
Freeze option: Before adding the mascarpone cheese, freeze cooled risotto mixture in freezer containers.

Portobello Risotto with Mascarpone

To use, partially thaw in refrigerator overnight. Heat through in a saucepan, stirring occasionally and adding a little broth or water if necessary. Garnish as servings as directed.
Note: With their large size and meaty texture, portobello mushrooms are well suited for grilling or broiling. Their meaty texture makes them popular as vegetarian burgers and in other vegetarian recipes.
¾ cup risotto mixture with heaping Tbsp. mascarpone cheese: 350 cal., 21g fat (10g sat. fat), 51mg chol., 393mg sod., 31g carb. (1g sugars, 1g fiber), 7g pro.

Test Kitchen Tip
Baby portobello mushrooms are also known as cremini mushrooms. They can be used instead of white mushrooms for a flavor boost.

Garden Pesto
Pasta Salad

GARDEN PESTO PASTA SALAD

My family and I live on a homestead in the Missouri Ozarks and produce much of our own food. In the summer, when the garden is bursting with fresh vegetables and it's too hot to cook, I like to use the season's veggies for pasta salads and other cool meals.
—Sarah Mathews, Ava, MO

PREP: 15 min. + chilling
MAKES: 10 servings

- 3 cups uncooked spiral pasta (about 9 oz.)
- ½ cup prepared pesto
- 3 Tbsp. white wine vinegar
- 1 Tbsp. lemon juice
- ½ tsp. salt
- ¼ tsp. pepper
- ¼ cup olive oil
- 1 medium zucchini, halved and sliced
- 1 medium sweet red pepper, chopped
- 1 medium tomato, seeded and chopped
- 1 small red onion, halved and thinly sliced
- ½ cup grated Parmesan cheese

1. Cook pasta according to package directions; drain. Rinse with cold water and drain well.
2. Meanwhile, whisk together pesto, vinegar, lemon juice, salt and pepper. Gradually whisk in oil until blended.
3. Combine vegetables and pasta. Drizzle with pesto dressing; toss to coat. Refrigerate salad, covered, until cold, about 1 hour. Serve with grated Parmesan cheese.
1 serving: 217 cal., 11g fat (2g sat. fat), 3mg chol., 339mg sod., 23g carb. (3g sugars, 2g fiber), 6g pro. **Diabetic exchanges:** 2 fat, 1½ starch.

Stuffed Hash Browns

STUFFED HASH BROWNS

Ever since we met, my husband has made me hash browns with bacon, pepper jack and sour cream. We share it when we have guests, too.
—Ann Ciszak Pazar, Anchorage, AK

PREP: 15 min. • **COOK:** 10 min./batch
MAKES: 4 servings

- 1 pkg. (20 oz.) refrigerated shredded hash brown potatoes
- ¼ cup finely chopped onion
- ½ tsp. salt
- ¼ tsp. pepper
- 4 Tbsp. olive oil, divided
- ½ cup pepper jack cheese
- ½ cup crumbled cooked bacon
- ½ cup sour cream
- 2 green onions, thinly sliced

1. In a large bowl, toss the potatoes with onion, salt and pepper. In a small cast-iron or other heavy skillet, heat 2 tsp. oil over medium heat. Add 1 cup potato mixture, pressing down to flatten with spatula. Cook, without stirring, until bottom is golden brown, 4-5 minutes. Drizzle with 1 tsp. oil; flip. Cook until bottom is golden brown, 4-5 minutes, sprinkling with 2 Tbsp. cheese and 2 Tbsp. bacon during the last minute of cooking.
2. Fold hash browns in half; slide onto plate and keep warm. Repeat with remaining ingredients. Top with sour cream and green onions.
1 serving: 410 cal., 27g fat (9g sat. fat), 26mg chol., 791mg sod., 30g carb. (3g sugars, 3g fiber), 13g pro.

🟢5i GREEN BEAN CASSEROLE

This classic green bean casserole has always been one of my favorite dishes. It's so easy to put together! You can make it before any guests arrive and keep it refrigerated until baking time.
—Anna Baker, Blaine, WA

PREP: 15 min. • **BAKE:** 35 min.
MAKES: 10 servings

- 2 cans (10¾ oz. each) condensed cream of mushroom soup, undiluted
- 1 cup whole milk
- 2 tsp. soy sauce
- ⅛ tsp. pepper
- 2 pkg. (16 oz. each) frozen green beans, cooked and drained
- 1 can (6 oz.) french-fried onions, divided

1. In a bowl, combine soup, milk, soy sauce and pepper. Gently stir in the beans. Spoon half of the mixture into a 13x9-in. baking dish. Sprinkle with half of the onions. Spoon remaining bean mixture over the top. Sprinkle with remaining onions.
2. Bake at 350° until heated through and the onions are brown and crispy, 30-35 minutes.
1 cup: 163 cal., 11g fat (3g sat. fat), 5mg chol., 485mg sod., 14g carb. (2g sugars, 1g fiber), 2g pro.

CAULIFLOWER AU GRATIN

This is a lower carb side dish that pairs well with pork, ham or beef. Even kids will ask for seconds! If you like a little crunch, sprinkle buttered bread crumbs over the top after 30 minutes of baking.
—Mary Zinchiak, Boardman, OH

PREP: 25 min. • **BAKE:** 45 min.
MAKES: 8 servings

- 1 large head cauliflower, cut into florets
- 2 Tbsp. olive oil
- 1 tsp. salt, divided
- 1 tsp. pepper, divided
- 4 Tbsp. butter, cubed
- 3 Tbsp. all-purpose flour
- 2 cups 2% milk
- 1 cup shredded Swiss cheese
- ½ cup grated Parmesan cheese
- ½ tsp. onion powder
- ½ tsp. ground mustard
- ½ tsp. Worcestershire sauce
- ⅛ tsp. cayenne pepper
  Chopped fresh thyme, optional

1. Preheat oven to 375°. Place the cauliflower on a rimmed baking sheet. Drizzle with oil; sprinkle with ½ tsp. salt and ½ tsp. pepper. Toss to coat. Bake 8 minutes. Stir; bake until crisp-tender and lightly browned, 7-8 minutes longer.
2. In a large saucepan, melt butter over medium heat. Stir in flour until smooth; gradually whisk in milk. Bring to a simmer, stirring constantly; cook and stir until thickened, 2-3 minutes. Remove from heat. Stir in the next 6 ingredients and remaining ½ tsp. salt and ½ tsp. pepper until smooth.
3. Pour ¾ cup cheese sauce into a greased 2-qt. baking dish. Top with cauliflower and remaining cheese sauce. Bake, uncovered, until bubbly and lightly browned, 30-35 minutes. If desired, top with chopped fresh thyme.
¾ cup: 196 cal., 14g fat (7g sat. fat), 34mg chol., 291mg sod., 11g carb. (5g sugars, 2g fiber), 9g pro.

Cauliflower au Gratin

Succotash

ROASTED BROCCOLI & CAULIFLOWER

When we make a time-consuming entree, we also do a quick side. These veggies are a good fit when you're watching calories.
—Debra Tolbert, Deville, LA

TAKES: 25 min. • **MAKES:** 8 servings

- 4 cups fresh cauliflowerets
- 4 cups fresh broccoli florets
- 10 garlic cloves, peeled and halved
- 2 Tbsp. olive oil
- ½ tsp. salt
- ½ tsp. pepper

Preheat oven to 425°. In a large bowl, combine all ingredients; toss to coat. Transfer to 2 greased 15x10x1-in. baking pans. Roast 15-20 minutes or until tender.

¾ cup: 58 cal., 4g fat (1g sat. fat), 0 chol., 173mg sod., 6g carb. (2g sugars, 2g fiber), 2g pro. **Diabetic exchanges:** 1 vegetable, ½ fat.

Health Tip

Low in calories and high in vitamins, cauliflower and broccoli offer many of the same nutrients. Broccoli does offer a few more of them, but overall these are two smart veggies to add to any health-conscious menu.

SUCCOTASH

You can't get more Southern than succotash. This recipe comes from my mother, who was a fantastic cook. This dish made her famous at least with everyone who ever tasted it.
—Rosa Boone, Mobile, AL

PREP: 1¾ hours + cooling • **COOK:** 1 hour
MAKES: 16 servings

- 1 smoked ham hock (about 1½ lbs.)
- 4 cups water
- 1 can (28 oz.) diced tomatoes, undrained
- 1½ cups frozen lima beans, thawed
- 1 pkg. (10 oz.) crowder peas, thawed, or 1 can (15½ oz.) black-eyed peas, drained
- 1 pkg. (10 oz.) frozen corn, thawed
- 1 medium green pepper, chopped
- 1 medium onion, chopped
- ⅓ cup ketchup
- 1½ tsp. salt
- 1½ tsp. dried basil
- 1 tsp. rubbed sage
- 1 tsp. paprika
- ½ tsp. pepper
- 1 bay leaf
- 1 cup sliced fresh or frozen okra
  Optional: Snipped fresh dill and chives

In a Dutch oven or large saucepan, simmer ham hock in water until tender, about 1½ hours. Cool; remove meat from the bone and return to pan. (Discard bone and broth or save for another use.) Add tomatoes, beans, peas, corn, green pepper, onion, ketchup and seasonings. Simmer, uncovered, for 45 minutes. Add the okra; simmer, uncovered, until tender, 15 minutes. Discard bay leaf before serving. Garnish with dill and chives if desired.

¾ cup: 79 cal., 0 fat (0 sat. fat), 2mg chol., 442mg sod., 16g carb. (5g sugars, 3g fiber), 4g pro. **Diabetic exchanges:** 1 starch.

Zesty Sugar Snap Peas

SPICY REFRIED BEANS

Jazz up a can of refried beans with jalapeno pepper, seasonings and cheese. Serve as a side or with tortilla chips as an appetizer.
—Taste of Home *Test Kitchen*

TAKES: 15 min. • **MAKES:** 2 cups

1   small onion, chopped
1   jalapeno pepper, seeded and chopped
1   garlic clove, minced
2   tsp. vegetable oil
1   can (16 oz.) refried beans
2   Tbsp. water
1   tsp. hot pepper sauce
¼   tsp. ground cumin
¼   tsp. chili powder
⅛   tsp. cayenne pepper
½   cup shredded Monterey Jack cheese

In a large skillet, saute onion, jalapeno and garlic in oil for 2-3 minutes or until tender. Stir in beans, water, hot pepper sauce, cumin, chili powder and cayenne. Cook and stir over medium-low heat until heated through. Transfer to a serving bowl; sprinkle with cheese.
Note: Wear disposable gloves when cutting hot peppers; the oils can burn skin. Avoid touching your face.
¼ cup: 95 cal., 4g fat (2g sat. fat), 11mg chol., 212mg sod., 10g carb. (2g sugars, 3g fiber), 5g pro. **Diabetic exchanges:** 1 fat, ½ starch.

WHY YOU'LL LOVE IT...

"I made this for a work luncheon and everyone loved it. A big hit for spicing up a can."
—AOWEN, TASTEOFHOME.COM

ZESTY SUGAR SNAP PEAS

Lemon-pepper seasoning and garlic make these crisp-tender sugar snap peas flavorful and an ideal accompaniment to a variety of entrees. You'll come to rely on this five-ingredient dish.
—Taste of Home *Test Kitchen*

TAKES: 15 min. • **MAKES:** 4 servings

1   lb. fresh or frozen sugar snap peas
1   Tbsp. butter
1   garlic clove, minced
¾   tsp. lemon-pepper seasoning
¼   tsp. salt

In a skillet, bring peas and ½ cup water to a boil. Reduce heat. Cover and cook until tender, 6-7 minutes. Drain. Add remaining ingredients. Cook and stir until well-coated, 2-3 minutes.
¾ cup: 74 cal., 3g fat (2g sat. fat), 8mg chol., 267mg sod., 8g carb. (4g sugars, 3g fiber), 4g pro. **Diabetic Exchanges:** 1 vegetable, ½ fat.

Spicy
Refried Beans

SLOW-COOKER RATATOUILLE

Not only does this classic recipe make a phenomenal side dish, you can also serve it with sliced French bread for a warm and easy appetizer. Try it in the summer with garden-fresh vegetables.
—Jolene Walters, North Miami, FL

PREP: 20 min. + standing
COOK: 3 hours • **MAKES:** 10 servings

- 1 large eggplant, peeled and cut into 1-in. cubes
- 2 tsp. salt, divided
- 3 medium tomatoes, chopped
- 3 medium zucchini, halved lengthwise and sliced
- 2 medium onions, chopped
- 1 large green pepper, chopped
- 1 large sweet yellow pepper, chopped
- 1 can (6 oz.) pitted ripe olives, drained and chopped
- 1 can (6 oz.) tomato paste
- ½ cup minced fresh basil
- 2 garlic cloves, minced
- ½ tsp. pepper
- 2 Tbsp. olive oil

1. Place eggplant in a colander over a plate; sprinkle with 1 tsp. salt and toss. Let stand for 30 minutes. Rinse and drain well. Transfer to a 5-qt. slow cooker coated with cooking spray.
2. Stir in tomatoes, zucchini, onions, green and yellow peppers, olives, tomato paste, basil, garlic, pepper and the remaining salt. Drizzle with oil. Cover and cook on high until vegetables are tender, 3-4 hours.
¾ cup: 116 cal., 5g fat (1g sat. fat), 0 chol., 468mg sod., 18g carb. (10g sugars, 6g fiber), 3g pro. **Diabetic exchanges:** 1 starch, 1 fat.

Slow-Cooker
Ratatouille

Buttered
Noodles

BUTTERED NOODLES

A few pantry ingredients jazz up egg noodles in this quick side dish that they'll ask for again and again.
—*Heather Nalley, Easley, SC*

TAKES: 20 min. • **MAKES:** 4 servings

- 2¼ cups uncooked egg noodles
- ¼ cup shredded part-skim mozzarella cheese
- 2 Tbsp. butter, melted
- 2 Tbsp. grated Parmesan cheese
- 2 tsp. minced fresh parsley
- ¼ tsp. salt
- ¼ tsp. garlic powder
- ⅛ tsp. pepper

Cook noodles according to package directions; drain. Transfer to a serving bowl. Immediately add the remaining ingredients and toss to coat.

¾ cup: 165 cal., 9g fat (5g sat. fat), 40mg chol., 290mg sod., 16g carb. (1g sugars, 1g fiber), 6g pro.

Oktoberfest
Red Cabbage

EASY FRIED RICE

This easy fried rice recipe really captures the flavor the version served in restaurants. Use leftover chicken for a satisfying meal that's easy to put together.
—Lori Schweer, Mapleton, MN

TAKES: 30 min. • **MAKES:** 4 servings

- 2   large eggs, beaten
- ¼   tsp. salt
- 3   Tbsp. vegetable oil, divided
- 4   cups cooked rice
- 1½ cups frozen stir-fry vegetable blend
- ½   cup sliced green onions
- 1   garlic clove, minced
- 1   cup diced cooked chicken
- 3   Tbsp. soy sauce
- 1   Tbsp. chicken broth
- ½   tsp. pepper
- ¼   tsp. ground ginger
- 4   bacon strips, cooked and crumbled

1. Combine the eggs and salt. In a large skillet or wok over medium heat, scramble eggs in 1 tsp. oil, breaking into small pieces. Remove from skillet and set aside.
2. Add remaining 2 Tbsp. plus 2 tsp. oil to skillet. Stir-fry rice over medium-high heat for 5 minutes. Add vegetables, onions and garlic; stir-fry for 5 minutes. Add the chicken; stir-fry until heated through, 3-5 minutes. Combine soy sauce, broth, pepper and ginger. Add to rice; stir to coat. Add bacon and eggs; heat through.
1½ cups: 476 cal., 19g fat (4g sat. fat), 133mg chol., 1077mg sod., 51g carb. (2g sugars, 2g fiber), 23g pro.

OKTOBERFEST RED CABBAGE

Four generations of our family celebrate Oktoberfest. We love this dish of red cabbage and apples, known as rotkohl, for the tart and sweet flavors.
—Diana Likes, Chandler, AZ

PREP: 20 min. • **COOK:** 50 min.
MAKES: 6 servings

- 3   Tbsp. bacon drippings or canola oil
- 1   small head red cabbage (about 1½ lbs.), shredded
- 2   medium tart apples, peeled and chopped
- 1   cup water
- ¼   cup sugar
- ¾   tsp. salt
- ¼   tsp. pepper
- ⅛   tsp. ground cloves
- ¼   cup white vinegar

1. In a Dutch oven, heat bacon drippings over medium heat. Add cabbage and apples; cook and stir 2-3 minutes. Stir in water, sugar, salt, pepper and cloves.
2. Bring to a boil. Reduce heat; simmer, covered, 40-45 minutes or until cabbage is tender, stirring occasionally. Stir in the vinegar.
¾ cup: 146 cal., 7g fat (3g sat. fat), 6mg chol., 331mg sod., 22g carb. (17g sugars, 3g fiber), 1g pro.

WHY YOU'LL LOVE IT...

"Fantastic! Loved the sweet-and-sour taste. My German nana taught me to make this, but I've never used cloves. They impart a great taste."
—ANNRMS, TASTEOFHOME.COM

Easy Fried Rice

HERBED RICE PILAF

This savory side dish has been a family favorite for years. Our 12-year-old daughter, Jennifer, is an expert with this recipe, which is a big help for a busy working mom like me. We enjoy this rice dish in the summer with a grilled entree.
—Jeri Dobrowski, Beach, ND

PREP: 15 min. • **COOK:** 15 min. + standing
MAKES: 6 servings

- 1 cup uncooked long grain rice
- 1 cup chopped celery
- ¾ cup chopped onion
- ¼ cup butter, cubed
- 2½ cups water
- 1 pkg. (2 to 2½ oz.) chicken noodle soup mix
- 1 tsp. dried thyme
- ¼ tsp. rubbed sage
- ¼ tsp. pepper
- 2 Tbsp. fresh minced parsley
- 1 Tbsp. chopped pimientos, optional

1. In a large skillet, cook the rice, celery and onion in butter, stirring constantly, until rice is browned. Stir in the next 5 ingredients; bring to a boil. Reduce heat; cover and simmer for 15 minutes. Sprinkle with parsley; stir in pimientos if desired.

2. Remove from heat and let stand, covered, for 10 minutes. Fluff with a fork.

¾ cup: 226 cal., 8g fat (5g sat. fat), 23mg chol., 426mg sod., 34g carb. (3g sugars, 2g fiber), 4g pro. **Diabetic exchanges:** 2 starch, 1½ fat.

STEAKHOUSE MUSHROOMS

I got this recipe from a friend back when we were in nursing school. Whenever my husband is cooking meat on the grill, you can bet I'll be in the kitchen preparing these tasty mushrooms.
—Kenda Burgett, Rattan, OK

TAKES: 20 min. • **MAKES:** 4 servings

- ¼ cup butter, cubed
- 1 lb. medium fresh mushrooms
- 2 tsp. dried basil
- ½ tsp. dried oregano
- ½ tsp. seasoned salt
- ¼ tsp. garlic powder
- 1 tsp. browning sauce, optional

In a large skillet, heat butter over medium-high heat. Add mushrooms; cook and stir until tender. Stir in seasonings and, if desired, browning sauce. Reduce heat to medium; cook, covered, 3-5 minutes to allow flavors to blend.

¾ cup: 131 cal., 12g fat (7g sat. fat), 30mg chol., 276mg sod., 5g carb. (2g sugars, 2g fiber), 4g pro.

Herbed Rice Pilaf

Spaghetti Squash with Tomatoes & Olives

SPAGHETTI SQUASH WITH TOMATOES & OLIVES

This squash is outstanding as a side dish, but you can also top it with canned tuna to create a simple, healthy main dish. It's easy and so tasty! I like to use my own canned tomatoes for the best flavor.
—Carol Chase, Sioux City, IA

PREP: 15 min. • **COOK:** 5¼ hours
MAKES: 10 servings

- 1 medium spaghetti squash, halved, seeds removed
- ¼ cup sliced green olives with pimientos, drained
- 1 can (14 oz.) diced tomatoes
- 1 tsp. dried oregano
- ½ tsp. salt
- ½ tsp. pepper
- ½ cup shredded cheddar cheese
- ¼ cup chopped fresh basil

1. Place squash in 6- or 7-qt. slow cooker, overlapping as needed to fit. Cook, covered, on low until tender, 5-7 hours.
2. Remove squash from slow cooker; drain any cooking liquid. Using a fork, separate the squash into strands resembling spaghetti, discarding skin. Return strands to slow cooker. Stir in the olives, tomatoes, oregano, salt and pepper; cook on low until heated through, about 15 minutes. Top with cheese and basil.
¾ cup: 92 cal., 3g fat (1g sat. fat), 6mg chol., 296mg sod., 15g carb. (1g sugars, 4g fiber), 3g pro. **Diabetic exchanges:** 1 starch, ½ fat.

Air-Fryer
French Fries

Caesar Salad

🔟 🍎 AIR-FRYER FRENCH FRIES

These low-calorie french fries are perfect because I can whip them up at a moment's notice with ingredients I have on hand. They are so crispy, you won't miss the deep fryer!
—Dawn Parker, Surrey, BC

PREP: 10 min. • **COOK:** 30 min.
MAKES: 4 servings

- 3 medium potatoes, cut into ½-in. strips
- 2 Tbsp. coconut or avocado oil
- ½ tsp. garlic powder
- ¼ tsp. salt
- ¼ tsp. pepper
  Chopped fresh parsley, optional

1. Preheat air fryer to 400°. Add the potatoes to a large bowl; add enough ice water to cover. Soak for 15 minutes. Drain the potatoes; place on towels and pat dry.
2. Combine potatoes, oil, garlic powder, salt and pepper in second large bowl; toss to coat. In batches, place potatoes in a single layer on tray in greased air-fryer basket. Cook until crisp and golden brown, 15-17 minutes, stirring and turning every 5-7 minutes. If desired, sprinkle with parsley.
¾ cup: 185 cal., 7g fat (6g sat. fat), 0 chol., 157mg sod., 28g carb. (1g sugars, 3g fiber), 3g pro. **Diabetic exchanges:** 2 starch, 1½ fat.

CAESAR SALAD

This refreshing salad has a zesty dressing that provides a burst of flavor with each bite. It's a wonderful way to perk up any meal.
—Schelby Thompson, Camden Wyoming, DE

TAKES: 10 min. • **MAKES:** 6 servings

- 1 large bunch romaine, torn
- ¾ cup olive oil
- 3 Tbsp. red wine vinegar
- 1 tsp. Worcestershire sauce
- ½ tsp. salt
- ¼ tsp. ground mustard
- 1 large garlic clove, minced
- ½ fresh lemon
  Dash pepper
- ¼ to ½ cup shredded Parmesan cheese
  Caesar-flavored or garlic croutons

1. Place lettuce in a large salad bowl. Combine the next 6 ingredients in a blender; process until smooth. Pour over lettuce and toss to coat.
2. Squeeze lemon juice over lettuce. Sprinkle with pepper, cheese and croutons.
1 cup: 265 cal., 28g fat (4g sat. fat), 2mg chol., 268mg sod., 3g carb. (1g sugars, 1g fiber), 2g pro.

SPAETZLE DUMPLINGS

These tender homemade spaetzle noodles take only minutes to make and are a natural accompaniment to chicken. You can serve them with chicken gravy or simply butter them and sprinkle with parsley.
—Pamela Eaton, Monclova, OH

TAKES: 15 min. • **MAKES:** 6 servings

- 2 cups all-purpose flour
- 4 large eggs, lightly beaten
- ⅓ cup 2% milk
- 2 tsp. salt
- 8 cups water
- 1 Tbsp. butter
  Minced fresh parsley, optional

1. In a large bowl, stir the flour, eggs, milk and salt until smooth (dough will be sticky). In a large saucepan over high heat, bring water to a boil. Pour dough into a colander or spaetzle maker coated with cooking spray; place over boiling water.

2. With a wooden spoon, press dough until small pieces drop into boiling water. Cook for 2 minutes or until the dumplings are tender and float. Remove with a slotted spoon; toss with butter. If desired, sprinkle with parsley.

1 cup: 223 cal., 6g fat (2g sat. fat), 130mg chol., 856mg sod., 33g carb. (1g sugars, 1g fiber), 9g pro.

Boston
Baked Beans

BOSTON BAKED BEANS

Simmered in molasses, these beans are perfect to take to your next potluck. They complement anything you serve with them.
—Darlene Duncan, Langhorne, PA

PREP: 20 min. + soaking • **COOK:** 10 hours
MAKES: 10 servings

- 1 lb. dried navy beans
- 6 cups water, divided
- ¼ lb. diced salt pork or 6 bacon strips, cooked and crumbled
- 1 large onion, chopped
- ½ cup packed brown sugar
- ½ cup molasses
- ¼ cup sugar
- 1 tsp. ground mustard
- 1 tsp. salt
- ½ tsp. ground cloves
- ½ tsp. pepper

1. Sort beans and rinse in cold water. Place beans in a 3- or 4-qt. slow cooker; add 4 cups water. Cover beans and let stand overnight.

2. Drain and rinse beans, discarding liquid. Return beans to slow cooker; add salt pork.

3. In a small bowl, combine the onion, brown sugar, molasses, sugar, mustard, salt, cloves, pepper and remaining water. Pour the mixture over beans; stir to combine.

4. Cover and cook beans on low for 10-12 hours or until beans are tender.

⅔ cup: 331 cal., 6g fat (2g sat. fat), 12mg chol., 511mg sod., 58g carb. (27g sugars, 7g fiber), 13g pro.

Health Tip

Making baked beans from scratch allows you to control the amount of sodium which is typically high in prepared baked beans. Decrease the salt if you are following a lower-sodium diet.

MOM'S SUPER STUPENDOUS POTATO SALAD

In college, my best friend and I debated whose mom made the best potato salad. Turns out the recipes were almost identical! Even though I've since tweaked our recipe, it still takes me home again.
—Ellie Martin Cliffe, Milwaukee, WI

PREP: 20 min. • **COOK:** 15 min. + chilling
MAKES: 12 servings

- 1 garlic clove, peeled
- 3 lbs. small red potatoes, quartered
- 2 Tbsp. cider vinegar, divided
- 1½ tsp. salt, divided
- 6 hard-boiled large eggs, divided use
- 1 cup mayonnaise
- ½ cup sour cream
- 1 Tbsp. Dijon mustard
- ½ tsp. paprika, plus extra for garnish, optional
- ¼ tsp. pepper
- 1 medium sweet onion, finely chopped
- 2 celery ribs, finely chopped
- 2 Tbsp. minced fresh parsley

1. Skewer garlic with a toothpick (to make it easy to find after cooking). Place potatoes, 1 Tbsp. vinegar, 1 tsp. salt and garlic in a Dutch oven; add water to cover. Bring to a boil. Reduce the heat; simmer until tender, 10-12 minutes. Drain the potatoes, reserving garlic; remove skewer and crush garlic.
2. Meanwhile, chop 5 eggs. Whisk together mayonnaise, sour cream, mustard, paprika, pepper, garlic and remaining vinegar and salt. Stir in potatoes, chopped eggs, onion and celery. Refrigerate 4 hours or until cold.
3. Just before serving, slice remaining egg. Top salad with the egg; sprinkle with the parsley and, if desired, additional paprika.
¾ cup: 281 cal., 19g fat (4g sat. fat), 107mg chol., 472mg sod., 20g carb. (2g sugars, 2g fiber), 6g pro.

Mom's Super Stupendous Potato Salad

GRILLED ZUCCHINI WITH ONIONS

Wondering what to do with all of your garden-grown zucchini in the summer? Give it a sizzle and a little heat with this healthy side. It's also an easy recipe to double or triple for summer cookouts.
—Alia Shuttleworth, Auburn, CA

TAKES: 20 min. • **MAKES:** 4 servings

- 6 small zucchini, halved lengthwise
- 4 tsp. olive oil, divided
- 2 green onions, thinly sliced
- 2 Tbsp. lemon juice
- ½ tsp. salt
- ⅛ tsp. crushed red pepper flakes

1. Drizzle the zucchini with 2 tsp. oil. Grill, covered, over medium heat for about 8-10 minutes or until tender, turning once.
2. Place in a large bowl. Add the green onions, lemon juice, salt, pepper flakes and remaining oil; toss to coat.
3 zucchini halves: 73 cal., 5g fat (1g sat. fat), 0 chol., 314mg sod., 7g carb. (3g sugars, 2g fiber), 2g pro. **Diabetic exchanges:** 1 vegetable, 1 fat.

Tra Vigne Green
Beans, page 55

Page 42

Page 36

5-Star Veggie Add-Ons

When it's time to whip up a savory side, vegetables are the ideal choice. Healthy, versatile, quick and easy, veggie dishes round out just about any menu. Turn here for the garden-fresh favorites today's home cooks rely on most.

Page 46

Page 52

ACORN SQUASH SLICES

Acorn squash is a favorite with my family. This recipe gets sweet maple flavor from syrup and an appealing nuttiness from pecans. It's easy, too, because you don't have to peel the squash.
—Richard Lamb, Williamsburg, IN

PREP: 15 min. • **BAKE:** 40 min.
MAKES: 6 servings

- 2 medium acorn squash (about 1½ lbs. each)
- ½ tsp. salt
- ¾ cup maple syrup
- 2 Tbsp. butter, melted
- ⅓ cup chopped pecans, optional

1. Cut squash in half lengthwise; remove and discard seeds and membrane. Cut each half widthwise into ½-in. slices; discard ends.
2. Place slices in a greased 13x9-in. baking dish. Sprinkle with salt. Combine syrup and butter; pour over squash. Sprinkle with pecans if desired.
3. Cover and bake at 350° until tender, for 40-45 minutes.
3 slices: 170 cal., 7g fat (0 sat. fat), 0 chol., 98mg sod., 31g carb. (0 sugars, 0 fiber), 2g pro. **Diabetic exchanges:** 1 starch, 1 fruit, 1 fat.

Did You Know?
Even though the skin separates from acorn squash very easily, it's completely edible. In fact, many enjoy the skins, particularly when the squash is roasted and the skin is sweetened a bit, as is the case with this tasty side dish.

Acorn Squash Slices

ASIAGO MASHED CAULIFLOWER

Asiago and fresh parsley help turn this healthier mashed potato alternative into a flavorful side dish that won't leave you feeling guilty or completely stuffed.
—Colleen Delawder, Herndon, VA

TAKES: 30 min. • **MAKES:** 4 servings

1 medium head cauliflower, cut into 1-in. pieces
1 tsp. sea salt, divided
4 oz. cream cheese, softened
½ cup shredded Asiago cheese
2 Tbsp. unsalted butter
2 Tbsp. coarsely chopped fresh parsley
¼ tsp. pepper

1. Place the cauliflower and ½ tsp. sea salt in a large saucepan; add water to cover. Bring to a boil. Cook, covered, until very tender, 12-15 minutes. Drain; cool slightly.
2. Transfer to a food processor. Add the cream cheese, Asiago cheese, butter, parsley, pepper and remaining sea salt. Process until blended.
½ cup: 239 cal., 20g fat (12g sat. fat), 56mg chol., 530mg sod., 10g carb. (4g sugars, 3g fiber), 9g pro.

5i 🍎
LEMON-ROASTED ASPARAGUS

When it comes to fixing asparagus, I think it's hard to go wrong. The springy flavors in this easy recipe burst with every bite.
—Jenn Tidwell, Fair Oaks, CA

TAKES: 20 min. • **MAKES:** 8 servings

2 lbs. fresh asparagus, trimmed
¼ cup olive oil
4 tsp. grated lemon zest
2 garlic cloves, minced
½ tsp. salt
½ tsp. pepper

Preheat oven to 425°. Place asparagus in a greased 15x10x1-in. baking pan. Mix remaining ingredients; drizzle over asparagus. Toss to coat. Roast until crisp-tender, 8-12 minutes.
1 serving: 75 cal., 7g fat (1g sat. fat), 0 chol., 154mg sod., 3g carb. (1g sugars, 1g fiber), 2g pro. **Diabetic exchanges:** 1½ fat, 1 vegetable.

Asiago Mashed Cauliflower

Grilled Cauliflower Wedges

STEWED ZUCCHINI & TOMATOES

A fresh take on traditional vegetable sides, this make-ahead dish stars fresh zucchini, tomatoes and green pepper. Bubbly cheddar cheese adds a down-home feel.
—*Barbara Smith, Salem, OR*

PREP: 20 min. • **COOK:** 3½ hours
MAKES: 6 servings

- 3 medium zucchini, cut into ¼-in. slices
- 1 tsp. salt, divided
- ½ tsp. pepper, divided
- 1 medium onion, thinly sliced
- 1 medium green pepper, thinly sliced
- 3 medium tomatoes, sliced
- ⅔ cup condensed tomato soup, undiluted
- 1 tsp. dried basil
- 1 cup shredded cheddar cheese
  Minced fresh basil, optional

1. Place zucchini in a greased 3-qt. slow cooker. Sprinkle with ½ tsp. salt and ¼ tsp. pepper. Layer with onion, green pepper and tomatoes. In a small bowl, combine the soup, basil and remaining salt and pepper; spread over tomatoes.
2. Cover and cook on low for 3-4 hours or until vegetables are tender. Sprinkle with cheese. Cover and cook 30 minutes longer or until the cheese is melted. If desired, top with fresh basil.
¾ cup: 126 cal., 6g fat (4g sat. fat), 20mg chol., 678mg sod., 14g carb. (8g sugars, 3g fiber), 7g pro. **Diabetic exchanges:** 1 vegetable, 1 fat, ½ starch.

GRILLED CAULIFLOWER WEDGES

This side is incredibly easy yet packed with flavor. Best of all, it looks like a dish from a five-star restaurant. The grill leaves the cauliflower cooked but crisp, and the red pepper flakes add bite.
—*Carmel Hall, San Francisco, CA*

TAKES: 30 min. • **MAKES:** 8 servings

- 1 large head cauliflower
- 1 tsp. ground turmeric
- ½ tsp. crushed red pepper flakes
- 2 Tbsp. olive oil
  Optional: Lemon juice, additional olive oil and pomegranate seeds

1. Remove the leaves and trim stem from cauliflower. Cut cauliflower into 8 wedges. Mix turmeric and pepper flakes. Brush wedges with oil; sprinkle with turmeric mixture.
2. Grill, covered, over medium-high heat or broil 4 in. from heat until cauliflower is tender, 8-10 minutes on each side. If desired, drizzle with lemon juice and additional olive oil, and serve with pomegranate seeds.
1 wedge: 57 cal., 4g fat (1g sat. fat), 0 chol., 32mg sod., 5g carb. (2g sugars, 2g fiber), 2g pro. **Diabetic exchanges:** 1 vegetable, 1 fat.

Stewed Zucchini
& Tomatoes

AIR-FRYER HERB & LEMON CAULIFLOWER

This standout side is easy to prepare with just a few ingredients. Crushed red pepper flakes add a touch of heat.
—Susan Hein, Burlington, WI

TAKES: 20 min. • **MAKES:** 4 servings

- 1 medium head cauliflower, cut into florets (about 6 cups)
- 4 Tbsp. olive oil, divided
- ¼ cup minced fresh parsley
- 1 Tbsp. minced fresh rosemary
- 1 Tbsp. minced fresh thyme
- 1 tsp. grated lemon zest
- 2 Tbsp. lemon juice
- ½ tsp. salt
- ¼ tsp. crushed red pepper flakes

Preheat air fryer to 350°. In a large bowl, combine cauliflower and 2 Tbsp. oil, toss to coat. In batches, arrange cauliflower in a single layer on tray in an air-fryer basket. Cook until florets are tender and edges are browned, 8-10 minutes, stirring halfway through. In a small bowl, combine remaining ingredients; stir in remaining 2 Tbsp. oil. Carefully transfer the cauliflower to a large bowl; drizzle with the herb mixture and toss to combine.

¾ cup: 161 cal., 14g fat (2g sat. fat), 0 chol., 342mg sod., 8g carb. (3g sugars, 3g fiber), 3g pro. **Diabetic exchanges:** 3 fat, 1 vegetable.

Test Kitchen Tip

Don't have an air fryer? You can also prepare this side dish in a 425° oven. Drizzle the cauliflower with 2 tablespoons oil and roast, uncovered, 20-25 minutes. Drizzle with herb mixture as directed and toss to combine.

Air-Fryer
Herb & Lemon
Cauliflower

Bohemian
Collards

🍎 BOHEMIAN COLLARDS

I've added unconventional ingredients to these collards that make them unique and exquisite on the palate and on the plate.
—Ally Phillips, Murrells Inlet, SC

PREP: 20 min. • **COOK:** 35 min.
MAKES: 8 servings

1	large bunch collard greens (about 2 lbs.)
6	bacon strips, chopped
1	Tbsp. olive oil
½	cup chicken broth
1½	cups fresh or frozen corn (about 7½ oz.)
1	cup chopped sweet red pepper
½	tsp. salt
¼	tsp. crushed red pepper flakes
¼	tsp. pepper

1. Trim thick stems from collard greens; coarsely chop leaves. In a Dutch oven, cook bacon over medium heat until crisp, stirring occasionally. Remove with a slotted spoon; drain on paper towels. Cook and stir collard greens in bacon drippings and oil just until coated. Add chicken broth; bring to a boil. Reduce heat; simmer, covered, until greens are very tender, 25-30 minutes.

2. Add corn, red pepper, salt, pepper flakes and pepper. Cook and stir until heated through. Sprinkle with bacon.

½ cup: 168 cal., 11g fat (3g sat. fat), 14mg chol., 369mg sod., 13g carb. (2g sugars, 5g fiber), 7g pro. **Diabetic exchanges:** 2 fat, 1 starch.

Better
Brussels Sprouts

5i

BETTER BRUSSELS SPROUTS

This is the only way my kids will eat Brussels sprouts! It's actually ideal for me because this dish is fast, easy and healthy, and it makes a lovely side. You can find Brussels sprout halves in the prepackaged salad aisle at the grocery store. They're a timesaver if you can find them, but you can always just buy whole ones and slice them in half.
—Teri Rasey, Cadillac, MI

TAKES: 20 min. • **MAKES:** 6 servings

- 3 Tbsp. coconut oil
- 1 pkg. (16 oz.) fresh halved
  Brussels sprouts
- ⅓ cup sliced onions
- ½ cup coarsely chopped cashews
- 1 tsp. granulated garlic
  Salt and pepper to taste

In a large heavy skillet or wok, heat coconut oil over medium heat. Add the Brussels sprouts; cook and stir 5 minutes. Add onion; cook 3 minutes longer, stirring every 20-30 seconds. Add cashews and garlic; cook 1 minute longer. Sprinkle with salt and pepper.
⅔ cup: 161 cal., 13g fat (7g sat. fat), 0 chol., 81mg sod., 11g carb. (1g sugars, 3g fiber), 5g pro.

SLOW COOKER TZIMMES

Tzimmes is a sweet Jewish dish consisting of a variety of fruits and vegetables, and it may or may not include meat. Traditionally (as it is here), it's tossed with honey and cinnamon and slowly cooked to blend all of the flavors.
—Lisa Renshaw, Kansas City, MO

PREP: 20 min. • **COOK:** 5 hours
MAKES: 12 servings (⅔ cup each)

- ½ medium butternut squash, peeled and cubed
- 2 medium sweet potatoes, peeled and cubed
- 6 medium carrots, sliced
- 2 medium tart apples, peeled and sliced
- 1 cup chopped sweet onion
- 1 cup chopped dried apricots
- 1 cup golden raisins
- ½ cup orange juice
- ¼ cup honey
- 2 Tbsp. finely chopped crystallized ginger
- 3 tsp. ground cinnamon
- 3 tsp. pumpkin pie spice
- 2 tsp. grated orange zest
- 1 tsp. salt

1. Place the first s7 ingredients in a 5- or 6-qt. slow cooker. Combine orange juice, honey, ginger, cinnamon, pumpkin spice, orange zest and salt; pour over top and mix well.
2. Cover and cook on low until vegetables are tender, 5-6 hours.
⅔ cup: 187 cal., 0 fat (0 sat. fat), 0 chol., 235mg sod., 48g carb. (29g sugars, 6g fiber), 2g pro.

Slow Cooker
Tzimmes

FRIED CABBAGE

When I was young, my family grew our own cabbage. It was fun to put them to use in the kitchen, just like I did with this comforting side. It's so good with potatoes, deviled eggs and corn bread.
—Bernice Morris, Marshfield, MO

TAKES: 20 min. • **MAKES:** 6 servings

- 2 Tbsp. butter
- 1 tsp. sugar
- ½ tsp. salt
- ¼ tsp. crushed red pepper flakes
- ⅛ tsp. pepper
- 6 cups coarsely chopped cabbage
- 1 Tbsp. water

In a large skillet, melt the butter over medium heat. Stir in sugar, salt, pepper flakes and pepper. Add the cabbage and water. Cook for 5-6 minutes or until tender, stirring occasionally.

1 cup: 59 cal., 4g fat (2g sat. fat), 10mg chol., 251mg sod., 6g carb. (3g sugars, 2g fiber), 1g pro. **Diabetic exchanges:** 1 vegetable, 1 fat.

Test Kitchen Tip

For a heartier dish, add chopped cooked bacon or sliced smoked sausage to this fried cabbage. For a German sauerkraut-style side, stir in some caraway seeds and a tablespoon of cider vinegar.

Fried Cabbage

EASY BAKED MUSHROOMS

I bet you've never had mushrooms quite like this! Skipping the deep fryer keeps them low in fat.
—Denise DiPace, Medford, NJ

TAKES: 30 min. • **MAKES:** 4 servings

- 1 lb. medium fresh mushrooms, halved
- 2 Tbsp. olive oil
- ¼ cup seasoned bread crumbs
- ¼ tsp. garlic powder
- ¼ tsp. pepper
  Fresh parsley, optional

1. Place the mushrooms on a baking sheet. Drizzle with oil; toss to coat. In a small bowl, combine the bread crumbs, garlic powder and pepper; sprinkle over the mushrooms.
2. Bake mushrooms, uncovered, at 425° for 18-20 minutes or until lightly browned. Garnish with fresh parsley if desired.
¾ cup: 116 cal., 8g fat (1g sat. fat), 0 chol., 112mg sod., 10g carb. (2g sugars, 2g fiber), 4g pro. **Diabetic exchanges:** 1½ fat, ½ starch.

BROCCOLI & CARROT CHEESE BAKE

A creamy sauce flavored with cheese makes vegetables so much more appealing to my crowd. This side dish will please even the pickiest veggie-phobics. It uses vegetables that are available year-round, so it works for spring as well as winter meals.
—Trisha Kruse, Eagle, ID

PREP: 25 min. • **BAKE:** 30 min. + standing
MAKES: 9 servings

- 2 cups thinly sliced fresh carrots
- 2 cups fresh broccoli florets
- 3 large eggs
- 2 cups 2% milk
- ¼ cup butter, melted
- ½ tsp. salt
- ¼ tsp. ground nutmeg
- ¼ tsp. pepper
- 1½ cups (6 oz.) grated Gruyere or Swiss cheese, divided
- 6 cups cubed egg bread

1. Place the carrots and broccoli in a steamer basket; place in a large saucepan over 1 in. of water. Bring to a boil; cover and steam 3-4 minutes or until crisp-tender.
2. Preheat oven to 325°. In a large bowl, whisk eggs, milk, butter, salt, nutmeg and pepper. Stir in vegetables and 1 cup cheese. Gently stir in bread.
3. Transfer to a greased 11x7-in. baking dish; sprinkle with remaining cheese. Bake, uncovered, until a knife inserted in center comes out clean, 30-35 minutes. Let stand 10 minutes before serving.
1 piece: 261 cal., 16g fat (8g sat. fat), 122mg chol., 428mg sod., 18g carb. (5g sugars, 2g fiber), 13g pro.

GREEN BEANS PROVENCALE

Garlic, tomatoes and olive oil are wonderful ingredients often found in southern French cooking. In this dish, they complement the green beans perfectly.
—Paula Wharton, El Paso, TX

TAKES: 30 min. • **MAKES:** 5 servings

- 1 lb. fresh green beans, trimmed and cut into 2-in. pieces
- 4 green onions, sliced
- 2 Tbsp. minced shallot
- 4 garlic cloves, minced
- 2 tsp. minced fresh rosemary or ½ tsp. dried rosemary, crushed
- 1 Tbsp. olive oil
- 1½ cups grape tomatoes, halved
- 2 Tbsp. minced fresh or 2 tsp. dried basil
- ½ tsp. salt
- ¼ tsp. pepper

1. Place beans in a steamer basket; place in a large saucepan over 1 in. of water. Bring to a boil; cover and steam for until crisp-tender, 4-5 minutes.
2. Meanwhile, in a large skillet, saute onions, shallot, garlic and rosemary in oil until vegetables are tender. Add the green beans, tomatoes, basil, salt and pepper; saute 2-3 minutes longer or until heated through.
¾ cup: 70 cal., 3g fat (0 sat. fat), 0 chol., 248mg sod., 10g carb. (4g sugars, 4g fiber), 2g pro. **Diabetic exchanges:** 2 vegetable, ½ fat.

Dill &
Chive Peas

COLCANNON POTATOES

Every Irish family has its own version of this classic dish. My recipe comes from my father's family in Ireland. It's part of my St. Patrick's Day menu, along with lamb chops, carrots and soda bread.
—Marilou Robinson, Portland, OR

PREP: 25 min. • **COOK:** 35 min.
MAKES: 12 servings

- 1 medium head cabbage (about 2 lbs.), shredded
- 4 lbs. medium potatoes (about 8), peeled and quartered
- 2 cups whole milk
- 1 cup chopped green onions
- 1½ tsp. salt
- ½ tsp. pepper
- ¼ cup butter, melted
  Minced fresh parsley
  Crumbled cooked bacon

1. Place cabbage and 2 cups water in a large saucepan; bring to a boil. Reduce heat; simmer, covered, until the cabbage is tender, about 10 minutes. Drain, reserving cooking liquid; keep cabbage warm in separate dish.
2. In same pan, combine potatoes and reserved cooking liquid. Add additional water to cover potatoes; bring to a boil. Reduce heat; cook, uncovered, until potatoes are tender, 15-20 minutes. Meanwhile, place milk, green onions, salt and pepper in a small saucepan; bring just to a boil and remove from the heat.
3. Drain potatoes; place in a large bowl and mash. Add milk mixture; beat just until blended. Stir in cabbage. To serve, drizzle with butter; top with the fresh parsley and bacon.
1 cup: 168 cal., 5g fat (3g sat. fat), 14mg chol., 361mg sod., 27g carb. (6g sugars, 4g fiber), 4g pro. **Diabetic exchanges:** 2 starch, 1 fat.

DILL & CHIVE PEAS

Growing my own vegetables and herbs helps keep things fresh in the kitchen, but when I can't use fresh, this side is a breeze.
—Tanna Richard, Cedar Rapids, IA

TAKES: 10 min. • **MAKES:** 4 servings

- 1 pkg. (16 oz.) frozen peas
- ¼ cup snipped fresh dill
- 2 Tbsp. minced fresh chives
- 1 Tbsp. butter
- 1 tsp. lemon-pepper seasoning
- ¼ tsp. kosher salt

Cook peas according to the package directions. Stir in remaining ingredients; serve immediately.
¾ cup: 113 cal., 3g fat (2g sat. fat), 8mg chol., 346mg sod., 16g carb. (6g sugars, 5g fiber), 6g pro. **Diabetic exchanges:** 1 starch, ½ fat.

WHY YOU'LL LOVE IT...

"My daughter made these for Christmas Eve, and they were so delicious, I will be making them for our Easter dinner. Thank you for a wonderful recipe."
—JANE BUCEY, TASTEOFHOME.COM

Colcannon
Potatoes

Roasted Cauliflower
with Tahini Yogurt Sauce

ROASTED CAULIFLOWER WITH TAHINI YOGURT SAUCE

I created my own cauliflower recipe in honor of my grandma, who taught me to love this delicious and healthy vegetable. She cooked with it all the time.
—Lidia Haddadian, Pasadena, CA

PREP: 15 min. • **BAKE:** 40 min.
MAKES: 4 servings

- ¼ cup grated Parmesan cheese
- 3 Tbsp. olive oil
- 2 garlic cloves, minced
- ¼ tsp. salt
- ¼ tsp. pepper
- 1 small head cauliflower (about 1½ lbs.), cut into 4 wedges

SAUCE
- ½ cup fat-free plain Greek yogurt
- 1 Tbsp. lemon juice
- 1 Tbsp. tahini
- ¼ tsp. salt
  Dash paprika
  Dash cayenne pepper
  Minced fresh parsley

1. Preheat oven to 375°. In a small bowl, mix the first 5 ingredients. Rub over cauliflower; arrange in a foil-lined 15x10x1-in. baking pan coated with cooking spray, cut sides up. Roast until golden and tender, 40-45 minutes.
2. For sauce, in a small bowl, mix yogurt, lemon juice, tahini, salt, paprika and pepper; serve over cauliflower. Sprinkle with parsley.
1 cauliflower wedge with about 2 Tbsp. sauce: 177 cal., 14g fat (3g sat. fat), 4mg chol., 421mg sod., 7g carb. (3g sugars, 2g fiber), 7g pro.

Creamed Corn

CREAMED CORN

Five ingredients are all you'll need for my popular dinner accompaniment. It's always wonderful no matter what the occasion. Try it on a barbecue buffet or holiday menu.
—Barbara Brizendine, Harrisonville, MO

PREP: 10 min. • **COOK:** 3 hours
MAKES: 5 servings

- 2 pkg. (one 16 oz., one 10 oz.) frozen corn
- 1 pkg. (8 oz.) cream cheese, softened and cubed
- ¼ cup butter, cubed
- 1 Tbsp. sugar
- ½ tsp. salt

In a 3-qt. slow cooker coated with cooking spray, combine all ingredients. Cover and cook on low until cheese is melted and corn is tender, 3-3½ hours. Stir just before serving.
¾ cup: 378 cal., 26g fat (16g sat. fat), 74mg chol., 439mg sod., 34g carb. (5g sugars, 4g fiber), 8g pro.

WHY YOU'LL LOVE IT...

"I love this recipe. I take it to work potlucks and to family dinners. It is now a tradition to bring it to Thanksgiving and Christmas dinner. It's loved by all, even the ones who don't like cream cheese."
—TRECONMOM, TASTEOFHOME.COM

Roasted Pumpkin
& Brussels Sprouts

Baked
Ratatouille

BAKED RATATOUILLE

Ratatouille is often a seasoned stew made of eggplant, tomatoes, green peppers, squash and sometimes meat. Bacon and cheese make my recipe exceptional. This version is heavenly when made with homegrown vegetables. It's so good, I sometimes make the casserole as a main course all for myself, then eat it for lunch a few days in a row.
—Catherine Lee, Chandler, AZ

PREP: 15 min. • **BAKE:** 50 min.
MAKES: 8 servings

4   bacon strips, cut into 2-in. pieces
1   cup sliced onion
1   can (14½ oz.) diced tomatoes, undrained
⅓   cup tomato paste
¼   cup olive oil
1   large garlic clove, minced
1   tsp. salt
1   tsp. Italian seasoning
1   large eggplant (about 1¼ lbs.), peeled and cubed
4   medium zucchini, sliced
1   large green pepper, cut into strips
8   to 12 oz. sliced Monterey Jack cheese

1. In a large skillet, cook bacon and onion over medium heat until bacon is crisp; drain. Stir in the tomatoes, tomato paste, oil, garlic, salt and Italian seasoning.
2. Spread half into a greased 13x9-in. baking dish. Layer with half of the eggplant, zucchini, green pepper and cheese. Repeat layers. Bake, uncovered, at 375° for 50-55 minutes or until hot and bubbly.
½ cup: 250 cal., 17g fat (7g sat. fat), 30mg chol., 607mg sod., 15g carb. (9g sugars, 5g fiber), 11g pro.

ROASTED PUMPKIN & BRUSSELS SPROUTS

While traveling to Taiwan, we visited a restaurant where fresh vegetables including pumpkin were served. That inspired me to roast pumpkin with Brussels sprouts for special occasions.
—Pam Correll, Brockport, PA

PREP: 15 min. • **BAKE:** 35 min.
MAKES: 8 servings

- 1 medium pie pumpkin (about 3 lbs.), peeled and cut into ¾-in. cubes
- 1 lb. fresh Brussels sprouts, trimmed and halved lengthwise
- 4 garlic cloves, thinly sliced
- ⅓ cup olive oil
- 2 Tbsp. balsamic vinegar
- 1 tsp. sea salt
- ½ tsp. coarsely ground pepper
- 2 Tbsp. minced fresh parsley

1. Preheat oven to 400°. In a large bowl, combine pumpkin, Brussels sprouts and garlic. In a small bowl, whisk oil, vinegar, salt and pepper; drizzle over vegetables and toss to coat.
2. Transfer to a greased 15x10x1-in. baking pan. Roast until vegetables are tender, 35-40 minutes, stirring once. Sprinkle with parsley.
¾ cup: 152 cal., 9g fat (1g sat. fat), 0 chol., 255mg sod., 17g carb. (4g sugars, 3g fiber), 4g pro. **Diabetic exchanges:** 2 fat, 1 starch.

Test Kitchen Tip
When making this colorful side dish, be sure to purchase a pie pumpkin and not a carving pumpkin. Pie pumpkins offer a dense flesh that isn't particularly stringy, so it's great for cooking and baking.

Tomato-Onion
Green Beans

CREAMY CELERY ROOT & PEARL ONIONS

I have made creamed onions for several recent Thanksgivings and wanted to change the recipe, so I decided to add celery root. It's perfect with the onions, and the creamy sauce is addicting!
—Tina Mirilovich, Johnstown, PA

PREP: 15 min. • **COOK:** 20 min.
MAKES: 8 servings

- 1 large celery root (about 1½ lbs.), peeled and cubed
- 3 Tbsp. butter
- 1 pkg. (14.4 oz.) pearl onions, thawed
- ¾ cup chicken broth
- 1 tsp. sugar
- ½ tsp. salt
- 1½ cups heavy whipping cream
- 2 Tbsp. minced fresh parsley
- ½ tsp. pepper

1. Place celery root in a 6-qt. stockpot; add water to cover. Bring to a boil. Reduce heat; simmer, uncovered, until tender, 4-6 minutes. Drain; set aside.
2. In a large skillet or Dutch oven, heat butter over medium heat. Add pearl onions, broth, sugar and salt. Cook onions, stirring often, until onions begin to brown, 12-15 minutes. Add celery root and cream; simmer until slightly thickened, 3-5 minutes. Stir in parsley and pepper.
⅔ cup: 250 cal., 21g fat (13g sat. fat), 63mg chol., 379mg sod., 14g carb. (6g sugars, 3g fiber), 3g pro.

🔟 🍎 TOMATO-ONION GREEN BEANS

Fresh green beans star in this healthy side. Serve with grilled chicken, pork tenderloin or seafood for a delicious ending to a busy day.
—David Feder, Buffalo Grove, IL

TAKES: 30 min. • **MAKES:** 6 servings

- 2 Tbsp. olive oil
- 1 large onion, finely chopped
- 1 lb. fresh green beans, trimmed
- 3 Tbsp. tomato paste
- ½ tsp. salt
- 2 Tbsp. minced fresh parsley

1. In a large skillet, heat the oil over medium-high heat. Add chopped onion; cook until tender and lightly browned, stirring occasionally.
2. Meanwhile, place the green beans in a large saucepan; add water to cover. Bring to a boil. Cook, covered, until crisp-tender, 5-7 minutes. Drain; add to onion. Stir in tomato paste and salt; heat through. Sprinkle with parsley.
⅔ cup: 81 cal., 5g fat (1g sat. fat), 0 chol., 208mg sod., 9g carb. (4g sugars, 3g fiber), 2g pro. **Diabetic exchanges:** 1 vegetable, 1 fat.

Creamy Celery
Root & Pearl Onions

ORANGE-SCENTED LEEKS & MUSHROOMS

This simple side is fantastic for seasonal celebrations. The sherry and orange juice add a unique flavor twist that makes this dish special.
—Carole Bess White, Portland, OR

PREP: 20 min. • **COOK:** 40 min.
MAKES: 7 servings

- 4 lbs. medium leeks (white and light green portions only), thinly sliced (about 8 cups)
- 1 lb. sliced fresh mushrooms
- 2 Tbsp. olive oil
- ¼ cup sherry or reduced-sodium chicken broth
- ½ cup reduced-sodium chicken broth
- 1 Tbsp. balsamic vinegar
- 1 tsp. orange juice
- ½ tsp. grated orange zest
- ¼ tsp. salt
- ¼ tsp. minced fresh thyme or dash dried thyme
- ⅛ tsp. pepper

1. In a Dutch oven, cook leeks and mushrooms in oil in batches over medium heat until tender, stirring occasionally, 15-20 minutes. Return all to the pan. Add sherry, stirring to loosen the browned bits from bottom of pan.

2. Stir in the remaining ingredients; cook and stir until liquid is almost evaporated, 10-15 minutes.

⅔ cup: 215 cal., 5g fat (1g sat. fat), 0 chol., 180mg sod., 40g carb. (12g sugars, 5g fiber), 6g pro.

CUCUMBERS IN CREAM

When I was a child, my family had an enormous vegetable garden, so we enjoyed freshly picked cucumbers during the summer. My mother would slice the cucumbers, soak them awhile in salt water and add thick cream, which she carefully scooped from the top of fresh milk.
—Phyllis Kirsling, Junction City, WI

PREP: 15 min. + standing
MAKES: 8 servings

- 3 medium cucumbers, peeled and thinly sliced
- 1 medium onion, sliced
- 2 cups water
- ½ tsp. salt
- ¾ cup heavy whipping cream
- ¼ cup sugar
- ¼ cup cider vinegar
  Minced fresh parsley, optional

In a bowl, combine cucumbers, onion, water and salt. Let stand for 1 hour; drain and rinse. In a serving bowl, beat cream, sugar and vinegar. Add cucumbers and onion; toss gently. Sprinkle with parsley if desired.

1 cup: 126 cal., 8g fat (5g sat. fat), 31mg chol., 157mg sod., 12g carb. (10g sugars, 2g fiber), 2g pro.

Orange-Scented
Leeks & Mushrooms

TRA VIGNE GREEN BEANS

The title of this recipe translates to "among the vines" in Italian. I was inspired by a restaurant in Napa Valley called, yes, you guessed it, Tra Vigne. The flavors in this dish to me represent the essence of its title.
—Jenn Tidwell, Fair Oaks, CA

PREP: 15 min. • **COOK:** 25 min.
MAKES: 9 servings

Tra Vigne Green Beans

- 2 lbs. fresh green beans, trimmed
- 12 bacon strips, chopped
- 2 shallots, minced
- 4 garlic cloves, minced
- ½ tsp. salt
- ½ tsp. pepper
- 2 cups white grape juice
- ¼ cup white wine vinegar
- ½ cup minced chives

1. In a large saucepan, bring 4 cups water to a boil. Add green beans; cover and cook for 5 minutes. Drain and immediately place green beans in ice water. Drain and pat dry.

2. Meanwhile, in a large skillet, cook bacon over medium heat until crisp. Carefully remove bacon to paper towels with a slotted spoon; drain, reserving 1 Tbsp. drippings.

3. In the same skillet saute shallots in bacon drippings until tender. Add garlic, salt and pepper; cook 1 minute longer. Stir in juice and vinegar. Bring to a boil; cook until liquid is reduced by half.

4. Add the green beans and the bacon, cook until heated through. Sprinkle with chives.

¾ cup: 130 cal., 5g fat (2g sat. fat), 11mg chol., 338mg sod., 17g carb. (10g sugars, 3g fiber), 5g pro.

Cherry
Tomato Salad

CHERRY TOMATO SALAD

This recipe evolved from a need to use the bumper crops of cherry tomatoes that we regularly grow. It's become a summer favorite, especially at cookouts.
—Sally Sibley, St. Augustine, FL

PREP: 15 min. + marinating
MAKES: 6 servings

- 1 qt. cherry tomatoes, halved
- ¼ cup canola oil
- 3 Tbsp. white vinegar
- ½ tsp. salt
- ½ tsp. sugar
- ¼ cup minced fresh parsley
- 1 to 2 tsp. minced fresh basil
- 1 to 2 tsp. minced fresh oregano

Place tomatoes in a shallow bowl. In a small bowl, whisk oil, vinegar, salt and sugar until blended; stir in herbs. Pour over tomatoes; gently toss to coat. Refrigerate, covered, overnight.

¾ cup: 103 cal., 10g fat (1g sat. fat), 0 chol., 203mg sod., 4g carb. (3g sugars, 1g fiber), 1g pro. **Diabetic exchanges:** 2 fat, 1 vegetable.

MARVELOUS MEDITERRANEAN VEGETABLES

With so many barbecues in the summer, I created this simple dish to complement nearly any entree. I like to prepare it earlier in the day and let it marinate, then I just throw it on the grill.
—Cathy Godberson, Oakville, ON

PREP: 25 min. + marinating • **GRILL:** 10 min.
MAKES: 9 servings

- 3 large portobello mushrooms, sliced
- 1 each medium sweet red, orange and yellow peppers, sliced
- 1 medium zucchini, sliced
- 10 fresh asparagus spears, cut into 2-in. lengths
- 1 small onion, sliced and separated into rings
- ¾ cup grape tomatoes

Marvelous Mediterranean Vegetables

- ½ cup fresh sugar snap peas
- ½ cup fresh broccoli florets
- ½ cup pitted Greek olives
- 1 bottle (14 oz.) Greek vinaigrette
- ½ cup crumbled feta cheese

1. In a bowl or shallow dish, combine mushrooms, peppers and zucchini. Add asparagus, onion, tomatoes, peas, broccoli and olives. Pour vinaigrette into bowl and turn to coat. Cover and refrigerate for at least 30 minutes.
2. Discard marinade. Transfer the vegetables to a grill wok or basket. Grill, uncovered, over medium heat until tender, 8-12 minutes, stirring frequently. Place on a serving plate; sprinkle with cheese.
Note: Also known as kalamata olives, they are almond-shaped and range in size from ½ to 1 in. long. Dark eggplant in color, kalamata olive is rich and fruity in flavor and can be found packed in either a vinegar brine or olive oil.

¾ cup: 196 cal., 16g fat (3g sat. fat), 3mg chol., 549mg sod., 11g carb. (4g sugars, 3g fiber), 4g pro.

Test Kitchen Tip

If you do not have a grill wok or basket, use a disposable foil pan. Simply poke holes in the bottom of the pan with a meat fork to allow liquid to drain.

ROASTED HERBED SQUASH WITH GOAT CHEESE

Cooking is a hobby I'm so happy to share with my toddler. She (and all our Christmas Eve party guests) heartily approved of this new potluck favorite. I think any type of winter squash would work well in this standout recipe.
—Lindsay Oberhausen, Lexington, KY

PREP: 25 min. • **COOK:** 30 min.
MAKES: 10 servings

- 2 medium acorn squash (about 1½ lbs. each), peeled and cut into 2-in. cubes
- 1 large butternut squash (5 to 6 lbs.), peeled and cut into 2-in. cubes
- 3 Tbsp. olive oil
- 2 Tbsp. minced fresh thyme
- 2 Tbsp. minced fresh rosemary
- 1 Tbsp. kosher salt
- 1 tsp. coarsely ground pepper
- 1 log (11 oz.) fresh goat cheese, crumbled
- 2 Tbsp. coarsely chopped fresh parsley
- 1 Tbsp. maple syrup, warmed slightly

1. Preheat oven to 425°. Toss squashes with oil and seasonings. Transfer to 2 foil-lined 15x10x1-in. baking pans.
2. Roast squash, stirring once, until soft and some pieces are caramelized, 30-35 minutes. Switch position of pans midway through roasting to ensure even doneness. If a darker color is desired, broil 3-4 in. from heat roughly 2-4 minutes.
3. Cool slightly. To serve, add goat cheese to squash; gently toss. Sprinkle with parsley; drizzle with maple syrup.
1 cup: 251 cal., 8g fat (3g sat. fat), 21mg chol., 715mg sod., 43g carb. (10g sugars, 10g fiber), 7g pro.

Test Kitchen Tip
To save time, first cut squash into rings, then peel each ring.

Roasted Herbed Squash with Goat Cheese

RED CABBAGE WITH APPLE

This delicious combination has a sweet and tart flavor with a hint of bacon and apple that goes perfectly with sauerbraten.
—Patricia Rutherford, Winchester, IL

PREP: 15 min. • **COOK:** 40 min.
MAKES: 6 servings

- 3 bacon strips, diced
- 1 medium onion, chopped
- 1 medium apple, peeled and chopped
- 1 small head red cabbage, chopped
- 1 cup water
- ¼ cup white wine vinegar
- 1 Tbsp. sugar
- ½ tsp. salt

1. In a large saucepan, cook bacon over medium heat until crisp. Using a slotted spoon, remove to paper towels to drain.
2. In the drippings, saute onion and apple until tender. Stir in the remaining ingredients. Bring to a boil. Reduce heat; cover and simmer for 30 minutes or until tender. Stir in reserved bacon.
¾ cup: 131 cal., 5g fat (2g sat. fat), 8mg chol., 333mg sod., 19g carb. (12g sugars, 4g fiber), 4g pro. **Diabetic exchanges:** 2 vegetable, 1 fat, ½ starch.

WHY YOU'LL LOVE IT...

"This is excellent! My family has added it as a must-have dish for Thanksgiving and Christmas."
—BETH KEATON, TASTEOFHOME.COM

JALAPENO GREEN BEANS

This simple green bean dish gets a bit of a kick from jalapeno pepper. If you don't like things too spicy, reduce the amount of jalapeno by half—or eliminate it completely.
—Deirdre Cox, Kansas City, MO

TAKES: 25 min. • **MAKES:** 4 servings

- 2 Tbsp. olive oil
- 1 jalapeno pepper, thinly sliced
- 1 shallot, thinly sliced
- 1 lb. fresh green beans, cut into 2-in. pieces
- ½ tsp. salt
- 2 Tbsp. lemon juice

In a large cast-iron or other heavy skillet, heat oil over medium-high heat. Add jalapeno and shallot; cook and stir until tender, 2-3 minutes. Add beans and salt; cook and stir until beans are tender, 8-10 minutes, reducing heat if necessary. Drizzle with lemon juice. Serve immediately.
Note: Wear disposable gloves when cutting hot peppers; the oils can burn skin. Avoid touching your face.
½ cup: 106 cal., 7g fat (1g sat. fat), 0 chol., 303mg sod., 11g carb. (4g sugars, 4g fiber), 2g pro. **Diabetic exchanges:** 1½ fat, 1 vegetable.

Jalapeno
Green Beans

SPAGHETTI SQUASH WITH APPLES, BACON & WALNUTS

I've always loved spaghetti squash as an alternative to pasta and enjoy it in the classic marinara style, but I wanted a new recipe so my family and I could enjoy it more often. Here, savory, salty and sour flavors combine perfectly with a hint of sweet spice. While the squash is baking, prep the rest: It will take you only a few minutes to finish after you shred the squash.
—Jeff Tori, Johnstown, CO

PREP: 1 hour • **COOK:** 20 min.
MAKES: 6 servings

- 1 medium spaghetti squash
- 1 tsp. ground cumin
- 8 bacon strips, chopped
- 8 green onions, sliced
- 2 Tbsp. butter
- 2 garlic cloves, minced
- ¼ tsp. crushed red pepper flakes
- 2 medium apple, peeled and chopped
- 1 cup apple cider or juice
- 2 Tbsp. maple syrup
- ½ tsp. salt
- 1 dash pepper
- ½ cup chopped walnuts, toasted
- 2 Tbsp. minced fresh parsley

1. Preheat oven to 400°. Cut squash lengthwise in half; remove and discard seeds. Sprinkle with ½ tsp. cumin. Place squash in a 15x10x1-in. baking pan, cut sides down. Bake until easily pierced with a fork, 35-45 minutes.
2. In a large skillet, cook bacon over medium heat until crisp, stirring occasionally. Carefully remove with a slotted spoon; drain on paper towels. Discard drippings.

3. Add green onions, 2 Tbsp. butter, garlic and pepper flakes; cook and stir over medium heat until tender, roughly 2-3 minutes. Stir in apples, cider, syrup, salt, pepper and remaining cumin. Bring to a boil; cook until slightly thickened, 4-6 minutes.
4. When squash is cool enough to handle, use a fork to separate strands. Add squash to skillet; cook until liquid is absorbed, 2-3 minutes. Stir in bacon, walnuts and parsley.
Note: To toast nuts, bake in a shallow pan in a 350° oven for 5-10 minutes or cook in a skillet over low heat until lightly browned, stirring occasionally.
¾ cup: 314 cal., 16g fat (5g sat. fat), 21mg chol., 482mg sod., 39g carb. (14g sugars, 7g fiber), 8g pro.

BACON & GARLIC SUGAR SNAP PEAS

This flavorful side dish calls for only four ingredients! Feel free to use fresh sugar snap peas if you'd like.
—Tami Kuehl, Loup City, NE

TAKES: 10 min. • **MAKES:** 4 servings

- 2 bacon strips, coarsely chopped
- 1 pkg. (14 oz.) frozen sugar snap peas, thawed
- 1 shallot or small onion, thinly sliced
- 2 garlic cloves, thinly sliced

In a large skillet, cook bacon over medium heat until crisp, stirring occasionally. Carefully remove with a slotted spoon; drain on paper towels. Cook and stir peas in bacon drippings until heated through. Add shallot and garlic; cook 1 minute longer. Sprinkle with reserved bacon.
½ cup: 126 cal., 6g fat (2g sat. fat), 9mg chol., 100mg sod., 13g carb. (5g sugars, 3g fiber), 5g pro. **Diabetic exchanges:** 1 starch, 1 fat.

Spaghetti Squash with Apples, Bacon & Walnuts

Bacon & Garlic
Sugar Snap Peas

Cornbread Pudding,
Page 78

Page 66

Page 76

Breakfast & Brunch Sides

Whether trying to amp up your breakfast routine, planning a special Sunday-morning buffet for friends or simply looking to start the day on a tasty note, this chapter offers plenty of eye-opening ideas sure to become new favorites.

Page 75

Page 85

5i

CORNFLAKE-COATED CRISPY BACON

I've loved my aunt's crispy-coated bacon ever since I was a child. Now I've shared the super simple recipe with my own children. We still enjoy a big panful every Christmas morning—and on many other days throughout the year!
—Brenda Severson, Norman, OK

PREP: 20 min. • **BAKE:** 25 min.
MAKES: 9 servings

- ½ cup evaporated milk
- 2 Tbsp. ketchup
- 1 Tbsp. Worcestershire sauce
  Dash pepper
- 18 bacon strips (1 lb.)
- 3 cups crushed cornflakes

Preheat oven to 375°. In a large bowl, combine milk, ketchup, Worcestershire sauce and pepper. Add bacon strips, turning to coat. Dip strips in crushed cornflakes, patting to help coating adhere. Place bacon on 2 racks; place each rack on an ungreased 15x10x1-in. baking pan. Bake until golden and crisp, rotating pans halfway through baking, 25-30 minutes.

2 bacon strips: 198 cal., 7g fat (3g sat. fat), 20mg chol., 547mg sod., 26g carb. (4g sugars, 0 fiber), 8g pro.

WHY YOU'LL LOVE IT...

"My husband was skeptical when he saw me coating bacon with crumbs, but when I set it out for breakfast, he was impressed! 'This is delicious' were the first words out of his mouth! There was a battle for the last piece."

—REDCOTTAGECHRONICALS, TASTEOFHOME.COM

Cornflake-Coated Crispy Bacon

SMOKY HASH BROWN CASSEROLE

Making this delicious, savory casserole in the slow cooker saves oven space, but you can bake it in the oven if you prefer.
—Susan Hein, Burlington, WI

PREP: 10 min. • **COOK:** 3½ hours
MAKES: 6 servings

- 1 tsp. butter
- 1 pkg. (28 oz.) frozen O'Brien potatoes, thawed
- 1 can (10¾ oz.) condensed cream of chicken soup, undiluted
- 4 oz. smoked cheddar cheese, shredded
- ½ tsp. pepper
- ¼ tsp. salt

Grease a 3-qt. slow cooker with butter. Combine potatoes, soup, cheese, pepper and salt. Transfer to prepared slow cooker. Cook, covered, on low until potatoes are tender, 3½-4½ hours.
Bake option: Preheat oven to 350°. Place potato mixture in a greased 13x9-in. baking dish. Bake, uncovered, until potatoes are tender, 45-55 minutes.
¾ cup: 227 cal., 10g fat (5g sat. fat), 25mg chol., 626mg sod., 25g carb. (2g sugars, 4g fiber), 7g pro.

Spring Onion Pimiento Cheese Grits

SPRING ONION PIMIENTO CHEESE GRITS

Grits were a breakfast staple when I was growing up. Even today, we still have them about three times a week. I think that the trick with grits is the more you whisk, the creamier they'll be.
—Melissa Pelkey Hass, Waleska, GA

PREP: 15 min. • **COOK:** 20 min.
MAKES: 16 servings

- 2 cups uncooked stone-ground yellow grits
- 1 pkg. (8 oz.) cream cheese, softened
- ½ cup mayonnaise
- 3 cups shredded Monterey Jack cheese
- 1 jar (4 oz.) diced pimientos, drained
- 3 green onions, diced
- 1 tsp. sugar
     Dash cayenne pepper
- ¼ cup butter, softened
     Salt and pepper to taste

1. Prepare grits according to package directions. Keep warm.
2. Meanwhile, using a mixer, beat cream cheese. Add mayonnaise; continue beating until creamy. Add the next 5 ingredients, mixing until well blended.
3. Stir butter and pimiento cheese mixture into the warm grits; season to taste. Mix well.
¾ cup: 281 cal., 20g fat (10g sat. fat), 41mg chol., 231mg sod., 19g carb. (1g sugars, 1g fiber), 8g pro.

SAGE TURKEY SAUSAGE PATTIES

Turkey sausage is a good option when you want to cut salt and saturated fat. You'll love the aroma of this recipe when it's sizzling in the pan.
—Sharman Schubert, Seattle, WA

TAKES: 30 min. • **MAKES:** 12 servings

- ¼ cup grated Parmesan cheese
- 3 Tbsp. minced fresh parsley or 1 Tbsp. dried parsley flakes
- 2 Tbsp. fresh sage or 2 tsp. dried sage leaves
- 2 garlic cloves, minced
- 1 tsp. fennel seed, crushed
- ¾ tsp. salt
- ½ tsp. pepper
- 1½ lbs. lean ground turkey
- 1 Tbsp. olive oil

1. In a large bowl, combine the first 7 ingredients. Crumble turkey over mixture and mix lightly but thoroughly. Shape into twelve 3-in. patties.
2. In a large cast-iron or other heavy skillet, cook patties in oil in batches over medium heat until meat is no longer pink, 3-5 minutes on each side. Drain on paper towels if necessary.
Freeze option: Place cooled, cooked patties on a waxed paper-lined baking sheet; cover and freeze until firm. Remove from pan and transfer to a resealable freezer container. To use, place patties on a baking sheet coated with cooking spray. Bake in a preheated 350° oven until heated through, about 15 minutes on each side.

1 patty: 104 cal., 6g fat (2g sat. fat), 46mg chol., 227mg sod., 0 carb. (0 sugars, 0 fiber), 11g pro. **Diabetic exchanges:** 1 lean meat, 1 fat.

Sage Turkey Sausage Patties

SWEET ONION PIE

Loaded with sweet onions, this creamy pie makes a scrumptious addition to the brunch buffet. By using less butter to cook the onions and swapping in some lighter ingredients, I cut calories and fat from the tasty dish.
—Barbara Reese, Catawissa, PA

PREP: 35 min. • **BAKE:** 30 min.
MAKES: 8 servings

- 2 sweet onions, halved and sliced
- 1 Tbsp. butter
- 1 frozen deep-dish pie crust (9 in.)
- 1 cup egg substitute
- 1 cup fat-free evaporated milk
- 1 tsp. salt
- ¼ tsp. pepper

1. In a large nonstick skillet, cook onions in butter over medium-low heat until very tender, 30 minutes. Meanwhile, line un-pricked crust with a double thickness of heavy-duty foil.
2. Bake crust at 450° for 6 minutes. Remove foil; cool on a wire rack. Reduce heat to 425°.
3. Spoon onions into crust. In a small bowl, whisk the egg substitute, milk, salt and pepper; pour over onions. Bake until a knife inserted in the center comes out clean, 30-35 minutes. Let pie stand for 5-10 minutes before cutting.

1 piece: 169 cal., 7g fat (2g sat. fat), 5mg chol., 487mg sod., 21g carb. (8g sugars, 1g fiber), 7g pro. **Diabetic exchanges:** 1 starch, 1 lean meat, 1 fat.

Sweet
Onion Pie

CAST-IRON LOADED BREAKFAST BISCUITS

These biscuits are full of hearty breakfast staples such as eggs, bacon, mushrooms and cheese! They are perfect to bake on the weekends, then freeze for a quick weekday breakfast. A gluten-free flour blend can be substituted for the all-purpose flour.
—Courtney Stultz, Weir, KS

PREP: 35 min. • **BAKE:** 20 min.
MAKES: 8 servings

- 4 bacon strips, chopped
- 1 cup chopped fresh mushrooms
- ⅓ cup chopped onion
- 1 garlic clove, minced
- 4 large eggs
- 2 cups all-purpose flour
- 3 tsp. baking powder
- ½ tsp. salt
- ½ cup cold butter, cubed
- 1 cup buttermilk
- ½ cup shredded cheddar cheese

1. Preheat the oven to 400°. In a 10-in. cast-iron or other ovenproof skillet, cook the bacon over medium heat until crisp, stirring occasionally. Remove with a slotted spoon; drain on paper towels. Cook and stir mushrooms, onion and garlic in bacon drippings until tender, 4-5 minutes. Remove from pan.
2. In a small bowl, whisk eggs until blended. Pour eggs into same pan; cook and stir over medium heat until eggs are thickened and no liquid egg remains. Remove from pan.
3. In a large bowl, whisk flour, baking powder and salt. Cut in the butter until mixture resembles coarse crumbs. Add buttermilk; stir just until moistened. Gently stir in mushroom mixture, eggs, bacon and cheese.
4. Drop dough by ½ cupfuls 1 in. apart into same skillet. Bake until bottoms are golden brown, 20-25 minutes.
1 biscuit: 356 cal., 22g fat (11g sat. fat), 141mg chol., 653mg sod., 27g carb. (2g sugars, 1g fiber), 11g pro.

Cast-Iron Loaded
Breakfast Biscuits

Crispy Mashed Potato
& Stuffing Patties

CRISPY MASHED POTATO & STUFFING PATTIES

Talk about a fun way to use holiday leftovers! Making this turkey and stuffing patty is so fast. The family looks forward to this breakfast treat every year.
—Kelli Ferea, Casa Grande, AZ

TAKES: 30 min. • **MAKES:** 12 patties

- 2 large eggs, lightly beaten
- 2 Tbsp. finely chopped onion
- ¼ tsp. pepper
- 2 cups leftover mashed potatoes
- 2 cups leftover chopped cooked turkey
- 2 cups leftover stuffing
- 2 Tbsp. butter
- 2 Tbsp. canola oil
  Unsweetened applesauce, optional

1. In a large bowl, whisk eggs, onion and pepper. Stir in potatoes, turkey and stuffing.
2. In a large skillet, heat butter and oil over medium-high heat. Working in batches, drop the potato mixture by ½ cupfuls into skillet; press to flatten slightly. Fry on each side until golden brown and heated through, 4-5 minutes. Drain on paper towels. If desired, serve with applesauce.
2 patties: 364 cal., 19g fat (6g sat. fat), 118mg chol., 628mg sod., 28g carb. (2g sugars, 2g fiber), 20g pro.

CORN PUDDING WITH BACON & CHEDDAR

This pudding can be prepared ahead and refrigerated overnight for easy meal planning. Remove from the refrigerator for 30 minutes before baking.
—Lynn Albright, Fremont, NE

PREP: 25 min. • **BAKE:** 40 min. + standing
MAKES: 6 servings

- 1 Tbsp. olive oil
- ¾ cup chopped sweet onion
- ¾ cup chopped sweet red pepper
- 4 large eggs, room temperature
- 1 cup heavy whipping cream
- 1 tsp. baking soda
- 1 tsp. hot pepper sauce
- ½ tsp. salt
- 2 cups fresh or frozen corn
- 2 cups crushed cornbread stuffing
- ½ lb. bacon strips, cooked and crumbled
- 1½ cups shredded sharp cheddar cheese, divided

1. Preheat oven to 350°. In a 10-in. cast-iron or other ovenproof skillet, heat oil over medium heat. Add onion and red pepper; cook and stir until crisp-tender, 6-8 minutes. Remove from skillet; set aside. In a large bowl, whisk eggs, cream, baking soda, hot pepper sauce and salt. Stir in the corn, stuffing, bacon, 1 cup cheese and onion mixture. Transfer to skillet.

2. Bake, uncovered, 35 minutes. Sprinkle with the remaining ½ cup cheese. Bake until puffed and golden brown, roughly 5-10 minutes longer. Let pudding stand 10 minutes before serving.

¾ cup: 516 cal., 36g fat (18g sat. fat), 211mg chol., 1117mg sod., 29g carb. (7g sugars, 3g fiber), 20g pro.

Corn Pudding with Bacon & Cheddar

GREEK SPINACH BAKE

Spanakopita is the Greek name for a traditional dish featuring spinach and feta cheese. You can serve my version as a side dish or meatless main dish.
—Sharon Olney, Galt, CA

PREP: 10 min. • **BAKE:** 1 hour
MAKES: 6 servings

- 2 cups 4% cottage cheese
- 1 pkg. (10 oz.) frozen chopped spinach, thawed and squeezed dry
- 8 oz. crumbled feta cheese
- 6 Tbsp. all-purpose flour
- ½ tsp. pepper
- ¼ tsp. salt
- 4 large eggs, lightly beaten

1. Preheat oven to 350°. In a large bowl, combine the cottage cheese, spinach and feta cheese. Stir in the flour, pepper and salt. Add eggs and mix well.

2. Spoon into a greased 9-in. square baking dish. Bake, uncovered, until a thermometer reads 160°, about 1 hour.

1 serving: 262 cal., 13g fat (7g sat. fat), 178mg chol., 838mg sod., 14g carb. (4g sugars, 3g fiber), 21g pro.

Greek Spinach Bake

SLOW-COOKER FRUIT COMPOTE

I use canned goods and my slow cooker to whip up an old-fashioned treat that's loaded with sweet fruits. It makes a cozy dessert or even an easy change-of-pace side dish for large parties.
—Mary Ann Jonns, Midlothian, IL

PREP: 10 min. • **COOK:** 2 hours
MAKES: 18 servings

- 2 cans (29 oz. each) sliced peaches, drained
- 2 cans (29 oz. each) pear halves, drained and sliced
- 1 can (20 oz.) pineapple chunks, drained
- 1 can (15¼ oz.) apricot halves, drained and sliced
- 1 can (21 oz.) cherry pie filling

In a 5-qt. slow cooker, combine the peaches, pears, pineapple and apricots. Top with pie filling. Cover and cook on high for 2 hours or until heated through. Serve with a slotted spoon.

½ cup: 190 cal., 0 fat (0 sat. fat), 0 chol., 18mg sod., 48g carb. (34g sugars, 3g fiber), 1g pro.

Test Kitchen Tip

Get creative with this compote. Feel free to replace any of the canned fruit with a different variety. Top servings with whipped cream, or use it as a colorful topping for vanilla ice cream when it's time for dessert.

Slow-Cooker
Fruit Compote

BREAKFAST SKEWERS

I think these spicy-sweet kabobs are an unexpected offering for a brunch. They're a perfect companion to any kind of egg dish.
—*Bobi Raab, St. Paul, MN*

TAKES: 20 min. • **MAKES:** 5 servings

- 1 pkg. (7 oz.) frozen fully cooked breakfast sausage links, thawed
- 1 can (20 oz.) pineapple chunks, drained
- 10 medium fresh mushrooms
- 2 Tbsp. butter, melted
  Maple syrup

1. Cut sausages in half; on 5 metal or soaked wooden skewers, alternately thread sausages, pineapple and mushrooms. Brush with the butter and syrup.
2. Grill, uncovered, over medium heat, turning and basting with syrup, for about 8 minutes or until sausages are browned and fruit is heated through.
1 skewer: 246 cal., 20g fat (8g sat. fat), 37mg chol., 431mg sod., 13g carb. (12g sugars, 1g fiber), 7g pro.

Savory Apple-Chicken Sausage

SAVORY APPLE-CHICKEN SAUSAGE

These easy, healthy sausages taste incredible, and they make an elegant brunch dish. The recipe is also versatile. It can be doubled or tripled for a crowd, and the sausage freezes well either cooked or raw.
—*Angela Buchanan, Longmont, CO*

TAKES: 25 min. • **MAKES:** 8 patties

- 1 large tart apple, peeled and diced
- 2 tsp. poultry seasoning
- 1 tsp. salt
- ¼ tsp. pepper
- 1 lb. ground chicken

1. In a large bowl, combine the first 4 ingredients. Crumble chicken over the mixture and mix lightly but thoroughly. Shape into eight 3-in. patties.
2. In a large, greased cast-iron or other heavy skillet, cook patties over medium heat until no longer pink, 5-6 minutes on each side. Drain if necessary.
1 sausage patty: 92 cal., 5g fat (1g sat. fat), 38mg chol., 328mg sod., 4g carb. (3g sugars, 1g fiber), 9g pro. **Diabetic exchanges:** 1 medium-fat meat.

CORN POTATO PANCAKES

I love combining different foods to see what I can come up with. In this case, I use leftover mashed potatoes to make these slightly crisp golden brown cakes.
—Carolyn Wilson, Lyndon, KS

TAKES: 20 min. • **MAKES:** about 1 dozen

- 2 cups mashed potatoes (with added milk and butter)
- ¼ cup all-purpose flour
- ¼ cup cream-style corn
- 1 egg, beaten
- 3 Tbsp. finely chopped onion
- 1 tsp. minced fresh parsley
- ½ tsp. salt
- ½ tsp. minced garlic
- ⅛ tsp. pepper
- 3 Tbsp. canola oil, divided

In a large bowl, combine the first 9 ingredients. In a skillet, heat 1 Tbsp. oil; drop four ¼ cupfuls of batter into skillet. Cook for 1-2 minutes on each side or until golden brown. Repeat with remaining oil and batter.

2 pancakes: 180 cal., 11g fat (3g sat. fat), 43mg chol., 461mg sod., 18g carb. (2g sugars, 1g fiber), 3g pro.

Hearty Sausage & Sweet Potatoes

HEARTY SAUSAGE & SWEET POTATOES

Sweet potatoes with sausage and sage make a happy dish. I get recipe requests when I serve this down-home hash.
—Courtney Stultz, Weir, KS

PREP: 20 min. • **COOK:** 25 min.
MAKES: 6 servings

- 2 large sweet potatoes, peeled and cut into ½-in. pieces.
- 2 Tbsp. olive oil, divided
- ½ tsp. salt
- 1 lb. bulk pork sausage
- 1 large tart apple, peeled and chopped
- 1 large carrot, cut into ½-in. pieces
- ½ tsp. dried sage leaves
- ½ tsp. ground cinnamon
- ½ tsp. pepper
- ⅛ tsp. pumpkin pie spice

1. In a large microwave-safe bowl, combine potatoes, 1 Tbsp. oil and salt. Microwave, covered, on high for 6-8 minutes or until tender, stirring every 2 minutes.
2. Meanwhile, in a large skillet, cook sausage over medium heat 6-8 minutes or until no longer pink, breaking into crumbles; remove with a slotted spoon.
3. In same skillet, heat remaining oil over medium-low heat. Add apple and carrot; cook, covered, until carrot is just tender, 5-7 minutes, stirring occasionally. Return sausage to pan.
4. Stir in sweet potatoes and seasonings; cook, covered, until carrot is tender, 10-12 minutes.
Note: This recipe was tested in a 1,100-watt microwave.

1 cup: 409 cal., 25g fat (7g sat. fat), 51mg chol., 793mg sod., 34g carb. (15g sugars, 4g fiber), 12g pro.

51

CANADIAN BACON WITH APPLES

At the holidays, I'd rather spend time with family than in the kitchen, so I like to rely on easy-to-fix recipes like this. No one can resist Canadian bacon and apples coated with a brown sugar glaze.
—Paula Marchesi, Lenhartsville, PA

TAKES: 20 min. • **MAKES:** 6 servings

- ½ cup packed brown sugar
- 1 Tbsp. lemon juice
- ⅛ tsp. pepper
- 1 large red apple, unpeeled
- 1 large green apple, unpeeled
- 1 lb. sliced Canadian bacon

1. In a large cast-iron or other heavy skillet, mix brown sugar, lemon juice and pepper. Cook and stir over medium heat until sugar is dissolved. Cut each apple into 16 wedges; add to the brown sugar mixture. Cook over medium heat until apples are tender, 5-7 minutes, stirring occasionally. Carefully remove the apples to a platter with a slotted spoon; keep warm.

2. Add the bacon to skillet; cook over medium heat, turning once, until heated through, about 3 minutes. Transfer to platter. Pour remaining brown sugar mixture over the apples and bacon.

1 serving: 199 cal., 4g fat (1g sat. fat), 28mg chol., 744mg sod., 30g carb. (27g sugars, 2g fiber), 12g pro.

OVERNIGHT ASPARAGUS STRATA

I've made this tasty egg dish for breakfast, brunch, even dinner as a side dish. This is not your run-of-the-mill strata.
—Lynn Licata, Sylvania, OH

PREP: 15 min. + chilling • **BAKE:** 40 min.
MAKES: 8 servings

- 1 lb. fresh asparagus, trimmed and cut into 1-in. pieces
- 4 English muffins, split and toasted
- 2 cups shredded Colby-Monterey Jack cheese, divided
- 1 cup cubed fully cooked ham
- ½ cup chopped sweet red pepper
- 8 large eggs
- 2 cups 2% milk
- 1 tsp. salt
- 1 tsp. ground mustard
- ¼ tsp. pepper

1. In a large saucepan, bring 8 cups water to a boil. Add asparagus; cook, uncovered, 2-3 minutes or just until crisp-tender. Drain and immediately drop into ice water. Drain and pat dry.

2. Arrange 6 English muffin halves in a greased 13x9-in. baking dish, cut side up. Trim remaining muffin halves to fill spaces. Layer with 1 cup cheese, asparagus, ham and red pepper.

3. In a large bowl, whisk eggs, milk, salt, mustard and pepper. Pour over top. Refrigerate, covered, overnight.

4. Preheat oven to 375°. Remove strata from refrigerator while oven heats. Sprinkle with remaining cheese. Bake, uncovered, until a knife inserted in the center comes out clean, 40-45 minutes. Let baked strata stand for 5 minutes before cutting.

1 piece: 318 cal., 17g fat (9g sat. fat), 255mg chol., 916mg sod., 20g carb. (5g sugars, 1g fiber), 21g pro.

Canadian Bacon with Apples

CORN & ONION SOUFFLE

I changed my dependable cheese souffle recipe to prepare it with fresh corn. If you're "souffle challenged," just remember to hold off on adding the whipped egg whites until just before you slip it in the oven.
—Lily Julow, Lawrenceville, GA

PREP: 25 min. • **BAKE:** 45 min.
MAKES: 10 servings

- 6 large eggs
- 2 Tbsp. plus ½ cup cornmeal, divided
- 2 cups fresh or frozen corn (about 10 oz.), thawed
- 2 cups 2% milk
- 1 Tbsp. sugar
- ¾ cup heavy whipping cream
- ½ cup butter, melted
- 1 Tbsp. canola oil
- 1 cup chopped sweet onion
- 3 oz. cream cheese, softened
- 1 tsp. plus ⅛ tsp. salt, divided
- ½ tsp. freshly ground pepper
- ⅛ tsp. baking soda

1. Separate eggs; let stand at room temperature 30 minutes. Grease a 2½-qt. souffle dish; dust lightly with 2 Tbsp. cornmeal.
2. Preheat oven to 350°. Place the corn, milk and sugar in a blender; cover and process until smooth. Add the cream and melted butter; cover and process 15-30 seconds longer.
3. In a large saucepan, heat oil over medium heat. Add onion; cook and stir 4-6 minutes or until tender. Stir in corn mixture, cream cheese, 1 tsp. salt, pepper and remaining cornmeal until heated through. Remove to a large bowl.
4. Whisk a small amount of the hot mixture into egg yolks; return all to bowl, whisking constantly.
5. In a large bowl, beat egg whites with baking soda and remaining salt on high speed until stiff but not dry. With a rubber spatula, gently stir a quarter of egg whites into corn mixture. Fold in remaining egg whites. Transfer to prepared dish.

6. Bake 45-50 minutes or until the top is deep golden brown and puffed and center appears set. Serve immediately.
1 serving: 325 cal., 25g fat (13g sat. fat), 174mg chol., 463mg sod., 19g carb. (7g sugars, 1g fiber), 8g pro.

ONION-GARLIC HASH BROWNS

Quick to assemble, these slow-cooked hash browns are one of my go-to sides. Stir in a little hot sauce if you like a bit of heat. I top my finished dish with a sprinkling of shredded cheddar cheese.
—Cindi Boger, Ardmore, AL

PREP: 20 min. • **COOK:** 3 hours
MAKES: 12 servings

- ¼ cup butter, cubed
- 1 Tbsp. olive oil
- 1 large red onion, chopped
- 1 small sweet red pepper, chopped
- 1 small green pepper, chopped
- 4 garlic cloves, minced
- 1 pkg. (30 oz.) frozen shredded hash brown potatoes
- ½ tsp. salt
- ½ tsp. pepper
- 3 drops hot pepper sauce, optional
- 2 tsp. minced fresh parsley

1. In a large skillet, heat butter and oil over medium heat. Add onion and peppers. Cook and stir until crisp-tender. Add garlic; cook 1 minute longer. Stir in hash browns, salt, pepper and, if desired, pepper sauce.
2. Transfer mixture to a 5-qt. slow cooker coated with cooking spray. Cook, covered, 3-4 hours or until heated through. Sprinkle with parsley just before serving.
½ cup: 110 cal., 5g fat (3g sat. fat), 10mg chol., 136mg sod., 15g carb. (1g sugars, 1g fiber), 2g pro. **Diabetic exchanges:** 1 starch, 1 fat.

Corn & Onion Souffle

Onion-Garlic
Hash Browns

CORNBREAD PUDDING

I love serving this satisfying corn bread pudding recipe with shrimp or other seafood. I actually adapted the dish from my mom's recipe, and it always reminds me of her.
—Bob Gebhardt, Wausau, WI

PREP: 5 min. • **BAKE:** 40 min.
MAKES: 12 servings

- 2 large eggs
- 1 cup sour cream
- 1 can (15¼ oz.) whole kernel corn, drained
- 1 can (14¾ oz.) cream-style corn
- ½ cup butter, melted
- 1 pkg. (8½ oz.) cornbread/muffin mix
- ¼ tsp. paprika

1. In a large bowl, combine the first 5 ingredients. Stir in cornbread mix just until blended. Pour into a greased 3-qt. baking dish. Sprinkle with paprika.
2. Bake, uncovered, at 350° until a knife inserted in the center comes out clean, 40-45 minutes. Serve warm.
1 serving: 249 cal., 14g fat (8g sat. fat), 73mg chol., 461mg sod., 26g carb. (8g sugars, 1g fiber), 4g pro.

WHY YOU'LL LOVE IT...

"This is everyone's favorite in my family. I don't make any changes. It's perfect. It's a holiday staple but requested all the time in my house!"
—AMBEROSU, TASTEOFHOME.COM

Pressure-Cooker
Hawaiian Breakfast Hash

Cornbread
Pudding

PRESSURE-COOKER HAWAIIAN BREAKFAST HASH

Breakfast is our favorite meal, and we love a wide variety of dishes. This hash brown recipe is full of flavor and possibilities. Top with some eggs or spinach for another twist!
—Courtney Stultz, Weir, KS

PREP: 30 min. • **COOK:** 5 min.
MAKES: 6 servings

- 4   bacon strips, chopped
- 1   Tbsp. canola or coconut oil
- 2   large sweet potatoes (about 1½ lbs.), peeled and cut into ½-in. pieces
- 2   cups cubed fresh pineapple (½-in. cubes)
- ½   tsp. salt
- ¼   tsp. chili powder
- ¼   tsp. paprika
- ¼   tsp. pepper
- ⅛   tsp. ground cinnamon

1. Select saute on a 6-qt. electric pressure cooker; adjust for medium heat. Add bacon; cook and stir until crisp. Carefully remove with a slotted spoon; drain on paper towels. Discard bacon drippings.

2. Add oil to pressure cooker. When oil is hot, brown potatoes in batches. Remove from pressure cooker. Add 1 cup water to pressure cooker. Cook 1 minute, stirring to loosen browned bits from pan. Press cancel. Place steamer basket in pressure cooker.

3. Stir pineapple and seasonings into potatoes; transfer to steamer basket. Lock lid; close pressure-release valve. Adjust to pressure cook on high for 2 minutes. Quick-release pressure. Sprinkle with bacon.

⅔ cup: 194 cal., 5g fat (1g sat. fat), 6mg chol., 309mg sod., 35g carb. (17g sugars, 4g fiber), 4g pro. **Diabetic exchanges:** 2 starch, 1 fat.

Fruity Pull-Apart Bread

FRUITY PULL-APART BREAD

Who doesn't love to start the day with monkey bread? This skillet version is just packed with bright berries and dolloped with irresistibly rich cream cheese. A little fresh basil brings it all together.
—Darla Andrews, Boerne, TX

PREP: 15 min. • **BAKE:** 35 min.
MAKES: 8 servings

- 1 tube (16.3 oz.) large refrigerated flaky honey butter biscuits
- ½ cup packed dark brown sugar
- ½ cup sugar
- ⅓ cup butter, melted
- 1 cup fresh blueberries
- 1 cup chopped fresh strawberries
- 4 oz. cream cheese, softened
- 1 Tbsp. minced fresh basil

1. Preheat oven to 350°. Separate dough into 8 biscuits; cut biscuits into fourths.
2. In a shallow bowl, combine sugars. Dip biscuits in melted butter, then in sugar mixture. Place biscuits in a greased 10¼-in. cast-iron skillet. Top with fresh berries; dollop with cream cheese. Bake until biscuits are golden brown and cooked through, 35-40 minutes. Sprinkle with basil.
1 serving: 383 cal., 20g fat (9g sat. fat), 30mg chol., 641mg sod., 49g carb. (28g sugars, 2g fiber), 5g pro.

APPLE-SAGE SAUSAGE PATTIES

Apple and sausage naturally go together. Add sage, and you've got a standout patty. They're freezer-friendly, so I make them ahead and grab when needed.
—Scarlett Elrod, Newnan, GA

PREP: 35 min. + chilling
COOK: 10 min./batch • **MAKES:** 16 servings

- 1 large apple
- 1 large egg, lightly beaten
- ½ cup chopped fresh parsley
- 3 to 4 Tbsp. minced fresh sage
- 2 garlic cloves, minced
- 1¼ tsp. salt
- ½ tsp. pepper
- ½ tsp. crushed red pepper flakes
- 1¼ lbs. lean ground turkey
- 6 tsp. olive oil, divided

1. Peel and coarsely shred apple; place apple in a colander over a plate. Let stand 15 minutes. Squeeze and blot dry with paper towels.
2. In a large bowl, combine egg, parsley, sage, garlic, seasonings and apple. Add turkey; mix lightly but thoroughly. Shape into sixteen 2-in. patties. Place patties on waxed paper-lined baking sheets. Refrigerate patties, covered, 8 hours or overnight.
3. In a large nonstick skillet, heat 2 tsp. oil over medium heat. In batches, cook patties 3-4 minutes on each side or until golden brown and a thermometer reads 165°, adding more oil as needed.
FREEZE OPTION: Place uncooked patties on waxed paper-lined baking sheets; wrap and freeze until firm. Remove from pans and transfer to a freezer container; return to freezer. To use, cook the frozen patties as directed, increasing time to 4-5 minutes on each side.
1 patty: 79 cal., 5g fat (1g sat. fat), 36mg chol., 211mg sod., 2g carb. (1g sugars, 0 fiber), 8g pro. **Diabetic exchanges:** 1 lean meat, ½ fat.

Apple-Sage
Sausage Patties

GLORIFIED HASH BROWNS

You'll be surprised at how quick and easy it is to put together this dressed-up potato casserole! When a friend made it for a church supper, I had to have the recipe. It's ideal for parties, brunches, potlucks and family reunions.
—Betty Kay Sitzman, Wray, CO

PREP: 10 min. • **BAKE:** 40 min.
MAKES: 10 servings

- 2 cans (10¾ oz. each) condensed cream of celery soup, undiluted
- 2 cartons (8 oz. each) spreadable chive and onion cream cheese
- 1 pkg. (2 lbs.) frozen cubed hash brown potatoes
- 1 cup shredded cheddar cheese

1. In a large microwave-safe bowl, combine the soup and cream cheese. Cover and cook on high for 3-4 minutes or until cream cheese is melted, stirring occasionally. Add the potatoes and stir until coated.
2. Spoon into a greased 13x9-in. baking dish. Bake, uncovered, at 350° until the potatoes are tender, 35-40 minutes. Sprinkle with cheddar cheese. Bake about 3-5 minutes longer or until cheese is melted.
Freeze option: Sprinkle cheddar cheese over the unbaked casserole. Cover and freeze. To use, partially thaw in refrigerator overnight. Remove from refrigerator 30 minutes before baking. Preheat oven to 350°. Bake casserole as directed, increasing time as necessary to heat through and for a thermometer inserted in center to read 165°.
1 serving: 215 cal., 12g fat (8g sat. fat), 35mg chol., 400mg sod., 20g carb. (2g sugars, 1g fiber), 6g pro.

ORANGE-GLAZED BACON

Just when you thought bacon couldn't get tastier, our Test Kitchen created this recipe.
—Taste of Home *Test Kitchen*

PREP: 20 min. • **BAKE:** 25 min.
MAKES: 8 servings

- ¾ cup orange juice
- ¼ cup honey
- 1 Tbsp. Dijon mustard
- ¼ tsp. ground ginger
- ⅛ tsp. pepper
- 1 lb. bacon strips

1. Preheat oven to 350°. In a small saucepan, combine first 5 ingredients. Bring to a boil; cook until the liquid is reduced to ⅓ cup.
2. Place bacon on a rack in an ungreased 15x10x1-in. baking pan. Bake for 10 minutes; drain.
3. Drizzle half of glaze over bacon. Bake for 10 minutes. Turn bacon and drizzle with remaining glaze. Bake until golden brown, 5-10 minutes longer. Place bacon on waxed paper until set. Serve bacon warm.
3 glazed bacon strips: 146 cal., 8g fat (3g sat. fat), 21mg chol., 407mg sod., 12g carb. (11g sugars, 0 fiber), 7g pro.

Orange-Glazed Bacon

Diner Corned Beef Hash

DINER CORNED BEEF HASH

I created my hash to taste like a dish from a northern Arizona restaurant we always loved. We round it out with eggs and toast.
—Denise Chelpka, Phoenix, AZ

PREP: 10 min. • **COOK:** 25 min.
MAKES: 4 servings

- 1¼ lbs. potatoes (about 3 medium), cut into ½-in. cubes
- 3 Tbsp. butter
- ¾ cup finely chopped celery
- ¾ lb. cooked corned beef, cut into ½-in. cubes (about 2½ cups)
- 4 green onions, chopped
- ¼ tsp. pepper
  Dash ground cloves
- 2 Tbsp. minced fresh cilantro

1. Place potatoes in a saucepan; add water to cover. Bring to a boil. Reduce heat; cook, uncovered, just until tender, 6-8 minutes. Drain.
2. In a large nonstick skillet, heat butter over medium-high heat. Add celery; cook and stir until crisp-tender, about 4-6 minutes. Add potatoes; cook until lightly browned, turning occasionally, 6-8 minutes . Stir in the corned beef; cook until heated through, 1-2 minutes. Sprinkle with green onions, pepper and cloves; cook 1-2 minutes longer. Stir in fresh cilantro.
1 cup: 407 cal., 25g fat (11g sat. fat), 106mg chol., 1059mg sod., 27g carb. (2g sugars, 4g fiber), 19g pro.

Test Kitchen Tip
Feel free to add some diced green pepper or stir in a little hot sauce if you like things spicy. You can also top the hash with a handful of shredded cheese shortly before serving.

Amish Apple
Scrapple

AMISH APPLE SCRAPPLE

Just the aroma of this cooking at breakfast takes me back to my days growing up in Pennsylvania. The recipe was a favorite at home and at church breakfasts.
—Marion Lowery, Medford, OR

PREP: 1 hour 20 min. + chilling
COOK: 10 min. • **MAKES:** 8 servings

- ¾ lb. bulk pork sausage
- ½ cup finely chopped onion
- 4 Tbsp. butter, divided
- ½ cup diced apple, unpeeled
- ¾ tsp. dried thyme
- ½ tsp. ground sage
- ¼ tsp. pepper
- 3 cups water, divided
- ¾ cup cornmeal
- 1 tsp. salt
- 2 Tbsp. all-purpose flour
  Maple syrup

1. In a large skillet, cook sausage and onion over medium-high heat until sausage is no longer pink and onion is tender. Remove from skillet; set aside.
2. Discard all but 2 Tbsp. drippings. Add 2 Tbsp. butter, apple, thyme, sage and pepper to drippings; cook over low heat until apple is tender, about 5 minutes. Remove from heat; stir in sausage mixture. Set aside.
3. In a large heavy saucepan, bring 2 cups water to a boil. Combine cornmeal, salt and remaining water; slowly pour into boiling water, stirring constantly. Return to a boil. Reduce heat; simmer, covered, for 1 hour, stirring occasionally. Stir in sausage mixture. Carefully pour into a greased 8x4-in. loaf pan. Refrigerate, covered, for 8 hours or overnight.
4. Slice ½ in. thick. Sprinkle flour over both sides of each slice. In a large skillet, heat remaining butter over medium heat. Add slices; cook until both sides are browned. Serve with syrup.
1 piece: 251 cal., 18g fat (7g sat. fat), 44mg chol., 667mg sod., 16g carb. (1g sugars, 1g fiber), 7g pro.

Spinach Pantry Souffle

SPINACH PANTRY SOUFFLE

We have always loved souffles, but I got tired of slaving over the white sauce. One day I substituted condensed soup for the white sauce, and we all thought it was great. When we started watching our fat intake, I switched to the reduced-fat, reduced-sodium soup, reduced-fat cheese and just two egg yolks, and it turned out amazing!
—Diane Conrad, North Bend, OR

PREP: 35 min. • **BAKE:** 30 min.
MAKES: 6 servings

- 6 large egg whites
- 2 Tbsp. grated Parmesan cheese
- 1 can (10¾ oz.) reduced-fat reduced-sodium condensed cream of mushroom soup, undiluted
- 1 cup shredded reduced-fat Mexican cheese blend
- 1 tsp. ground mustard
- 1 pkg. (10 oz.) frozen chopped spinach, thawed and squeezed dry
- 2 large egg yolks, beaten

1. Let egg whites stand at room temperature for 30 minutes. Coat a 2-qt. souffle dish with cooking spray and lightly sprinkle with Parmesan cheese; set aside.
2. In a small saucepan, combine soup, cheese blend and mustard; cook and stir over medium heat for 5 minutes or until cheese is melted. Transfer to a large bowl; stir in spinach. Stir a small amount of soup mixture into egg yolks; return all to the bowl, stirring constantly.
3. In a small bowl with clean beaters, beat egg whites until stiff peaks form. With a spatula, stir a fourth of the egg whites into spinach mixture until no white streaks remain. Fold in remaining egg whites until combined. Transfer to prepared dish.
4. Bake at 375° until top is puffed and center appears set, for 30-35 minutes. Serve immediately.
1 serving: 140 cal., 8g fat (3g sat. fat), 90mg chol., 453mg sod., 7g carb. (1g sugars, 1g fiber), 12g pro. **Diabetic exchanges:** 2 medium-fat meat, ½ starch.

Apple Maple Pecan
Salad, Page 102

Page 104

Page 92

Leafy Greens, Crispy Slaws & Crunchy Bites

When it's time to round out menus, nothing fills the bill like a salad. Turn here for delicious, quick and easy ideas that complement any entree.

Page 108

Page 94

PERFECT WINTER SALAD

This is my most-requested salad recipe. It is delicious as a main dish with grilled chicken breast or as a side salad. I think it's so good, I sometimes eat it at the end of the meal, instead of dessert!
—DeNae Shewmake, Burnsville, MN

TAKES: 20 min. • **MAKES:** 12 servings

- ¼ cup reduced-fat mayonnaise
- ¼ cup maple syrup
- 3 Tbsp. white wine vinegar
- 2 Tbsp. minced shallot
- 2 tsp. sugar
- ½ cup canola oil
- 2 pkg. (5 oz. each) spring mix salad greens
- 2 medium tart apples, thinly sliced
- 1 cup dried cherries
- 1 cup pecan halves
- ¼ cup thinly sliced red onion

1. In a small bowl, mix the first 5 ingredients; gradually whisk in oil until blended. Refrigerate, covered, until serving.

2. To serve, place remaining ingredients in a large bowl; toss with dressing.

1 cup: 235 cal., 18g fat (1g sat. fat), 2mg chol., 47mg sod., 20g carb. (15g sugars, 2g fiber), 2g pro.

Test Kitchen Tip
For a change of pace, try swapping out the apples with 2 pears or replace the pecans with a cup of walnut halves.

Perfect Winter Salad

BOK CHOY & RADISHES

This is such a great-tasting, good-for-you recipe. With bok choy and radishes, the simple dish truly capitalizes on all the flavors of spring.
—Ann Baker, Texarkana, TX

TAKES: 25 min. • **MAKES:** 8 servings

- 1 head bok choy
- 2 Tbsp. butter
- 1 Tbsp. olive oil
- 12 radishes, thinly sliced
- 1 shallot, sliced
- 1 tsp. lemon-pepper seasoning
- ¾ tsp. salt

1. Cut off and discard root end of bok choy, leaving stalks with leaves. Cut green leaves from stalks and cut the leaves into 1-in. slices; set aside. Cut white stalks into 1-in. pieces.
2. In a large cast-iron or other heavy skillet, cook bok choy stalks in butter and oil until crisp-tender, 3-5 minutes. Add the radishes, shallot, lemon pepper, salt and reserved leaves; cook and stir until heated through, 3 minutes.
0.750 cup: 59 cal., 5g fat (2g sat. fat), 8mg chol., 371mg sod., 3g carb. (2g sugars, 1g fiber), 2g pro. **Diabetic exchanges:** 1 vegetable, 1 fat.

Apple Walnut Slaw

APPLE WALNUT SLAW

After a co-worker shared this recipe with me, it became a family favorite of my own. Apples, walnuts and raisins are a fun way to dress up coleslaw.
—Joan Hallford, North Richland Hills, TX

TAKES: 15 min. • **MAKES:** 12 servings

- ¾ cup mayonnaise
- ¾ cup buttermilk
- 4 to 5 Tbsp. sugar
- 4½ tsp. lemon juice
- ¾ tsp. salt
- ¼ to ½ tsp. pepper
- 6 cups shredded cabbage (about 1 small head)
- 1½ cups shredded carrots (2-3 medium carrots)
- ⅓ cup finely chopped red onion
- 1 cup coarsely chopped walnuts, toasted
- ¾ cup raisins
- 2 medium apples, chopped

1. Whisk together first 6 ingredients. In a large bowl, combine vegetables, walnuts and raisins; toss with dressing. Fold in apples.
2. Refrigerate, covered, until serving.
Note: To toast nuts, bake in a shallow pan in a 350° oven for 5-10 minutes or cook in a skillet over low heat until lightly browned, stirring occasionally.
¾ cup: 233 cal., 17g fat (2g sat. fat), 2mg chol., 264mg sod., 21g carb. (14g sugars, 3g fiber), 3g pro.

CILANTRO BLUE CHEESE SLAW

Serve this slaw as a side dish to any meal, or use it to top your favorite fish taco recipe instead of lettuce and the usual toppings. It may seem like a lot of ingredients, but the slaw comes together pretty quickly.
—Christi Dalton, Hartsville, TN

TAKES: 25 min. • **MAKES:** 8 servings

- 8 cups shredded cabbage
- 1 small red onion, halved and thinly sliced
- ⅓ cup minced fresh cilantro
- 1 jalapeno pepper, seeded and minced
- ¼ cup crumbled blue cheese
- ¼ cup fat-free mayonnaise
- ¼ cup reduced-fat sour cream
- 2 Tbsp. rice vinegar
- 2 Tbsp. lime juice
- 1 garlic clove, minced
- 1 tsp. sugar
- 1 tsp. grated lime zest
- ¾ tsp. salt
- ½ tsp. coarsely ground pepper

In a large bowl, combine the cabbage, onion, cilantro and jalapeno. In a small bowl, combine remaining ingredients; pour over salad and toss to coat.
Note: Wear disposable gloves when cutting hot peppers; the oils can burn skin. Avoid touching your face.
¾ cup: 63 cal., 2g fat (1g sat. fat), 6mg chol., 362mg sod., 9g carb. (5g sugars, 3g fiber), 3g pro. **Diabetic exchanges:** 1 vegetable, ½ fat.

Cilantro Blue
Cheese Slaw

Bacon &
Broccoli Salad

BACON & BROCCOLI SALAD

You'll want to serve this family-friendly side dish year-round. The broccoli gets a big-time flavor boost from bacon, toasted pecans, dried berries and a mayo dressing.
—Cindi Read, Hendersonville, TN

TAKES: 30 min. • **MAKES:** 16 servings

- 3 bunches broccoli, cut into florets (about 10 cups)
- 1 lb. bacon strips, cooked and crumbled
- 1 cup chopped pecans, toasted
- 1 cup dried blueberries
- 1 cup dried cherries
- ¼ cup finely chopped red onion

DRESSING
- 1 cup mayonnaise
- ¼ cup sugar
- ¼ cup cider vinegar

In a large bowl, combine the first 6 ingredients. For dressing, in a small bowl, whisk mayonnaise, sugar and vinegar. Pour over broccoli mixture; toss to coat.
¾ cup: 300 cal., 19g fat (3g sat. fat), 11mg chol., 290mg sod., 26g carb. (15g sugars, 5g fiber), 8g pro.

Ham & Swiss Layered Salad

HONEY-MUSTARD BRUSSELS SPROUTS SALAD

Even if you dislike Brussels sprouts salad, you will love this dish. The dressing is truly tasty, and it pairs so nicely with the apples, grapes and walnuts. You can also add whatever cheese, nuts or fruit you prefer.
—Sheila Sturrock, Coldwater, ON

TAKES: 25 min. • **MAKES:** 10 servings

- 1 lb. fresh Brussels sprouts, trimmed and shredded
- 2 medium tart apples, chopped
- 1 medium red onion, chopped
- 1 small sweet orange pepper, chopped
- ½ cup chopped walnuts
- ½ cup green grapes, sliced
- ½ cup shredded cheddar cheese
- 3 bacon strips, cooked and crumbled
- ¼ cup olive oil
- 2 Tbsp. red wine vinegar
- 2 Tbsp. honey mustard
- 1 garlic clove, minced
- ¼ tsp. salt
- ¼ tsp. pepper

In a large bowl, combine the first 8 ingredients. In a small bowl, whisk remaining ingredients; pour over salad. Toss to coat.

1 cup: 170 cal., 12g fat (3g sat. fat), 8mg chol., 177mg sod., 13g carb. (7g sugars, 3g fiber), 5g pro. **Diabetic exchanges:** 2 fat, 1 starch.

WHY YOU'LL LOVE IT...

"This is my new favorite salad and side dish! It's the perfect combination of sweet, savory, crunchy and tangy. I didn't have honey mustard on hand for the dressing, so I used equal amounts of Dijon mustard and honey, and it was delicious."
—CAROLEIGHFULCHER, TASTEOFHOME.COM

HAM & SWISS LAYERED SALAD

Layered salads rank among the classics in the potluck hall of fame. In this one, the combination of ham, cheese, egg and bacon is like a deconstructed sandwich, making it hearty enough for a main course.
—Stacy Huggins, Valley Center, CA

TAKES: 30 min. • **MAKES:** 12 servings

- 2 cups mayonnaise
- 1 cup sour cream
- ½ tsp. sugar
- ⅛ tsp. salt
- ⅛ tsp. pepper
- 8 cups fresh baby spinach (about 6 oz.)
- 6 hard-boiled large eggs, chopped
- ½ lb. sliced fully cooked ham, cut into strips
- 4 cups torn iceberg lettuce (about ½ head)
- 2½ cups frozen petite peas (about 10 oz.), thawed, optional
- 1 small red onion, halved and thinly sliced
- 8 oz. sliced Swiss cheese, cut into strips
- ½ lb. bacon strips, cooked and crumbled

For dressing, mix first 5 ingredients. In a 3-qt. or larger glass bowl, layer spinach, eggs, ham, lettuce, peas if desired and onion. Spread with the dressing. Sprinkle with the cheese and bacon. Refrigerate, covered, until serving.

1 cup: 501 cal., 43g fat (12g sat. fat), 137mg chol., 665mg sod., 11g carb. (5g sugars, 3g fiber), 19g pro.

Honey-Mustard Brussels
Sprouts Salad

TURNIP GREENS SALAD

This is a recipe that was created using items from my garden. Because most people cook turnip greens, I wanted to present those same greens in a way that would retain the nutrient content. This salad also can have various kinds of meat added for taste. I have used cooked shrimp, chicken or beef.
—James McCarroll, Murfreesboro, TN

TAKES: 30 min. • **MAKES:** 8 servings

- 1 **bunch fresh turnip greens (about 10 oz.)**
- 5 **oz. fresh baby spinach (about 8 cups)**
- 1 **medium cucumber, halved and thinly sliced**
- 1 **cup cherry tomatoes, halved**
- ¾ **cup dried cranberries**
- ½ **medium red onion, thinly sliced**
- ⅓ **cup crumbled feta cheese**
- 1 **garlic clove**
- ½ **tsp. kosher salt**
- ⅓ **cup extra virgin olive oil**
- 2 **Tbsp. sherry vinegar**
- 1 **tsp. Dijon mustard**
- ¼ **tsp. pepper**
- ⅛ **tsp. cayenne pepper**

1. Trim and discard root end of turnip greens. Coarsely chop leaves and cut stalks into 1-in. pieces. Place in a large bowl. Add spinach, cucumber, tomatoes, cranberries, red onion and feta.
2. Place garlic on a cutting board; sprinkle with salt. Using the flat side of a knife, mash garlic. Continue to mash until it reaches a paste consistency. Transfer to a small bowl. Whisk in oil, vinegar, mustard, pepper and cayenne until blended. Drizzle over salad; toss to coat. Serve immediately.
1¼ cups: 161 cal., 10g fat (2g sat. fat), 3mg chol., 203mg sod., 17g carb. (12g sugars, 3g fiber), 3g pro. **Diabetic exchanges:** 2 vegetable, 2 fat, ½ starch.

Turnip
Greens Salad

SUMMER SALAD BY THE LAKE

I came up with this recipe to show my true appreciation to all the teachers at my son's school. The dish had to be as special as the teachers, who always go the extra mile for their students. I think this salad did the trick! It's hearty, earthy, sweet and loaded with nothing but good stuff.
—Ramya Ramamurthy, Fremont, CA

PREP: 35 min. • **COOK:** 15 min.
MAKES: 10 servings

15 garlic cloves, peeled and halved lengthwise
2 medium sweet peppers, sliced
2 Tbsp. olive oil
½ tsp. salt
½ tsp. pepper
SALAD
2½ cups water
1 Tbsp. olive oil
1½ tsp. salt
1 cup uncooked pearl (Israeli) couscous
½ cup red quinoa, rinsed
2 large tomatoes, cut into 1-in. pieces
2 cups fresh arugula or baby spinach
1 cup cubed fresh pineapple
½ cup fresh shelled peas or frozen peas
½ cup crumbled feta cheese
½ cup sunflower kernels, toasted
¼ cup minced fresh parsley
DRESSING
¼ cup olive oil
3 Tbsp. balsamic vinegar
2 tsp. honey
1 tsp. grated lemon zest
½ tsp. salt
½ tsp. pepper

1. Preheat oven to 425°. Toss together garlic, sweet peppers, oil, salt and pepper; transfer to a parchment-lined 15x10x1-in. baking pan. Bake until dark golden brown, about 15 minutes. Transfer to a large bowl.
2. Meanwhile, in a small saucepan, bring water, oil and salt to a boil. Stir in couscous and quinoa. Reduce heat; simmer, covered, 15 minutes or until liquid is absorbed. Remove from heat; let stand, covered, 5 minutes.
3. Transfer the couscous and quinoa to the bowl with roasted pepper mixture. Stir in the remaining salad ingredients. In a small bowl, whisk dressing ingredients until blended. Pour over salad; gently toss to coat.
¾ cup: 269 cal., 15g fat (2g sat. fat), 3mg chol., 700mg sod., 29g carb. (7g sugars, 3g fiber), 7g pro. **Diabetic exchanges:** 2 starch, 2 fat.

Summer Salad
by the Lake

Test Kitchen Tip

This is a versatile salad for which you can use any summer veggies and fruits. Try peaches or nectarines instead of pineapple; add cherry tomatoes instead of heirloom; or use spinach instead of arugula. The possibilities are endless. In fall and winter, consider root veggies such as grilled or roasted carrots, broccoli or even squash.

**Hearty Spinach Salad
with Hot Bacon Dressing**

HEARTY SPINACH SALAD WITH HOT BACON DRESSING

This warm and hearty spinach and bacon salad offers comfort at any meal. The glossy dressing features a hint of celery seed for a special touch.
—Taste of Home *Test Kitchen*

TAKES: 30 min. • **MAKES:** 6 servings

- 8 cups torn fresh spinach
- 3 bacon strips, diced
- ½ cup chopped red onion
- 2 Tbsp. brown sugar
- 2 Tbsp. cider vinegar
- ¼ tsp. salt
- ¼ tsp. ground mustard
- ⅛ tsp. celery seed
- ⅛ tsp. pepper
- 1 tsp. cornstarch
- ⅓ cup cold water

1. Place spinach in a large salad bowl. In a small nonstick skillet, cook bacon over medium heat until crisp. Using a slotted spoon, remove to paper towels to drain.
2. In the drippings, saute onion until tender. Stir in the brown sugar, vinegar, salt, mustard, celery seed and pepper. Combine the cornstarch and water until smooth; slowly stir into skillet. Bring to a boil; cook and stir until thickened, about 1-2 minutes.
3. Remove from the heat; pour over spinach and toss to coat. Sprinkle with bacon. Serve immediately.
¾ cup: 97 cal., 7g fat (2g sat. fat), 8mg chol., 215mg sod., 8g carb. (6g sugars, 1g fiber), 2g pro. **Diabetic exchanges:** 1½ fat, 1 vegetable.

Tangy Cilantro Lime Confetti Salad

TANGY CILANTRO LIME CONFETTI SALAD

I love standout salads that burst with flavor—the kind that make you feel as if you're splurging without having to eat that piece of chocolate cake. This is one of my very favorites, and everyone I serve it to loves it as well.
—Jasey McBurnett, Rock Springs, WY

TAKES: 25 min. • **MAKES:** 6 servings

- 2 medium sweet orange peppers, chopped
- 2 medium ripe avocados, peeled and cubed
- 1 container (10½ oz.) cherry tomatoes, halved
- 1 cup fresh or frozen corn, thawed
- ½ medium red onion, finely chopped

DRESSING
- ¼ cup seasoned rice vinegar
- 3 Tbsp. lime juice
- 2 Tbsp. olive oil
- ½ cup fresh cilantro leaves
- 2 garlic cloves, halved
- 2 tsp. sugar
- ½ tsp. kosher salt
- ¼ tsp. pepper

Place the first 5 ingredients in a large bowl. Place dressing ingredients in a blender; cover and process until creamy and light in color. Pour over vegetable mixture; toss to coat. Refrigerate, covered, up to 3 hours.
1 cup: 187 cal., 12g fat (2g sat. fat), 0 chol., 526mg sod., 20g carb. (10g sugars, 5g fiber), 3g pro. **Diabetic exchanges:** 2 vegetable, 2 fat, ½ starch.

MEXICAN LAYERED SALAD

I like to prepare this dish in advance, adding the avocado, cheese and chips just before serving. I think it's a different twist on a layered salad.
—Joan Hallford, North Richland Hills, TX

TAKES: 20 min. • **MAKES:** 10 servings

- 4 cups torn romaine
- 1 medium red onion, thinly sliced, optional
- 1 large cucumber, halved and sliced
- 3 medium tomatoes, chopped
- 1 each large green and sweet red pepper, chopped or sliced
- 2 medium ripe avocados, peeled and sliced or cut into ½-in. pieces
- 1½ cups mayonnaise
- ¼ cup canned chopped green chiles
- 2 tsp. chili powder
- ½ tsp. onion powder
- ¼ tsp. salt
- ¼ tsp. garlic powder
- 1 cup crushed tortilla chips
- ½ cup shredded cheddar cheese

In a 2-qt. trifle bowl or glass serving bowl, layer fresh vegetables and avocado. In a small bowl, mix the mayonnaise, chiles and seasonings; spread over top. Sprinkle with chips and cheese.

¾ cup: 371 cal., 35g fat (6g sat. fat), 18mg chol., 325mg sod., 13g carb. (3g sugars, 5g fiber), 4g pro.

Dad's Greek Salad

DAD'S GREEK SALAD

The heart of a Greek salad is in the olives, feta and fresh veggies. Dress it with oil and vinegar, then add more olives and cheese.
—Arge Salvatori, Waldwick, NJ

TAKES: 20 min. • **MAKES:** 8 servings

- 4 large tomatoes, seeded and coarsely chopped
- 2½ cups thinly sliced English cucumbers
- 1 small red onion, halved and thinly sliced
- ¼ cup olive oil
- 3 Tbsp. red wine vinegar
- ¼ tsp. salt
- ⅛ tsp. pepper
- ¼ tsp. dried oregano, optional
- ¾ cup pitted Greek olives
- ¾ cup crumbled feta cheese

Place tomatoes, cucumbers and onion in a large bowl. In a small bowl, whisk oil, vinegar, salt and pepper and, if desired, oregano until blended. Drizzle over salad; toss to coat. Top with olives and cheese.

¾ cup: 148 cal., 12g fat (2g sat. fat), 6mg chol., 389mg sod., 7g carb. (3g sugars, 2g fiber), 3g pro. **Diabetic exchanges:** 2 vegetable, 2 fat.

CRUNCHY RAMEN SALAD

For potlucks and picnics, this ramen noodle salad is a knockout. I tote the veggies in a bowl, dressing in a jar and noodles in a bag. Then I shake them up together when it is time to eat.
—LJ Porter, Bauxite, AR

TAKES: 25 min. • **MAKES:** 16 servings

- 1 Tbsp. plus ½ cup olive oil, divided
- ½ cup slivered almonds
- ½ cup sunflower kernels
- 2 pkg. (14 oz. each) coleslaw mix
- 12 green onions, chopped (about 1½ cups)
- 1 medium sweet red pepper, chopped
- ⅓ cup cider vinegar
- ¼ cup sugar
- ⅛ tsp. pepper
- 2 pkg. (3 oz. each) chicken ramen noodles

1. In a large skillet, heat 1 Tbsp. oil over medium heat. Add the almonds and sunflower kernels; cook until toasted, about 4 minutes. Cool.

2. In a large bowl, combine coleslaw mix, onions and red pepper. In a small bowl, whisk vinegar, sugar, pepper, contents of ramen seasoning packets and remaining oil. Pour over salad; toss to coat. Refrigerate until serving. Break noodles into small pieces. Just before serving, stir in noodles, almonds and sunflower kernels.

¾ cup: 189 cal., 13g fat (2g sat. fat), 0 chol., 250mg sod., 16g carb. (6g sugars, 3g fiber), 4g pro.

Did You Know?

The term coleslaw is derived from the Dutch word koolsla, literally translated as cabbage salad.
The term has evolved to refer to many types of crunchy, shredded-vegetable salads that hold up well after being dressed.

Crunchy Ramen Salad

HONEY-ORANGE BROCCOLI SLAW

When you need coleslaw quickly, here's a great choice. Hints of honey and citrus make it feel special.
—Debbie Cassar, Rockford, MI

TAKES: 15 min. • **MAKES:** 6 servings

- 1 pkg. (12 oz.) broccoli coleslaw mix
- ⅓ cup sliced almonds
- ⅓ cup raisins
- 2 to 3 Tbsp. honey
- 2 Tbsp. olive oil
- 2 Tbsp. orange juice
- 4 tsp. grated orange zest
- ¼ tsp. salt

In a large bowl, combine the coleslaw mix, almonds and raisins. In a small bowl, whisk the remaining ingredients. Pour over salad; toss to coat.

⅔ cup: 136 cal., 7g fat (1g sat. fat), 0 chol., 103mg sod., 18g carb. (13g sugars, 3g fiber), 3g pro. **Diabetic exchanges:** 1½ fat, 1 starch.

Mom's Chopped Coleslaw

RAINBOW VEGGIE SALAD

Every salad should be colorful and crunchy like this one with its bright tomatoes, carrots, peppers and sassy spring mix. Toss with your best dressing.
—Liz Bellville, Tonasket, WA

PREP: 25 min. • **MAKES:** 8 servings

- ½ English cucumber, cut lengthwise in half and sliced
- 2 medium carrots, thinly sliced
- 1 cup each red and yellow cherry tomatoes, halved
- ¾ cup pitted ripe olives, halved
- 1 celery rib, thinly sliced
- ¼ cup each chopped sweet yellow, orange and red pepper
- ¼ cup thinly sliced red onion
- ⅛ tsp. garlic salt
  Dash coarsely ground pepper
- 1 pkg. (5 oz.) spring mix salad greens
- ⅔ cup reduced-fat buttermilk ranch salad dressing

1. Place cucumber, carrots, tomatoes, olives, celery, sweet peppers, onion, garlic salt and pepper in a large bowl; toss to combine.
2. Just before serving, add the salad greens. Drizzle with dressing and toss gently to combine.
1 cup: 64 cal., 3g fat (1g sat. fat), 0 chol., 232mg sod., 7g carb. (3g sugars, 2g fiber), 2g pro. **Diabetic exchanges:** 1 vegetable, ½ fat.

MOM'S CHOPPED COLESLAW

For our Friday fish dinners, my mother treated us to her homemade coleslaw on the side. That creamy, tangy flavor is still a family tradition.
—Cynthia McDowell, Banning, CA

TAKES: 20 min. • **MAKES:** 6 servings

- ½ medium head cabbage (about 1¼ lbs.)
- ½ cup finely chopped celery
- ½ cup finely chopped sweet red or green pepper
- ⅓ cup finely chopped sweet onion

DRESSING
- ½ cup mayonnaise
- ¼ cup sugar
- ¼ cup 2% milk
- ¼ cup buttermilk
- 2 tsp. white vinegar
- ¼ tsp. hot pepper sauce
  Dash pepper

1. Cut the cabbage into 1½- to 2-in. pieces. Place half of the cabbage in a food processor; pulse until chopped. Transfer chopped cabbage to a large bowl; repeat with remaining cabbage.
2. Add remaining vegetables to cabbage. In a small bowl, whisk dressing ingredients until blended. Pour over coleslaw and toss to coat. Refrigerate until serving.
¾ cup: 203 cal., 15g fat (2g sat. fat), 8mg chol., 147mg sod., 16g carb. (13g sugars, 2g fiber), 2g pro.

Rainbow
Veggie Salad

APPLE MAPLE PECAN SALAD

A well-made salad has good taste and pleasing crunch. With cabbage, apples and pecans, this one gets high marks in both with extra points for a light springy color.
—Emily Tyra, Lake Ann, MI

PREP: 15 min. + standing
MAKES: 12 servings

- ¼ cup lemon juice
- ¼ cup canola oil
- ¼ cup maple syrup
- 1½ tsp. Dijon mustard
- ½ tsp. coarsely ground pepper
- 4 cups shredded cabbage
- 3 large Granny Smith apples, julienned
- ½ cup crumbled Gorgonzola cheese
- 1 cup chopped pecans, toasted

Whisk the first 5 ingredients until blended. Combine cabbage, apples and Gorgonzola; toss with dressing to coat. Let stand 30 minutes before serving. Sprinkle with pecans.

Note: To toast nuts, bake in a shallow pan in a 350° oven for 5-10 minutes or cook in a skillet over low heat until lightly browned, stirring occasionally.

¾ cup: 169 cal., 13g fat (2g sat. fat), 4mg chol., 84mg sod., 14g carb. (9g sugars, 3g fiber), 2g pro. **Diabetic exchanges:** 2½ fat, 1 starch.

Apple Maple
Pecan Salad

PICNIC SWEET POTATO SALAD

A homemade vinaigrette coats this colorful salad chock-full of sweet potato cubes. It's ideal for warm-weather picnics and patio parties, but my family loves it year-round!
—Mary Leverette, Columbia, SC

TAKES: 30 min.
MAKES: 13 servings (¾ cup each)

- 4 medium sweet potatoes, peeled and cubed
- 3 medium apples, chopped
- 6 bacon strips, cooked and crumbled
- ¼ cup chopped onion
- 3 Tbsp. minced fresh parsley
- ½ tsp. salt
- ¼ tsp. pepper
- ⅔ cup canola oil
- 2 Tbsp. red wine vinegar

1. Place sweet potatoes in a Dutch oven and cover with water. Bring to a boil. Reduce heat; cover and cook for 10-15 minutes or just until tender. Drain.
2. Transfer to a large bowl; cool to room temperature. Add the apples, bacon, onion, parsley, salt and pepper to the potatoes. In a small bowl, whisk oil and vinegar. Pour over salad; toss gently to coat. Chill until serving.

¾ cup: 169 cal., 12g fat (2g sat. fat), 3mg chol., 163mg sod., 13g carb. (7g sugars, 2g fiber), 2g pro. **Diabetic exchanges:** 2 fat, 1 starch.

RIBBON SALAD WITH ORANGE VINAIGRETTE

Zucchini, cucumbers and carrots are peeled into ribbons for this citrusy salad. We like to serve it for parties and special occasions.
—Nancy Heishman, Las Vegas, NV

TAKES: 30 min. • **MAKES:** 8 servings

- 1 medium zucchini
- 1 medium cucumber
- 1 medium carrot
- 3 medium oranges

Ribbon Salad with Orange Vinaigrette

- 3 cups fresh baby spinach
- 4 green onions, finely chopped
- ½ cup chopped walnuts
- ½ tsp. salt
- ½ tsp. pepper
- ½ cup golden raisins, optional

VINAIGRETTE
- ¼ cup olive oil
- 4 tsp. white wine vinegar
- 1 Tbsp. finely chopped green onion
- 2 tsp. honey
- ¼ tsp. salt
- ¼ tsp. pepper

1. Using a vegetable peeler, shave zucchini, cucumber and carrot lengthwise into very thin strips.
2. Finely grate enough zest from oranges to measure 2 Tbsp.. Cut 1 orange crosswise in half; squeeze juice from orange to measure ½ cup. Reserve zest and juice for vinaigrette. Cut a thin slice from the top and bottom of remaining oranges; stand oranges upright on a cutting board. With a knife, cut off peel and outer membrane from orange. Cut along the membrane of each segment to remove fruit.
3. In a large bowl, combine the spinach, orange sections, green onions, walnuts, salt, pepper and, if desired, raisins. Add the vegetable ribbons; gently toss to combine. In a small bowl, combine vinaigrette ingredients. Add reserved orange zest and juice; whisk until blended. Drizzle half of the vinaigrette over salad; toss to coat. Serve with remaining vinaigrette.

1½ cups: 162 cal., 12g fat (1g sat. fat), 0 chol., 240mg sod., 14g carb. (9g sugars, 2g fiber), 3g pro. **Diabetic exchanges:** 2 fat, 1 vegetable, ½ starch.

Red, White & Blue
Summer Salad

RED, WHITE & BLUE SUMMER SALAD

Caprese and fresh fruit always remind me of summer. In this salad, I combine traditional Caprese flavors with summer blueberries and peaches. I also add a little prosciutto for saltiness, creating a balanced, flavor-packed side dish.
—Emily Falke, Santa Barbara, CA

TAKES: 25 min. • **MAKES:** 12 servings

- ⅔ cup extra virgin olive oil
- ½ cup julienned fresh basil
- ⅓ cup white balsamic vinegar
- ¼ cup julienned fresh mint leaves
- 2 garlic cloves, minced
- 2 tsp. Dijon mustard
- 1 tsp. sea salt
- 1 tsp. sugar
- 1 tsp. pepper
- 2 cups cherry tomatoes
- 8 cups fresh arugula
- 1 carton (8 oz.) fresh mozzarella cheese pearls, drained
- 2 medium peaches, sliced
- 2 cups fresh blueberries
- 6 oz. thinly sliced prosciutto, julienned
  Additional mint leaves

1. In a small bowl, whisk together the first 9 ingredients. Add tomatoes; let stand while preparing salad.
2. In a large bowl, combine arugula, mozzarella, peach slices, blueberries and prosciutto. Pour tomato mixture over the top; toss to coat. Garnish with additional mint leaves. Serve immediately.
1 cup: 233 cal., 18g fat (5g sat. fat), 27mg chol., 486mg sod., 10g carb. (8g sugars, 2g fiber), 8g pro.

Test Kitchen Tip
White balsamic vinegar adds flavor and keeps colors bright in this sweet-salty salad.

Bok Choy Salad

BOK CHOY SALAD

Depending on what I have in the kitchen at home, I sometimes use only the sunflower kernels or almonds in this salad. The recipe makes a lot, perfect for cookouts or reunions.
—Stephanie Marchese, Whitefish Bay, WI

TAKES: 25 min. • **MAKES:** 10 servings

- 1 head bok choy, finely chopped
- 2 bunches green onions, thinly sliced
- 2 pkg. (3 oz. each) ramen noodles, broken
- ¼ cup slivered almonds
- 2 Tbsp. sunflower kernels
- ¼ cup butter
DRESSING
- ⅓ to ½ cup sugar
- ½ cup canola oil
- 2 Tbsp. cider vinegar
- 1 Tbsp. soy sauce

1. In a large bowl, combine bok choy and green onions. Save seasoning packet from ramen noodles for another use. In a large skillet, saute the noodles, almonds and sunflower kernels in butter until browned, about 7 minutes. Remove from the heat; cool to room temperature. Add to bok choy mixture.
2. In a jar with a tight-fitting lid, combine the dressing ingredients; shake well. Just before serving, drizzle over salad and toss to coat.
¾ cup: 240 cal., 19g fat (5g sat. fat), 12mg chol., 386mg sod., 16g carb. (8g sugars, 2g fiber), 4g pro.

Emily's Honey
Lime Coleslaw

EMILY'S HONEY LIME COLESLAW

Here's a refreshing take on slaw with a honey-lime vinaigrette rather than the traditional mayo. It's a great take-along for all those summer picnics.
—Emily Tyra, Lake Ann, MI

PREP: 20 min. + chilling
MAKES: 8 servings

- 1½ tsp. grated lime zest
- ¼ cup lime juice
- 2 Tbsp. honey
- 1 garlic clove, minced
- ½ tsp. salt
- ¼ tsp. pepper
- ¼ tsp. crushed red pepper flakes
- 3 Tbsp. canola oil
- 1 small head red cabbage (about ¾ lb.), shredded
- 1 cup shredded carrots (about 2 medium carrots)
- 2 green onions, thinly sliced
- ½ cup fresh cilantro leaves

Whisk together the first 7 ingredients until smooth. Gradually whisk in oil until blended. Combine the cabbage, carrots and green onions; toss with lime mixture to lightly coat. Refrigerate, covered, 2 hours. Sprinkle with cilantro.
½ cup: 86 cal., 5g fat (0 sat. fat), 0 chol., 170mg sod., 10g carb. (7g sugars, 2g fiber), 1g pro. **Diabetic exchanges:** 1 vegetable, 1 fat.

SPINACH & BACON SALAD WITH PEACHES

Peaches and bacon? Oh, yeah. I made this family favorite for a big summer party. It was so easy to prep the parts separately, then toss it all together right before chow time.
—Megan Riofski, Frankfort, IL

TAKES: 25 min.
MAKES: 8 servings (1½ cups dressing)

- 1 cup olive oil
- ⅓ cup cider vinegar
- ¼ cup sugar
- 1 tsp. celery seed
- 1 tsp. ground mustard
- ½ tsp. salt

SALAD

- 6 cups fresh baby spinach (about 6 oz.)
- 2 medium peaches, sliced
- 1¾ cups sliced fresh mushrooms
- 3 large hard-boiled large eggs, halved and sliced
- ½ lb. bacon strips, cooked and crumbled
- 1 small red onion, halved and thinly sliced
- ¼ cup sliced almonds, toasted
  Grated Parmesan cheese

Place the first 6 ingredients in a blender; cover and process until blended. In a large bowl, combine spinach, peaches, mushrooms, eggs, bacon, onion and almonds. Serve with the dressing and cheese.

Note: To toast nuts, bake in a shallow pan in a 350° oven for 5-10 minutes or cook in a skillet over low heat until lightly browned, stirring occasionally.

1½ cups salad with 3 Tbsp. dressing: 391 cal., 35g fat (6g sat. fat), 80mg chol., 372mg sod., 13g carb. (10g sugars, 2g fiber), 8g pro.

Spinach & Bacon Salad with Peaches

KALE SLAW SPRING SALAD

My parents and in-laws are retired and like to spend winters in Florida. This tangy spring salad brings the snowbirds back for our Easter celebration!
—Jennifer Gilbert, Brighton, MI

TAKES: 25 min. • **MAKES:** 10 servings

- 5 cups chopped fresh kale
- 3 cups torn romaine
- 1 pkg. (14 oz.) coleslaw mix
- 1 medium fennel bulb, thinly sliced
- 1 cup chopped fresh broccoli
- ½ cup shredded red cabbage
- 1 cup crumbled feta cheese
- ¼ cup sesame seeds, toasted
- ⅓ cup extra virgin olive oil
- 3 Tbsp. sesame oil
- 2 Tbsp. honey
- 2 Tbsp. cider vinegar
- 2 Tbsp. lemon juice
- ⅓ cup pureed strawberries
  Sliced fresh strawberries

1. Combine kale and romaine. Add coleslaw mix, fennel, broccoli and red cabbage; sprinkle with feta cheese and sesame seeds. Toss to combine.
2. Stir together olive oil and sesame oil. Whisk in honey, vinegar and lemon juice. Add pureed strawberries. Whisk until combined. Dress salad just before serving; top with sliced strawberries.
1⅓ cups: 192 cal., 15g fat (3g sat. fat), 6mg chol., 140mg sod., 12g carb. (7g sugars, 3g fiber), 4g pro. **Diabetic exchanges:** 3 fat, 1 starch.

THAI SALAD WITH CILANTRO LIME DRESSING

I created this salad to replicate one I tried on a cruise several years ago. It goes over well at potlucks year-round. We love the Thai chile, but if you're not into spice, leave it out.
—Donna Gribbins, Shelbyville, KY

PREP: 35 min. • **MAKES:** 22 servings

- 2 medium limes
- 1 bunch fresh cilantro leaves, stems removed (about 2 cups)
- 1 cup sugar
- 1 Thai red chile pepper, seeded and chopped
- 2 garlic cloves, halved
- ½ tsp. salt
- ½ tsp. pepper
- 2 cups canola oil
- 1 head Chinese or napa cabbage, finely shredded
- 1 small head red cabbage, finely shredded
- 1 English cucumber, chopped
- 1 pkg. (10 oz.) frozen shelled edamame, thawed
- 2 medium ripe avocados, peeled and cubed
- 1 cup shredded carrots
- 3 green onions, sliced

1. Finely grate enough zest from limes to measure 1 Tbsp. Cut limes crosswise in half; squeeze juice from limes. Place zest and juice in a blender; add cilantro, sugar, red chile pepper, garlic, salt and pepper. While processing, gradually add oil in a steady stream.
2. In a large bowl, combine cabbages, cucumber, edamame, avocados, carrots and green onions. Drizzle with dressing; toss to coat.
Note: Wear disposable gloves when cutting hot peppers; the oils can burn skin. Avoid touching your face.
1 cup: 271 cal., 23g fat (2g sat. fat), 0 chol., 69mg sod., 16g carb. (11g sugars, 2g fiber), 2g pro.

BROCCOLI & APPLE SALAD

Even my picky daughter loves this one! My yogurt dressing on crunchy veggie salad makes a cool and creamy side dish.
—Lynn Cluff, Littlefield, AZ

TAKES: 15 min. • **MAKES:** 6 servings

- 3 cups small fresh broccoli florets
- 3 medium apples, chopped
- ½ cup chopped mixed dried fruit
- 1 Tbsp. chopped red onion
- ½ cup reduced-fat plain yogurt
- 4 bacon strips, cooked and crumbled

In a large bowl, combine the broccoli, apples, dried fruit and onion. Add the yogurt; toss to coat. Sprinkle with the bacon. Refrigerate until serving.
1 cup: 124 cal., 3g fat (1g sat. fat), 7mg chol., 134mg sod., 22g carb. (17g sugars, 3g fiber), 4g pro. **Diabetic exchanges:** 1½ starch, ½ fat.

**Thai Salad with
Cilantro Lime Dressing**

YUMMY CORN CHIP SALAD

Corn chips give a special crunch and an unexpected flavor to this potluck favorite. Bacon adds a hint of smokiness, while the cranberries bring a touch of sweetness. It's the perfect picnic companion!
—Nora Friesen, Aberdeen, MS

TAKES: 25 min. • **MAKES:** 12 servings

- ¾ cup canola oil
- ¼ cup cider vinegar
- ¼ cup mayonnaise
- 2 Tbsp. yellow mustard
- ½ tsp. salt
- ¾ cup sugar
- ½ small onion
- ¾ tsp. poppy seeds

SALAD

- 2 bunches leaf lettuce, chopped (about 20 cups)
- 1 pkg. (9¼ oz.) corn chips
- 8 bacon strips, cooked and crumbled
- 1 cup shredded part-skim mozzarella cheese
- 1 cup dried cranberries

1. For dressing, place first 7 ingredients in a blender. Cover; process until smooth. Stir in poppy seeds.
2. Place salad ingredients in a large bowl; toss with dressing. Serve immediately.
1⅓ cups: 436 cal., 30g fat (4g sat. fat), 12mg chol., 456mg sod., 38g carb. (24g sugars, 2g fiber), 7g pro.

Summertime Tomato Salad

SUMMERTIME TOMATO SALAD

My crazy good salad has cherry tomatoes, squash and blueberries together in one bowl. Then I layer on the flavor with fresh corn, red onion and mint.
—Thomas Faglon, Somerset, NJ

PREP: 25 min. + chilling
MAKES: 12 servings

- 4 medium ears sweet corn, husked
- 2 lbs. cherry tomatoes (about 6 cups), halved
- 1 small yellow summer squash, halved lengthwise and sliced
- 1 cup fresh blueberries
- 1 small red onion, halved and thinly sliced
- ¼ cup olive oil
- 2 Tbsp. lemon juice
- 1 Tbsp. minced fresh mint
- ½ tsp. salt
- ½ tsp. freshly ground pepper

1. In a 6-qt. stockpot, bring 8 cups water to a boil. Add corn; cook, uncovered, until crisp-tender, 2-4 minutes. Remove corn and immediately drop into ice water to cool; drain well.
2. Cut corn from cobs and place in a bowl. Add remaining ingredients; toss to combine. Refrigerate, covered, until cold, about 30 minutes.
¾ cup: 95 cal., 5g fat (1g sat. fat), 0 chol., 108mg sod., 12g carb. (6g sugars, 2g fiber), 2g pro. **Diabetic exchanges:** 1 vegetable, 1 fat, ½ starch.

GRILLED CHICKEN RAMEN SALAD

This is pretty much a complete meal in one bowl, and when it goes on the table, everyone says, "Yeah!"
—Karen Carlson, San Luis Obispo, CA

TAKES: 30 min. • **MAKES:** 8 servings

- 2 Tbsp. canola oil
- 2 pkg. (3 oz. each) ramen noodles, crumbled
- ⅔ cup canola oil
- 2 tsp. sesame oil
- ⅓ cup seasoned rice vinegar
- 1 Tbsp. sugar
- 2 Tbsp. reduced-sodium soy sauce
- 1½ lbs. boneless skinless chicken breast halves
- ½ tsp. pepper
- ¼ tsp. salt
- 1 pkg. (14 oz.) coleslaw mix
- ½ cup minced fresh cilantro
- 3 cups fresh snow peas, thinly sliced lengthwise
- 2 cups shredded carrots
- 4 cups torn mixed salad greens
- 3 thinly sliced green onions
- ⅓ cup crumbled cooked bacon, optional

1. In a large saucepan, heat oil over medium-low heat. Add ramen noodles; cook and stir until toasted, 5-8 minutes. Remove from pan; set aside.

2. In a bowl, whisk oils, vinegar, sugar and soy sauce until blended; set aside.

3. Sprinkle chicken with pepper and salt. Place chicken on a lightly oiled grill rack. Grill, covered, over medium heat or broil 4-5 in. from heat until a thermometer reads 165°, 8-10 minutes on each side. Cool slightly and chop into ½-in. pieces.

4. In a large bowl, combine coleslaw mix and cilantro. Layer coleslaw mixture, peas, chicken, carrots, salad greens, noodles and green onions in an 8- to 10-qt. dish. Sprinkle with bacon; serve with vinaigrette.

1 serving: 458 cal., 29g fat (4g sat. fat), 47mg chol., 738mg sod., 28g carb. (10g sugars, 4g fiber), 22g pro.

Grilled Chicken Ramen Salad

Bacon Pear Salad with
Parmesan Dressing

BACON PEAR SALAD WITH PARMESAN DRESSING

This simple salad is an elegant side dish for any menu. With a blend of fresh pears and warm, comforting flavors, it's perfect for special meals.
—Rachel Lewis, Danville, VA

TAKES: 15 min. • **MAKES:** 6 servings

- 2 cups chopped leaf lettuce
- 2 cups chopped fresh kale
- 2 medium pears, thinly sliced
- 1 cup shredded pepper jack cheese
- 4 bacon strips, cooked and crumbled

PARMESAN GARLIC DRESSING

- ¼ cup mayonnaise
- 1 Tbsp. Dijon mustard
- 2 tsp. grated Parmesan cheese
- ½ tsp. garlic powder
- ⅛ tsp. pepper
- 2 to 3 Tbsp. 2% milk

In a large bowl, combine the lettuce and kale. Top with pears, pepper jack cheese and bacon. In a small bowl, whisk the mayonnaise, mustard, Parmesan cheese, garlic powder and pepper. Gradually whisk in enough milk to reach desired consistency. Drizzle over salad; toss to coat.

1 cup: 206 cal., 15g fat (5g sat. fat), 27mg chol., 335mg sod., 11g carb. (6g sugars, 2g fiber), 7g pro.

WHY YOU'LL LOVE IT...

"Absolutely loved this recipe! My husband even ate it, and he doesn't like salad. Better yet, he said, 'Make it again.' Thanks for sharing!"
—KENNEDY22, TASTEOFHOME.COM

Strawberry Kale Salad

STRAWBERRY KALE SALAD

This fresh, zingy salad is super easy and always a crowd-pleaser! The lovely sliced strawberries and fresh mint give it an extra summery feel, and crumbled bacon and toasted almonds add the perfect amount of crunch.
—Luanne Asta, Hampton Bays, NY

TAKES: 25 min. • **MAKES:** 10 servings

- ½ cup olive oil
- ⅓ cup cider vinegar
- 1 tsp. honey
- ¼ tsp. salt
- ⅛ tsp. pepper
- 1 bunch kale (about 12 oz.), trimmed and chopped (about 14 cups)
- 2 cups sliced fresh strawberries
- ¾ lb. bacon strips, cooked and crumbled
- ¼ cup minced fresh mint
- 1 cup crumbled feta cheese
- ¼ cup slivered almonds, toasted

1. For dressing, whisk together first 5 ingredients.

2. To serve, place kale, strawberries, bacon and mint in a large bowl; toss with dressing. Sprinkle with cheese and almonds.

Note: To toast nuts, bake in a shallow pan in a 350° oven for 5-10 minutes or cook in a skillet over low heat until lightly browned, stirring occasionally.

1⅓ cups: 231 cal., 19g fat (4g sat. fat), 18mg chol., 399mg sod., 8g carb. (2g sugars, 2g fiber), 8g pro.

Orzo with Caramelized
Butternut Squash & Bacon,
Page 120

Page 118

Page 122

Pasta & Noodles

Jazz up your dinner routine with popular pasta! These change-of-pace sides take menus to new heights with flavor and fun. From stovetop greats to oven-baked specialties, the hearty recipes found here add flair to any meal.

Page 129

Page 127

ASIAN QUINOA

I love to cook, and to come up with new recipes. I serve this dish at least once a month. For a different twist, I'll occasionally add a scrambled egg or use soy sauce instead of rice vinegar.
—Sonya Labbe, West Hollywood, CA

PREP: 20 min. • **COOK:** 20 min. + standing
MAKES: 4 servings

- 1   cup water
- 2   Tbsp. rice vinegar
- 2   Tbsp. plum sauce
- 2   garlic cloves, minced
- 1   tsp. minced fresh gingerroot
- 1   tsp. sesame oil
- ¼   tsp. salt
- ¼   tsp. crushed red pepper flakes
- ½   cup quinoa, rinsed
- 1   medium sweet red pepper, chopped
- ½   cup sliced water chestnuts, chopped
- ½   cup fresh sugar snap peas, trimmed and halved
- 2   green onions, thinly sliced

1. In a large saucepan, combine the first 8 ingredients; bring to a boil. Add quinoa. Reduce heat; cover and simmer until water is absorbed, 12-15 minutes.
2. Remove from heat. Add the red pepper, water chestnuts, peas and onions; fluff with a fork. Cover and let stand for 10 minutes.

⅔ cup: 138 cal., 3g fat (0 sat. fat), 0 chol., 205mg sod., 25g carb. (5g sugars, 3g fiber), 4g pro. **Diabetic exchanges:** 1 starch, 1 vegetable.

Asian
Quinoa

CREAMY PASTA WITH BACON

My son loves bacon, so this side is a hit with him. Sometimes, I even add chicken to make it a main dish.
—Kim Uhrich, Cabot, AR

TAKES: 20 min. • **MAKES:** 6 servings

- 1 pkg. (9 oz.) refrigerated linguine
- 1 medium onion, chopped
- 1 Tbsp. canola oil
- 2 garlic cloves, minced
- 2 Tbsp. all-purpose flour
- 1½ cups heavy whipping cream
- 3 large eggs, lightly beaten
- 8 cooked bacon strips, chopped
- ½ cup grated Parmesan cheese

1. Cook linguine according to package directions. Meanwhile, in a large skillet, saute onion in oil until tender. Add garlic; cook 1 minute longer.

2. In a small bowl, whisk flour and cream until smooth; stir into the pan. Bring to a boil, stirring constantly. Reduce heat; cook and stir for 1 minute or until thickened. Remove from the heat. Stir a small amount of hot mixture into eggs; return all to the pan, stirring constantly. Bring to a gentle boil; cook and stir 2 minutes longer.

3. Drain linguine; add to the pan. Stir in bacon and cheese; heat through.

¾ cup: 474 cal., 33g fat (17g sat. fat), 202mg chol., 440mg sod., 29g carb. (2g sugars, 2g fiber), 15g pro.

Test Kitchen Tip

Save some of the water you cook the pasta in and add it to the finished pasta if you like your sauce a little bit thinner.

Penne with Kale & Onion

🗊 PENNE WITH KALE & ONION

I love kale; my husband hates it. But when I swapped it into a favorite penne-with-spinach recipe, it was so delicious that he asked for seconds!
—Kimberly Hammond, Kingwood, TX

PREP: 15 min. • **COOK:** 20 min.
MAKES: 6 servings

- 1 medium onion, sliced
- 2 Tbsp. olive oil, divided
- 8 garlic cloves, thinly sliced
- 3 cups uncooked penne pasta
- 6 cups chopped fresh kale
- ½ tsp. salt

1. In a large skillet, cook the onion in 1 Tbsp. oil over medium heat until the onion is golden brown, 15-20 minutes, stirring frequently. Add the garlic; cook until fragrant.

2. Meanwhile, in a large saucepan, cook penne according to package directions. In a Dutch oven, bring 1 in. of water to a boil. Add kale; cover and cook until tender, 10-15 minutes. Drain.

3. Drain penne; drizzle with remaining oil. Stir the salt, penne and kale into the onion mixture; heat through.

1 cup: 189 cal., 5g fat (1g sat. fat), 0 chol., 206mg sod., 31g carb. (2g sugars, 2g fiber), 6g pro. **Diabetic exchanges:** 1.5 starch, 1 vegetable, 1 fat.

GARDEN PRIMAVERA FETTUCCINE

I created this side while trying to make broccoli Alfredo. I kept adding fresh vegetables, and the result was this creamy pasta dish!
—Tammy Perrault, Lancaster, OH

TAKES: 30 min. • **MAKES:** 10 servings

- 1   pkg. (12 oz.) fettuccine
- 1   cup fresh cauliflowerets
- 1   cup fresh broccoli florets
- ½   cup julienned carrot
- 1   small sweet red pepper, julienned
- ½   small yellow summer squash, sliced
- ½   small zucchini, sliced
- 1   cup Alfredo sauce
- 1   tsp. dried basil
     Shredded Parmesan cheese, optional

1. In a large saucepan, cook fettuccine according to package directions, adding vegetables during the last 4 minutes. Drain and return to the pan.
2. Add Alfredo sauce and basil; toss to coat. Cook over low heat until heated through, 1-2 minutes. Sprinkle with cheese if desired.

¾ cup: 165 cal., 3g fat (2g sat. fat), 7mg chol., 121mg sod., 28g carb. (2g sugars, 3g fiber), 7g pro. **Diabetic exchanges:** 2 starch, ½ fat.

PENNE WITH CARAMELIZED ONIONS

This recipe is a favorite of my fly-fishing buddies when we take our annual trip to British Columbia. The pine nuts are a delicious surprise.
—Paul Humphrey DDS, Allyn, WA

TAKES: 30 min. • **MAKES:** 4 servings

- 2   cups uncooked penne pasta
- ¼   cup pine nuts
- 2   garlic cloves, minced
- 1   Tbsp. butter
- 1   large onion, chopped
- 2   Tbsp. olive oil
- 16 pitted Greek olives, coarsely chopped
- ¼   tsp. salt
- ¼   tsp. dried basil
- ¼   tsp. dried oregano
- ¼   tsp. pepper
- ¾   cup crumbled feta cheese

1. Cook pasta according to package directions. Meanwhile, in a small skillet, saute pine nuts and garlic in butter until golden brown; set aside.
2. In a large skillet, cook onion in oil over medium heat 10-15 minutes or until golden brown, stirring frequently. Reduce heat to low. Stir in the olives, salt, basil, oregano and pepper. Drain pasta; add to onion mixture. Stir in feta cheese and pine nut mixture.

1 cup: 374 cal., 22g fat (6g sat. fat), 19mg chol., 627mg sod., 33g carb. (4g sugars, 3g fiber), 11g pro.

Test Kitchen Tip

Frequently used in Italian dishes and sauces such as pesto, pine nuts are often toasted to enhance their flavor.

CRANBERRY RICOTTA GNOCCHI WITH BROWN BUTTER SAUCE

To make light, airy gnocchi, work quickly and handle the dough as little as possible. You'll be pleased with the pillowy dumplings.
—Sally Sibthorpe, Shelby Township, MI

PREP: 30 min. + standing • **COOK:** 15 min.
MAKES: 8 servings

- ¾   cup dried cranberries, divided
- 2   cups ricotta cheese
- 1   cup all-purpose flour
- ½   cup grated Parmesan cheese
- 1   large egg, lightly beaten
- ¾   tsp. salt, divided
- ¾   cup butter, cubed
- 2   Tbsp. minced fresh sage
- ½   cup chopped walnuts, toasted
- ⅛   tsp. white pepper

1. Finely chop ¼ cup cranberries. In a large bowl, combine ricotta, flour, Parmesan cheese, egg, ½ tsp. salt and chopped cranberries; mix until blended. On a lightly floured surface, knead 10-12 times, forming a soft dough. Cover and let rest for 10 minutes.
2. Divide dough into 4 portions. On a floured surface, roll each portion into a ¾-in.-thick rope; cut into ¾-in. pieces. Press and roll each piece with a lightly floured fork.
3. In a Dutch oven, bring 4 qt. water to a boil. Cook gnocchi in batches for roughly 30-60 seconds or until they float to the top. Remove gnocchi with a slotted spoon; keep warm.
4. In a large heavy saucepan, cook butter over medium heat 5 minutes. Add sage; cook 3-5 minutes longer or until butter is golden brown, stirring occasionally. Stir in walnuts, white pepper, and the remaining cranberries and salt. Add gnocchi; stir gently to coat.

¾ cup: 411 cal., 30g fat (16g sat. fat), 101mg chol., 503mg sod., 26g carb. (11g sugars, 1g fiber), 13g pro.

Cranberry Ricotta Gnocchi
with Brown Butter Sauce

ORZO WITH CARAMELIZED BUTTERNUT SQUASH & BACON

The year my garden produced a bumper crop of butternut squash, I made so many new dishes trying to use up my bounty! This is a tasty, easy side with pretty colors, and it makes plenty to fill your hungry family. To make it into a main, simply add cooked shrimp or shredded chicken.
—Kallee Krong-Mccreery, Escondido, CA

PREP: 20 min. • **COOK:** 20 min.
MAKES: 6 servings

- 1½ cups uncooked orzo pasta
- 4 bacon strips, chopped
- 2 cups cubed peeled butternut squash (½-in. cubes)
- ½ cup chopped onion
- 1 cup cut fresh or frozen cut green beans, thawed
- 1 garlic clove, minced
- 1 Tbsp. butter
- 1 tsp. garlic salt
- ¼ tsp. pepper
- ¼ cup grated Parmesan cheese
  Minced fresh parsley

1. In a large saucepan, cook orzo according to package directions.
2. Meanwhile, in a large skillet, cook bacon over medium heat until crisp, stirring occasionally. Remove with a slotted spoon; drain on paper towels. Cook and stir the squash and the onion in bacon drippings until tender, about 8-10 minutes. Add beans and garlic; cook 1 minute longer.
3. Drain orzo; stir into squash mixture. Add butter, garlic salt, pepper and reserved bacon; heat through. Sprinkle with Parmesan and parsley.
¾ cup: 329 cal., 11g fat (4g sat. fat), 20mg chol., 533mg sod., 47g carb. (4g sugars, 3g fiber), 11g pro.

Orzo with Caramelized
Butternut Squash & Bacon

Lemon Pasta
with Spinach

LEMON PASTA WITH SPINACH

Healthy spinach, garlic and lemon combine to coat angel hair pasta for a lovely side that'll freshen any meal.
—Charlene Anderson, Bonney Lake, WA

TAKES: 25 min. • **MAKES:** 6 servings

- 8 oz. uncooked angel hair pasta
- 2 garlic cloves, minced
- 2 Tbsp. butter
- 1 pkg. (6 oz.) fresh baby spinach
- 3 Tbsp. lemon juice
- 2 tsp. grated lemon zest
- ½ tsp. salt
- ¼ tsp. pepper

1. Cook pasta according to the package directions.
2. Meanwhile, in a large skillet, saute garlic in butter until tender. Add spinach, lemon juice and zest, salt and pepper; cook 2-3 minutes longer or until spinach is wilted.
3. Drain the pasta. Add to skillet; toss to coat.

¾ cup: 184 cal., 4g fat (3g sat. fat), 10mg chol., 249mg sod., 30g carb. (1g sugars, 2g fiber), 6g pro. **Diabetic exchanges:** 2 starch, 1 fat.

COUSCOUS WITH MUSHROOMS

Fluffy couscous takes only minutes to prepare. I use the versatile pasta a lot because it cooks quickly and you can add almost any vegetable to it.
—Claudia Ruiss, Massapequa, NY

TAKES: 15 min. • **MAKES:** 4 servings

- 1¼ cups water
- 2 Tbsp. butter
- 2 tsp. chicken bouillon granules
- ¼ tsp. salt
- ¼ tsp. pepper
- 1 cup uncooked couscous
- 1 can (7 oz.) mushroom stems and pieces, drained

In a small saucepan, combine the first 5 ingredients; bring to a boil. Stir in couscous and mushrooms. Remove from the heat; let stand, covered, until liquid is absorbed, 5-10 minutes. Fluff with a fork.

¾ cup: 230 cal., 6g fat (4g sat. fat), 15mg chol., 794mg sod., 37g carb. (2g sugars, 3g fiber), 8g pro.

Did You Know?
A lot of people believe couscous is a grain but it's actually a type of pasta that's made of dough from water and semolina.

SWISS ANGEL HAIR & ASPARAGUS

I found this recipe in an old community cookbook that I paid 50 cents for at a garage sale. My husband just loves it!
—Michele Cornish, Blairstown, NJ

TAKES: 30 min. • **MAKES:** 10 servings

- 12 oz. uncooked angel hair pasta
- 1 lb. fresh asparagus, trimmed and cut into 2-in. pieces
- ½ lb. sliced fresh mushrooms
- 1 tsp. minced chives
- 3 Tbsp. butter
- 2 Tbsp. all-purpose flour
- 2¼ tsp. salt-free seasoning blend
- ½ tsp. salt
- 2¼ cups whole milk
- 1½ cups shredded Swiss cheese
  Grated Parmesan cheese, optional

1. Cook pasta according to package directions. Meanwhile, place asparagus in a steamer basket; place in a large saucepan over 1 in. of water. Bring to a boil; cover and steam for 3-5 minutes or until crisp-tender.
2. In a saucepan, saute mushrooms and chives in butter until tender. Stir in flour, seasoning blend and salt; gradually add milk. Bring to a boil; cook and stir for about 1-2 minutes or until thickened. Add the Swiss cheese; cook and stir until melted.
3. Drain pasta and place in a large bowl. Add asparagus and cheese sauce; toss to coat. Garnish with Parmesan cheese if desired.

¾ cup: 267 cal., 10g fat (6g sat. fat), 29mg chol., 212mg sod., 32g carb. (5g sugars, 2g fiber), 12g pro.

PEAS PLEASE ASIAN NOODLES

My Asian-inspired pasta salad doubles up on the peas for some serious crunch and sweetness. It's a tasty side or meatless main.
—Catherine Cassidy, Milwaukee, WI

TAKES: 20 min. • **MAKES:** 8 servings

- 12 oz. uncooked Japanese soba noodles or whole wheat spaghetti
- ¼ cup water
- 1 cup fresh snow peas or sugar snap peas, trimmed
- 3 cups ice water
- ¾ cup frozen green peas, thawed
- 1 small cucumber, chopped
- 3 green onions, finely chopped

SAUCE
- ¼ cup creamy peanut butter
- 3 Tbsp. orange juice
- 3 Tbsp. white or rice vinegar
- 3 Tbsp. soy sauce
- 4 tsp. sesame oil or tahini
- 4 tsp. canola oil
- 1 Tbsp. garlic powder
- 2 to 3 tsp. hot pepper sauce
- 2¼ tsp. sugar

TOPPINGS
- ½ cup chopped fresh cilantro
  Sesame seeds, toasted

1. Cook noodles according to package directions. Meanwhile, in a small saucepan, bring ¼ cup water to a boil over medium-high heat. Add snow peas; cook, uncovered, just until crisp-tender, 1-2 minutes. Drain; immediately drop snow peas into ice water. Remove and pat dry.
2. Drain noodles; rinse with cold water and drain again. Combine noodles with snow peas, green peas, cucumber and green onions.
3. In another bowl, whisk together the sauce ingredients until blended; pour over noodles and vegetables. Toss to coat. To serve, sprinkle with cilantro and sesame seeds.

1 cup: 264 cal., 9g fat (1g sat. fat), 0 chol., 740mg sod., 39g carb. (4g sugars, 2g fiber), 10g pro.

Peas Please
Asian Noodles

PASTA WITH FRESH VEGETABLES

Looking for a recipe with summer flavor? This delicious vegetable pasta dish is so easy to prepare and a wonderful way to use up your garden-fresh veggies. It's also hearty and nutritious but still lower in fat and calories! Try it with a grilled entree.
—Laurie Couture, Swanton, VT

PREP: 15 min. • **COOK:** 20 min.
MAKES: 6 servings

- 8 oz. uncooked penne pasta
- 1 cup sliced fresh carrots
- 1 Tbsp. olive oil
- ½ tsp. minced garlic
- 1 cup fresh broccoli florets
- 1 cup sliced yellow summer squash
- 1 cup chopped green pepper
- 1 Tbsp. minced fresh basil or 1 tsp. dried basil
- 1 tsp. minced fresh thyme or ¼ tsp. dried thyme
- 1 tsp. minced fresh oregano or ¼ tsp. dried oregano
- ½ tsp. salt
- ¼ tsp. pepper
- 3 cups chopped fresh plum tomatoes
  Grated Parmesan cheese

1. Cook pasta according to package directions; drain.
2. Meanwhile, in a large nonstick skillet, saute carrots in oil until crisp-tender. Add garlic; cook 1 minute longer. Stir in tomatoes, broccoli, squash, green pepper and seasonings. Bring to a boil. Reduce heat; simmer, uncovered, until vegetables are tender, 8-10 minutes.
3. Stir in the pasta; sprinkle with cheese.
1¼ cups: 205 cal., 4g fat (1g sat. fat), 1mg chol., 244mg sod., 37g carb. (6g sugars, 4g fiber), 7g pro.

Pasta with Fresh
Vegetables

COLORFUL COUSCOUS

We love it when side dishes pop with color, such as the bright accents in this light and fluffy couscous. It's a scrumptious and welcome switch from potatoes or rice.
—Taste of Home *Test Kitchen*

TAKES: 25 min. • **MAKES:** 6 servings

- 2   Tbsp. olive oil
- 5   miniature sweet peppers, julienned
- ⅓   cup finely chopped onion
- 2   garlic cloves, minced
- 1   can (14½ oz.) chicken broth
- ¼   cup water
- ½   tsp. salt
- ¼   tsp. pepper
- 1   pkg. (10 oz.) couscous

In a large saucepan, heat the oil over medium-high heat; saute peppers, onion and garlic until tender, roughly 2-3 minutes. Stir in broth, water, salt and pepper; bring to a boil. Stir in couscous. Remove from heat; let stand, covered, 5 minutes. Fluff with a fork.
¾ cup: 220 cal., 5g fat (1g sat. fat), 2mg chol., 498mg sod., 37g carb. (2g sugars, 2g fiber), 7g pro.

Homemade Fettuccine

HOMEMADE FETTUCCINE

This fresh fettuccine recipe will give you a real taste of Italy.
—Taste of Home *Test Kitchen*

PREP: 1¼ hours + standing
MAKES: 1¼ lbs.

- 3½   to 4 cups semolina flour
- 1   tsp. salt
- 1   cup warm water

1. Combine 3½ cups flour and salt in a large bowl. Make a well in the center. Pour water into well and stir together, forming a ball.
2. Turn onto a floured surface; knead until smooth and elastic, 8-10 minutes, adding remaining flour if necessary to keep dough from sticking to surface and hands (dough will be stiff). Shape dough into a rectangle; cover and let rest for 30 minutes.
3. Divide dough into fourths. On a floured surface, roll each portion into a 16x8-in. rectangle. Dust dough with flour to prevent sticking while rolling. Cut crosswise into ⅛-in. slices. Separate the noodles onto clean towels; let dry overnight (let dry in the shape the noodles will be stored in). Package dry pasta.
4. To cook fettuccine: Fill a Dutch oven three-fourths full with water. Bring to a boil. Add noodles; cook, uncovered, until tender, 8-10 minutes. Drain.
2 oz.: 210 cal., 1g fat (0 sat. fat), 0 chol., 237mg sod., 43g carb. (1g sugars, 2g fiber), 7g pro.

Test Kitchen Tip
Add chopped fresh herbs for a flavor punch. For a more traditional Italian pasta, substitute 2 eggs for ½ cup of the water.

Gnocchi with
Mushrooms & Onion

GNOCCHI WITH MUSHROOMS & ONION

Tender potato gnocchi is so delicious with sauteed mushrooms and onions. It's one of my family's go-to side dishes.
—Kris Berezansky, Clymer, PA

TAKES: 20 min. • **MAKES:** 5 servings

- 1 pkg. (16 oz.) potato gnocchi
- ½ lb. sliced fresh mushrooms
- ¾ cup chopped sweet onion
- ¼ cup butter, cubed
- ¼ tsp. salt
- ¼ tsp. Italian seasoning
- ¼ tsp. crushed red pepper flakes
  Grated Parmesan cheese

1. Cook gnocchi according to package directions. Meanwhile, in a large cast-iron skillet, saute mushrooms and onion in butter until tender.
2. Drain gnocchi. Add the gnocchi, salt, Italian seasoning and pepper flakes to the skillet; heat through. Sprinkle with the cheese.
Note: Look for potato gnocchi in the pasta or frozen foods section.
¾ cup: 287 cal., 11g fat (6g sat. fat), 31mg chol., 583mg sod., 41g carb. (7g sugars, 3g fiber), 8g pro.

CREAMY RANCH PASTA

I came up with this after making recipes for a bridal shower. It was party day and I needed to take some shortcuts! Everyone loves the simple Parmesan ranch white sauce, and it's easy to throw in veggies you have on hand.
—Merry Graham, Newhall, CA

PREP: 25 min. • **BAKE:** 30 min.
MAKES: 8 servings

- 2½ cups uncooked bow tie pasta
- 2 cups (8 oz.) shredded Italian cheese blend
- 1¼ cups grated Parmesan cheese, divided
- 1 cup (8 oz.) sour cream
- 1 cup ranch salad dressing

Creamy Ranch Pasta

- 1 pkg. (10 oz.) frozen chopped spinach, thawed and squeezed dry or 2 cups chopped fresh spinach
- 2 slices day-old French bread (½ in. thick)
- 1 Tbsp. olive oil
- 1 tsp. grated lemon zest
- 1 tsp. dried parsley flakes
- ¼ tsp. garlic salt

1. Preheat oven to 350°. Cook pasta according to package directions.
2. In a large bowl, mix Italian cheese blend, 1 cup Parmesan cheese, sour cream and salad dressing. Drain pasta; add to cheese mixture. Fold in the spinach. Transfer to a greased 13x9-in. baking dish.
3. Tear French bread into pieces; place in a food processor. Cover and pulse until crumbs form. Toss bread crumbs with oil, lemon zest, parsley, garlic salt and remaining ¼ cup Parmesan cheese. Sprinkle over pasta mixture.
4. Bake, covered, 25 minutes. Uncover; bake until golden brown and bubbly, 5-10 minutes.
¾ cup: 436 cal., 30g fat (12g sat. fat), 40mg chol., 841mg sod., 25g carb. (3g sugars, 2g fiber), 15g pro.

Test Kitchen Tip
Turn this dish into a delicious main course by adding in 2 cups cooked chicken, ham or shrimp while folding in the spinach.

Confetti Quinoa

5i 🍎
CONFETTI QUINOA

*If you have never tried quinoa, start with my
easy side, brimming with colorful veggies.
I serve it with orange-glazed chicken.*
—Kim Ciepluch, Kenosha, WI

TAKES: 30 min. • **MAKES:** 4 servings

- 2 cups water
- 1 cup quinoa, rinsed
- ½ cup chopped fresh broccoli
- ½ cup coarsely chopped zucchini
- ¼ cup shredded carrots
- ½ tsp. salt
- 1 Tbsp. lemon juice
- 1 Tbsp. olive oil

1. In a large saucepan, bring water to a
boil. Add the next 5 ingredients. Reduce
heat; simmer, covered, until liquid is
absorbed, 12-15 minutes.
2. Stir in lemon juice and oil. Remove
from heat; fluff with a fork.
⅔ cup: 196 cal., 6g fat (1g sat. fat), 0 chol.,
307mg sod., 29g carb. (1g sugars, 4g
fiber), 7g pro. **Diabetic exchanges:**
2 starch, ½ fat.

Health Tip
Quinoa is a smart alternative to
white rice, as it offers more fiber
and protein.

NUTTY KALE PESTO PASTA WITH CARAMELIZED ONION

My bountiful garden and vegetarian daughter both inspired me to create this nutritious, calcium-rich pasta sauce. In summer, everything I make begins with my garden onions, tomatoes, kale and basil. No one would ever guess that this hearty dish is brimming with produce and is prepared in about 30 minutes. For a gluten-free version, substitute quinoa pasta.
—Cindy Beberman, Orland Park, IL

PREP: 20 min. • **COOK:** 15 min.
MAKES: 8 servings

⅓ cup hazelnuts, toasted and skins removed
2 cups roughly chopped fresh kale, stems removed
¼ cup plus 2 Tbsp. grated Parmesan cheese, divided
¼ cup loosely packed basil leaves
¼ cup plus 2 Tbsp. olive oil, divided
½ tsp. salt, divided
12 oz. uncooked whole wheat linguine
1 large sweet onion, thinly sliced
3 garlic cloves, minced
1 Tbsp. honey
3 large tomatoes, chopped

1. Pulse hazelnuts in food processor until finely ground. Add kale, ¼ cup Parmesan cheese, basil, ¼ cup olive oil and ¼ tsp. salt; pulse until smooth and creamy, adding oil if pesto seems dry.
2. In a large stockpot, cook linguine according to package directions. Meanwhile, in a large skillet, heat the remaining 2 Tbsp. oil over medium heat. Add onion; cook and stir until tender, about 5 minutes. Reduce heat to low; add garlic and honey. Cook, stirring occasionally, until onion caramelizes, about 5 minutes more.
3. Drain linguine, reserving ½ cup pasta water. In a large serving bowl, combine kale pesto, onion mixture, linguine, chopped tomato and remaining salt. Toss until well coated, adding reserved pasta water if needed to reach desired consistency. Top with remaining Parmesan cheese. Serve warm.
Note: To toast nuts, bake in a shallow pan in a 350° oven for 5-10 minutes or cook in a skillet over low heat until lightly browned, stirring occasionally.
1 cup: 314 cal., 15g fat (2g sat. fat), 3mg chol., 224mg sod., 42g carb. (7g sugars, 7g fiber), 8g pro.

Nutty Kale Pesto Pasta
with Caramelized Onion

Orzo Timbales with
Fontina Cheese

VEGGIE MACARONI & CHEESE

This creamy mac and cheese definitely doesn't come from a box! Fresh veggies add crunch and color and will leave everyone saying, "More, please!"
—Marsha Morril, Harrisburg, OR

PREP: 30 min. • **BAKE:** 15 min.
MAKES: 12 servings

- 1½ cups uncooked elbow macaroni
- 3 cups fresh broccoli florets
- 2 cups fresh cauliflowerets
- 3 large carrots, halved lengthwise and thinly sliced
- 2 celery ribs, sliced
- 1 Tbsp. butter
- 1 medium onion, chopped
- ¼ cup all-purpose flour
- 1 cup 2% milk
- 1 cup chicken broth
- 3 cups shredded sharp cheddar cheese
- 1 Tbsp. Dijon mustard
- ¼ tsp. salt
- ⅛ tsp. pepper
- ¼ tsp. paprika

1. Preheat oven to 350°. In a 6-qt. stockpot, cook macaroni according to package directions, adding broccoli, cauliflower, carrots and celery during the last 6 minutes of cooking time. Drain; transfer to a greased 13x9-in. baking dish.
2. Meanwhile, in a large saucepan, heat butter over medium-high heat; saute onion until tender. Stir in flour until blended. Gradually stir in milk and broth; bring to a boil. Cook and stir until thickened, about 2 minutes; stir in cheese, mustard, salt and pepper.
3. Add to macaroni mixture, stirring to coat; sprinkle with paprika. Bake, uncovered, until heated through, 15-20 minutes.
1 cup: 200 cal., 11g fat (6g sat. fat), 33mg chol., 391mg sod., 15g carb. (3g sugars, 2g fiber), 10g pro.

ORZO TIMBALES WITH FONTINA CHEESE

Take mac and cheese to a new level using orzo pasta and fontina. With a pop of color from sweet red peppers, these timbales bake in ramekins for perfectly impressive individual servings.
—Gilda Lester, Millsboro, DE

PREP: 20 min. • **BAKE:** 30 min.
MAKES: 6 servings

- 1 cup uncooked orzo pasta
- 1½ cups shredded fontina cheese
- ½ cup finely chopped roasted sweet red peppers
- 1 can (2¼ oz.) sliced ripe olives, drained
- 2 large eggs
- 1½ cups 2% milk
- ¼ tsp. salt
- ⅛ tsp. ground nutmeg
  Minced fresh parsley, optional

1. Preheat oven to 350°. Cook orzo according to package directions for al dente; drain. Transfer to a bowl. Stir in cheese, peppers and olives. Divide among 6 greased 10-oz. ramekins or custard cups. Place ramekins on a baking sheet.
2. In a small bowl, whisk eggs, milk, salt and nutmeg; pour over orzo mixture. Bake 30-35 minutes or until golden brown. Let stand 5 minutes before serving. If desired, run a knife around sides of ramekins and invert onto serving plates. If desired, sprinkle with parsley.
1 serving: 301 cal., 13g fat (7g sat. fat), 98mg chol., 521mg sod., 29g carb. (5g sugars, 1g fiber), 15g pro.

Veggie Macaroni
& Cheese

GARDEN ORZO RISOTTO

No one will believe this rich, creamy dish was prepared in less than 30 minutes! I developed the recipe when my garden tomatoes, zucchini and basil were coming on strong. Using orzo instead of Arborio rice makes the risotto so much easier to prepare.
—Cindy Beberman, Orland Park, IL

TAKES: 30 min. • **MAKES:** 6 servings

- 1 small zucchini, chopped
- 1 shallot, chopped
- 2 Tbsp. olive oil
- 2 garlic cloves, minced
- 1 cup uncooked whole wheat orzo pasta
- 2 cups vegetable broth
- 1 cup 2% milk
- 1 pkg. (6 oz.) fresh baby spinach
- 2 medium tomatoes, seeded and chopped
- ¼ cup minced fresh basil
- ⅓ cup grated Parmesan cheese
  Salt and pepper to taste

1. In a large saucepan over medium-high heat, saute zucchini and shallot in oil until almost tender. Add garlic; cook 1 minute longer. Add the orzo, broth and milk. Bring to a boil over medium-high heat. Reduce heat to medium-low; cook and stir until liquid is almost absorbed, 10-15 minutes.
2. Stir in the spinach, tomatoes and basil; cook and stir until spinach is wilted. Remove from the heat; stir in the cheese, salt and pepper.
⅔ cup: 202 cal., 7g fat (2g sat. fat), 7mg chol., 429mg sod., 27g carb. (5g sugars, 6g fiber), 8g pro. **Diabetic exchanges:** 1 starch, 1 vegetable, 1 fat.

TORTELLINI SALAD WITH ARTICHOKES & SWEET PEPPERS

I've been making this for almost 10 years, and someone asks me for the recipe every time I bring it to a party. It's really easy to make. It reminds me of summer cookouts with good friends.
—Westyn Layne, Scranton, PA

TAKES: 25 min. • **MAKES:** 10 servings

- 1 pkg. (20 oz.) refrigerated cheese tortellini
- ¼ cup olive oil
- 3 Tbsp. lemon juice
- 2 Tbsp. minced fresh parsley
- ½ tsp. salt
- ½ tsp. freshly ground pepper
- 2 cans (14 oz. each) water-packed artichoke hearts, well drained and finely chopped
- 1 medium sweet red pepper, finely chopped
- ½ cup shredded Parmesan cheese

1. Cook tortellini according to package directions for al dente. Drain tortellini; cool slightly.
2. Meanwhile, in a large bowl, whisk oil, lemon juice, parsley, salt and pepper until blended. Add tortellini, artichokes and pepper; toss to coat. Cover and refrigerate until serving. Just before serving, stir in cheese.
¾ cup: 274 cal., 11g fat (4g sat. fat), 27mg chol., 595mg sod., 32g carb. (2g sugars, 2g fiber), 11g pro.

Tortellini Salad with
Artichokes & Sweet Peppers

Creamy
Pumpkin Tortellini

CREAMY PUMPKIN TORTELLINI

My kids love the creamy, rich sauce on these tortellinis so much that they don't even know it's made with pumpkin. Use freshly grated Parmesan cheese for the best, nutty and delicious flavor.
—Trisha Kruse, Eagle, ID

TAKES: 30 min. • **MAKES:** 6 servings

- 2 pkg. (9 oz. each) refrigerated cheese tortellini
- 1 Tbsp. butter
- 3 Tbsp. finely chopped onion
- 1 cup canned pumpkin
  Pinch ground nutmeg
- 1 cup half-and-half cream
- ¼ cup grated Parmesan cheese
- ½ tsp. salt
- ¼ tsp. pepper
- 1 Tbsp. minced fresh parsley
  Additional grated or shredded Parmesan, optional

1. Cook tortellini according to package directions; drain, reserving ½ cup cooking liquid. Meanwhile, in a large nonstick skillet, heat butter over medium heat. Add onion; cook and stir 1-2 minutes or until tender. Add the pumpkin and nutmeg; cook and stir 1 minute. Stir in cream; bring to a boil. Reduce heat to medium-low; simmer, uncovered, 4-5 minutes or until thickened, stirring occasionally. Remove from heat; stir in cheese, salt and pepper.

2. Add tortellini; toss with sauce, adding enough reserved pasta water to coat pasta. Sprinkle with parsley and, if desired, additional cheese.

1 cup: 363 cal., 14g fat (8g sat. fat), 65mg chol., 610mg sod., 45g carb. (5g sugars, 3g fiber), 14g pro.

Lemon Couscous
with Broccoli

LEMON COUSCOUS WITH BROCCOLI

I combined two recipes to create this side with broccoli and pasta. The splash of lemon adds nice flavor. Instead of toasted almonds, you could also sprinkle servings with grated Parmesan cheese.
—Beth Dauenhauer, Pueblo, CO

TAKES: 25 min. • **MAKES:** 6 servings

- 1 Tbsp. olive oil
- 4 cups fresh broccoli florets, cut into small pieces
- 1 cup uncooked whole wheat couscous
- 2 garlic cloves, minced
- 1¼ cups reduced-sodium chicken broth
- 1 tsp. grated lemon zest
- 1 tsp. lemon juice
- ½ tsp. salt
- ½ tsp. dried basil
- ¼ tsp. coarsely ground pepper
- 1 Tbsp. slivered almonds, toasted

1. In a large cast-iron or other heavy skillet, heat oil over medium-high heat. Add broccoli; cook and stir until crisp-tender.

2. Add couscous and garlic; cook and stir 1-2 minutes longer. Stir in broth, lemon zest, lemon juice and seasonings; bring to a boil. Remove from heat; let stand, covered, until broth is absorbed, 5-10 minutes. Fluff with a fork. Sprinkle with almonds.

⅔ cup: 115 cal., 3g fat (0 sat. fat), 0 chol., 328mg sod., 18g carb. (1g sugars, 4g fiber), 5g pro. **Diabetic exchanges:** 1 starch, ½ fat.

Parmesan Fettuccine

PARMESAN FETTUCCINE

This simple side dish makes a pretty presentation. With only four ingredients, it's ready in no time. Try it with steak for a super treat!
—Sundra Hauck, Bogalusa, LA

TAKES: 20 min. • **MAKES:** 4 servings

- 8 oz. uncooked fettuccine
- ⅓ cup butter, cubed
- ⅓ cup grated Parmesan cheese
- ⅛ tsp. pepper

1. Cook fettuccine according to package directions; drain.

2. In a large skillet, melt butter over low heat. Add fettuccine and stir until coated. Sprinkle with cheese and pepper; toss to coat.

¾ cup: 359 cal., 19g fat (11g sat. fat), 46mg chol., 260mg sod., 41g carb. (2g sugars, 2g fiber), 10g pro.

BACON MAC & CHEESE CORNBREAD SKILLET

My cast-iron skillet is a workhorse in my kitchen. I just love it for cooking and baking. This cast-iron mac and cheese recipe can be served as a main dish or as a smaller side.
—Lisa Keys, Kennet Square, PA

PREP: 35 min. • **BAKE:** 30 min. + standing
MAKES: 8 servings

Bacon Mac & Cheese
Cornbread Skillet

1¾ cups uncooked elbow macaroni
8 bacon strips, chopped
1 cup shredded smoked Gouda or cheddar cheese
1 cup shredded pepper jack cheese
4 oz. cream cheese, cubed
6 large eggs, divided
3 cups 2% milk, divided
4 green onions, chopped
1 tsp. kosher salt, divided
½ tsp. pepper, divided
1 pkg. (8½ oz.) cornbread/muffin mix
½ tsp. smoked paprika
Additional green onions

1. Preheat oven to 400°. Cook macaroni according to the package directions. Meanwhile, in a 12-in. cast-iron or other ovenproof skillet, cook bacon over medium heat until crisp, stirring occasionally. Remove with a slotted spoon; drain on paper towels. Discard drippings, reserving 1 Tbsp. in pan.
2. Drain macaroni; add macaroni to drippings. Stir in shredded cheeses and cream cheese; cook and stir over medium heat until cheese is melted, about 2-3 minutes. Whisk 2 eggs, 1 cup milk, green onions, ½ tsp. kosher salt and ¼ tsp. pepper; pour into skillet. Cook and stir until slightly thickened, 3-4 minutes. Remove from heat.
3. Reserve ¼ cup bacon for topping; sprinkle remaining chopped bacon over macaroni. Place cornbread mix, paprika and the remaining 4 eggs, 2 cups milk, ½ tsp. kosher salt and ¼ tsp. pepper in a blender; cover and process until smooth. Pour over bacon.
4. Bake until puffed and golden brown,

30-35 minutes. Let stand 10 minutes before serving. Sprinkle with reserved bacon and additional green onions.
1 cup: 497 cal., 27g fat (13g sat. fat), 203mg chol., 978mg sod., 40g carb. (12g sugars, 3g fiber), 23g pro.

Test Kitchen Tip
Give this recipe some seasonal flair: Add cooked green peas for a touch of spring or tasty pieces of butternut squash for a fall twist.

FIVE-CHEESE RIGATONI

Who can resist cheesy pasta hot from the oven? This ooey-gooey rigatoni boasts a homemade creamy Swiss sauce that comes together in just a few minutes.
—*Shirley Foltz, Dexter, KS*

PREP: 25 min. • **BAKE:** 25 min.
MAKES: 9 servings

- 1 pkg. (16 oz.) rigatoni or large tube pasta
- 2 Tbsp. butter
- 3 Tbsp. all-purpose flour
- 1 tsp. salt
- ½ tsp. pepper
- 2½ cups whole milk
- ½ cup shredded Swiss cheese
- ½ cup shredded fontina cheese
- ½ cup shredded part-skim mozzarella cheese
- ½ cup grated Parmesan cheese, divided
- ½ cup grated Romano cheese, divided

1. Cook rigatoni according to the package directions.
2. Preheat the oven to 375°. In a large saucepan, melt butter. Stir in the flour, salt and pepper until smooth. Gradually stir in milk; bring to a boil. Cook and stir until thickened, 1-2 minutes. Stir in shredded Swiss, fontina, mozzarella, ¼ cup Parmesan and ¼ cup Romano cheeses until melted.
3. Drain rigatoni; stir in cheese sauce. Transfer to a greased 13x9-in. baking dish. Sprinkle with remaining Parmesan and Romano cheeses. Cover and bake 20 minutes. Uncover; bake until bubbly, 5-10 minutes longer.
¾ cup: 362 cal., 14g fat (8g sat. fat), 40mg chol., 586mg sod., 42g carb. (5g sugars, 2g fiber), 18g pro.

Five-Cheese Rigatoni

Cheese Tortellini with Tomatoes & Corn

HERBED NOODLES WITH EDAMAME

Serve this side dish to give your meal a pop of flavor! All the fresh herbs make it feel extra-special, and frozen edamame makes it quick and easy.
—Marie Rizzio, Interlochen, MI

TAKES: 30 min. • **MAKES:** 4 servings

- 3½ cups uncooked egg noodles
- 2 Tbsp. butter
- 1 green onion, sliced
- 1 Tbsp. finely chopped sweet red pepper
- ½ cup frozen shelled edamame, thawed
- ¼ cup reduced-sodium chicken broth
- 1 Tbsp. minced fresh parsley
- 1½ tsp. minced fresh marjoram
- 1½ tsp. minced fresh chives
- 1 Tbsp. olive oil
- ¼ cup grated Romano cheese

1. Cook noodles according to package directions. Meanwhile, in a large skillet, heat butter over medium-high heat. Add onion and red pepper; cook and stir until tender. Stir in edamame and broth; heat through. Add herbs.
2. Drain the noodles and add to skillet; toss to combine. Transfer to a serving plate. Drizzle with oil and sprinkle with the cheese.

1 cup: 264 cal., 14g fat (6g sat. fat), 50mg chol., 214mg sod., 26g carb. (1g sugars, 2g fiber), 10g pro.

CHEESE TORTELLINI WITH TOMATOES & CORN

Fresh corn and basil make this dish taste like summer. I think it's a good one for bringing to picnics or gatherings, but it's also fantastic alongside any entree for weeknight dinners!
—Sally Maloney, Dallas, GA

TAKES: 25 min. • **MAKES:** 4 servings

- 1 pkg. (9 oz.) refrigerated cheese tortellini
- 3⅓ cups fresh or frozen corn (about 16 oz.)
- 2 cups cherry tomatoes, quartered
- 2 green onions, thinly sliced
- ¼ cup minced fresh basil
- 2 Tbsp. grated Parmesan cheese
- 4 tsp. olive oil
- ¼ tsp. garlic powder
- ⅛ tsp. pepper

In a 6-qt. stockpot, cook the tortellini according to package directions, adding corn during last 5 minutes of cooking. Drain; transfer to a large bowl. Add remaining ingredients; toss to coat.
1¾ cups: 366 cal., 12g fat (4g sat. fat), 30mg chol., 286mg sod., 57g carb. (6g sugars, 5g fiber), 14g pro.

WHY YOU'LL LOVE IT...

"My family loves this recipe. I always use fresh corn and put it on the grill until I get some nice grill marks. Then I cut it off the cob and add it to the other ingredients. It's a favorite."
—SPINMOM, TASTEOFHOME.COM

Herbed Noodles
with Edamame

PASTA PUTTANESCA

This pasta is perfect for a big gathering. It works well as a side dish or as a meatless main course. One peeled, diced carrot may be used in place of the sugar for a milder and healthier substitute.
—Kathryn White, Pinehurst, NC

PREP: 25 min. • **COOK:** 15 min.
MAKES: 8 servings

- 1 pkg. (16 oz.) penne pasta
- 1 Tbsp. olive oil
- 1 medium carrot, finely chopped
- 3 anchovy fillets
- ¼ cup pitted Greek olives, chopped
- ¼ cup oil-packed sun-dried tomatoes, drained
- 5 garlic cloves, minced
- 2 Tbsp. capers, drained
- 2 tsp. dried oregano
- 2 tsp. dried thyme
- 2 tsp. fennel seed, crushed
- 1 to 1½ tsp. crushed red pepper flakes
- 1 can (28 oz.) diced tomatoes, undrained
- 1 Tbsp. tomato paste
- ½ tsp. sugar
- 6 fresh basil leaves, thinly sliced
- 3 Tbsp. grated Parmesan cheese

1. Cook pasta according to package directions.

2. Meanwhile, heat Dutch oven over medium-high heat. Add oil; cook and stir the carrot and anchovy fillets until the carrot is tender. Stir in olives, sun-dried tomatoes, garlic, capers, dried oregano, thyme, fennel and pepper flakes; cook 1 minute longer. Stir in diced tomatoes, tomato paste and sugar. Bring to a boil. Reduce heat; simmer, uncovered, until thickened, about 10-15 minutes.

3. Drain pasta. Add pasta and basil to sauce mixture; toss to coat. Sprinkle with cheese.

1 cup: 283 cal., 5g fat (1g sat. fat), 3mg chol., 362mg sod., 50g carb. (6g sugars, 5g fiber), 10g pro.

Pasta Puttanesca

Lemon
Mushroom Orzo

LEMON MUSHROOM ORZO

Sometimes I serve this tasty side dish chilled and other times we enjoy it hot. It has a pleasant tinge of lemon and a nice crunch from the pecans.
—*Shelly Nelson, Akeley, MN*

TAKES: 25 min. • **MAKES:** 12 servings

- 1   pkg. (16 oz.) orzo pasta
- 3   Tbsp. olive oil, divided
- ¾   lb. sliced fresh mushrooms
- ¾   cup chopped pecans, toasted
- ½   cup minced fresh parsley
- 1   tsp. grated lemon zest
- 3   Tbsp. lemon juice
- 1   tsp. salt
- ½   tsp. pepper

1. Cook orzo according to package directions. Meanwhile, in a large cast-iron or other heavy skillet, heat 2 Tbsp. oil over medium-high heat. Add mushrooms; cook and stir until tender and lightly browned. Drain orzo.
2. In a large bowl, place orzo, mushroom mixture, pecans, parsley, lemon zest, lemon juice, salt, pepper and remaining oil; toss to combine.
¾ cup: 225 cal., 9g fat (1g sat. fat), 0 chol., 202mg sod., 31g carb. (2g sugars, 2g fiber), 6g pro. **Diabetic exchanges:** 2 starch, 1½ fat.

Granny's Apple Scalloped
Potatoes, Page 152

Page 153

Page 165

Potatoes & Sweet Potatoes

Whether they're roasted, fried, mashed, scalloped, sprinkled with cheese or simply swirled with butter, the versatility of humble potatoes is what makes them so popular in today's kitchens. Turn to these recipes to find a new spin on spuds.

Page 156

Page 160

ROASTED SMASHED POTATOES WITH ARTICHOKES

I'm usually not a fan of artichokes, but this combination worked nicely when I tried it at a restaurant. I had to try it at home. Keep an eye on the pan while baking; you may need to stir the mixture a few times to keep the artichokes from getting too brown and the potatoes from sticking.
—Susan Bickta, Kutztown, PA

PREP: 30 min. **ROAST:** 20 min.
MAKES: 4 servings

- 1 lb. small red potatoes
- 2 jars (7½ oz. each) marinated quartered artichoke hearts
- ½ tsp. salt
- ¼ tsp. pepper
  Minced fresh chives, optional

Preheat oven to 400°. Place potatoes in a large saucepan; add water to cover. Bring to a boil. Reduce the heat; cook, uncovered, until tender, 15-20 minutes. Drain. Drain artichokes, reserving ¼ cup oil. Drizzle oil in a 12-in. cast-iron or other ovenproof skillet; arrange the potatoes and artichokes over oil. Using a potato masher, flatten potatoes to ½-in. thickness; sprinkle with salt and pepper. Roast until crispy and golden brown, 20-25 minutes. If desired, top with minced fresh chives.

1 serving: 334 cal., 27g fat (5g sat. fat), 0 chol., 834mg sod., 25g carb. (1g sugars, 9g fiber), 2g pro.

Roasted Smashed Potatoes with Artichokes

SUPER SIMPLE SCALLOPED POTATOES

I've made many types of scalloped potatoes but I always come back to this rich, creamy, foolproof recipe.
—Kallee Krong-Mccreery, Escondido, CA

PREP: 20 min. • **BAKE:** 45 min. + standing
MAKES: 10 servings

- 3 cups heavy whipping cream
- 1½ tsp. salt
- ½ tsp. pepper
- 1 tsp. minced fresh thyme, optional
- 3 lbs. russet potatoes, thinly sliced (about 10 cups)
  Minced fresh parsley, optional

1. Preheat oven to 350°. In a large bowl, combine the cream, salt, pepper and, if desired, thyme. Arrange potatoes in a greased 13x9-in. baking dish. Pour cream mixture over top.
2. Bake, uncovered, 45-55 minutes or until potatoes are tender and top is lightly browned. Let stand 10 minutes before serving. If desired, sprinkle dish with parsley.
¾ cup: 353 cal., 27g fat (17g sat. fat), 99mg chol., 390mg sod., 26g carb. (3g sugars, 3g fiber), 4g pro.

Pressure-Cooker Buffalo Wing Potatoes

PRESSURE-COOKER BUFFALO WING POTATOES

I was getting tired of standard mashed potatoes and baked spuds, so I decided to create something new. This potluck-ready recipe is an easy and delicious twist on the usual potato dish.
—Summer Feaker, Ankeny, IA

TAKES: 20 min. • **MAKES:** 6 servings

- 2 lbs. Yukon Gold potatoes, cut into 1-in. cubes
- 1 small sweet yellow pepper, chopped
- ½ small red onion, chopped
- ¼ cup Buffalo wing sauce
- ½ cup shredded cheddar cheese
  Optional toppings: Crumbled cooked bacon, sliced green onions and sour cream

1. Place steamer basket and 1 cup water in a 6-qt. electric pressure cooker. Place potatoes, yellow pepper and onion in basket. Lock lid; close pressure-release valve. Adjust to pressure-cook on high for 3 minutes. Quick-release pressure.
2. Remove vegetables to a serving bowl; discard cooking liquid. Add Buffalo wing sauce to vegetables; gently stir to coat. Sprinkle with the cheese. Cover and let stand until the cheese is melted, roughly 1-2 minutes. If desired, top with bacon, green onions and sour cream.
¾ cup: 182 cal., 4g fat (2g sat. fat), 9mg chol., 382mg sod., 32g carb. (3g sugars, 3g fiber), 6g pro. **Diabetic exchanges:** 2 starch, ½ fat.

Loaded Mashed
Potato Bites

LOADED MASHED
POTATO BITES

*Put leftover mashed potatoes to good use!
Turn them into fried appetizer bites loaded
with bacon, cheese and onions.*
—Becky Hardin, St. Peters, MO

PREP: 15 min. + chilling • **COOK:** 10 min.
MAKES: 1½ dozen

- 3 cups mashed potatoes
- 1½ cups shredded sharp cheddar
  cheese
- ¾ cup crumbled cooked bacon
- ½ cup chopped green onions
- 2 oz. Colby-Monterey Jack cheese, cut
  into eighteen ½-in. cubes
- ½ cup panko bread crumbs
- ½ cup grated Parmesan cheese
- ½ tsp. salt
- ½ tsp. pepper
- 1 large egg, beaten
  Oil for deep-fat frying

1. In a large bowl, combine potatoes,
shredded cheese, bacon and green
onions. Divide into eighteen ¼-cup
portions. Shape each portion around
a cheese cube to cover completely,
forming a ball. Refrigerate, covered,
at least 30 minutes.
2. In a shallow bowl, mix bread crumbs,
Parmesan cheese, salt and pepper.
Place egg in a separate shallow bowl.
Dip potato balls in egg, then in crumb
mixture, patting to help coating adhere.
3. In an electric skillet or a deep-fat
fryer, heat oil to 375°. Fry potato balls, a
few at a time, until golden brown, about
2 minutes. Drain on paper towels.
1 piece: 227 cal., 19g fat (5g sat. fat),
30mg chol., 420mg sod., 8g carb. (1g
sugars, 1g fiber), 7g pro.

PESTO MASHED
RED POTATOES

*Rich and creamy mashed potatoes get a pop
of flavor with a swirl of pesto. It's a fabulous
way to amp up a tried-and-true side dish.*
—Taste of Home *Test Kitchen*

TAKES: 30 min. • **MAKES:** 12 servings

- 4½ lbs. red potatoes, cut into 1-in. pieces
- 6 Tbsp. butter, cubed
- 1½ tsp. salt
- ¾ tsp. pepper
- 1 to 1⅓ cups heavy whipping cream,
  warmed
- ⅓ cup prepared pesto
- ¼ cup extra virgin olive oil

Place potatoes in a large saucepan or
Dutch oven and cover with water. Bring
to a boil. Reduce heat; cover and cook
for 10-15 minutes or until tender. Drain.
Mash potatoes with butter, salt, pepper
and enough cream to achieve desired
consistency. Transfer potatoes to a
serving dish; swirl pesto into potatoes.
Drizzle with olive oil; serve immediately.
¾ cup: 307 cal., 20g fat (9g sat. fat), 38mg
chol., 436mg sod., 28g carb. (2g sugars,
3g fiber), 4g pro.

WHY YOU'LL LOVE IT...

*"The potatoes are so good!
I always make traditional garlic
mashed potatoes but I wanted to
try something different and came
across this recipe. It has such great
flavor and is definitely a crowd
pleaser! I will for sure be making
this again!"*
—HKAROW9713, TASTEOFHOME.COM

Pesto Mashed
Red Potatoes

SPEEDY STUFFED POTATOES

These twice-baked potatoes are always a hit. They're delicious and easy to prepare. I use my own garlic and chives from my garden.
—Marie Hattrup, Sonoma, CA

TAKES: 30 min. • **MAKES:** 8 servings

- 4 large baking potatoes
- 3 Tbsp. butter, softened
- ⅔ cup sour cream
- ½ tsp. minced garlic
- ¾ tsp. salt
- ¼ tsp. pepper
- ½ cup shredded cheddar cheese
- Optional: Paprika and chopped green onions

1. Scrub and pierce potatoes; place on a microwave-safe plate. Microwave, uncovered, on high for 10-12 minutes or until tender, turning once.

2. When cool enough to handle, cut the potatoes in half lengthwise. Scoop out pulp, leaving a thin shell. In a large bowl, mash the pulp with butter. Stir in the sour cream, garlic, salt and pepper. Spoon into potato shells.

3. Place on a microwave-safe plate. Sprinkle with cheese. Microwave, uncovered, on high for 1-2 minutes or until heated through. If desired, top with paprika, additional pepper, and chopped green onions.

1 serving: 212 cal., 6g fat (4g sat. fat), 19mg chol., 317mg sod., 35g carb. (4g sugars, 3g fiber), 7g pro. **Diabetic exchanges:** 2 starch, 1 fat.

Maple Miso Sweet
Potato Casserole

MAPLE MISO SWEET POTATO CASSEROLE

This recipe takes a beloved holiday side dish and gives it a savory twist to complement its traditionally sweet flavors.
—Sara Schwabe, Bloomington, IN

PREP: 35 min. • **BAKE:** 30 min.
MAKES: 6 servings

- 2 Tbsp. tahini
- 2 lbs. sweet potatoes (about 2 large), peeled and cubed

TOPPING
- ¼ cup all-purpose flour
- ¼ cup packed brown sugar
- 2 Tbsp. cold butter
- 2 Tbsp. sesame seeds

FILLING
- 3 Tbsp. butter
- 3 Tbsp. maple syrup
- 2 Tbsp. white miso paste
- 1 Tbsp. rice vinegar
- ½ tsp. ground cinnamon
- ½ tsp. ground ginger

1. Preheat oven to 375°. Place tahini in freezer for 20 minutes. Place sweet potatoes in a 6-qt. stockpot; add water to cover. Bring to a boil. Reduce heat; cook, uncovered, until tender, roughly 10-12 minutes. Meanwhile, make the topping by combining flour and sugar; cut in the butter and chilled tahini until crumbly. Stir in sesame seeds.
2. Drain potatoes; return to pan. Beat until mashed. Add butter, maple syrup, miso paste, rice vinegar, cinnamon and ginger. Transfer mixture to a greased 13x9-in. baking dish. Sprinkle topping over mixture.
3. Bake, covered, 15 minutes. Uncover, bake until the topping is golden brown, 15-20 minutes.

⅔ cup: 386 cal., 15g fat (7g sat. fat), 25mg chol., 383mg sod., 60g carb. (32g sugars, 6g fiber), 5g pro.

Test Kitchen Tip

It's easy to prep this sweet potato casserole in advance. Prepare the mashed potato filling the day before and refrigerate overnight. Top with the streusel topping and bake the casserole the next day.

Speedy
Stuffed Potatoes

Potato Kugel

ROASTED BALSAMIC SWEET POTATOES

The standard cold potato salad belongs to the summer months, but this warm, spicy dish is perfect for the cozy season!
—Karen Vande Slunt, Watertown, WI

PREP: 30 min. • **COOK:** 30 min.
MAKES: 12 servings

- 6 medium sweet potatoes, cubed
- 1 tsp. olive oil
- ½ tsp. salt
- ½ tsp. pepper
- 1 lb. bacon strips, chopped
- 4 celery ribs, chopped
- 1 medium onion, thinly sliced
- 3 garlic cloves, minced
- 1 cup beef stock
- ⅔ cup balsamic vinegar
- 4 tsp. paprika
- ¾ tsp. ground cumin, optional
- 6 green onions, chopped
  Minced fresh parsley, optional

1. Preheat oven to 375°. Place sweet potatoes in a 15x10x1-in. pan; drizzle with olive oil and sprinkle with salt and pepper. Turn to coat. Bake until tender, 30-35 minutes.
2. Meanwhile, in a large skillet, cook bacon over medium-low heat until crisp; drain. Discard all but 4 tsp. drippings.
3. Cook celery and onion in drippings over medium heat until tender, roughly 6-8 minutes. Stir in the garlic; cook for about 1 minute. Add beef stock and balsamic vinegar; simmer until liquid is reduced by half, 5-8 minutes. Add paprika and, if desired, cumin; cook 1 minute longer.
4. Pour balsamic mixture over sweet potatoes; add bacon. Toss to coat. Top with the green onions and, if desired, minced fresh parsley; serve sweet potatoes immediately.
½ cup: 287 cal., 16g fat (5g sat. fat), 25mg chol., 413mg sod., 30g carb. (15g sugars, 4g fiber), 7g pro.

POTATO KUGEL

The secret to keeping your potatoes their whitest is to switch back and forth when grating the potatoes and onion in your food processor or box grater.
—Ellen Ruzinsky, Yorktown Heights, NY

PREP: 20 min. • **BAKE:** 40 min.
MAKES: 12 servings

- 2 large eggs
- ¼ cup matzo meal
- 2 tsp. kosher salt
  Dash pepper
- 6 large potatoes (about 4¾ lbs.), peeled
- 1 large onion, cut into 6 wedges
- ¼ cup canola oil

1. Preheat oven to 375°. In a large bowl, whisk eggs, matzo meal, salt and pepper.
2. In a food processor fitted with the grating attachment, alternately grate potatoes and onion. Add to egg mixture; toss to coat. In a small saucepan, heat oil over medium heat until warmed. Stir into the potato mixture. Transfer to a greased 13x9-in. baking dish. Bake 40-50 minutes or until golden brown.
1 serving: 210 cal., 6g fat (1g sat. fat), 35mg chol., 515mg sod., 36g carb. (3g sugars, 3g fiber), 5g pro.

Roasted Balsamic
Sweet Potatoes

GRANNY'S APPLE SCALLOPED POTATOES

I created this dish because I love scalloped potatoes and apples. This recipe is perfectly sized for the two of us , but you could easily double it.
—Shirley Rickis, The Villages, FL

PREP: 25 min. • **BAKE:** 55 min. + standing
MAKES: 4 servings

- 1 medium Granny Smith apple, peeled and thinly sliced
- 1 tsp. sugar
- 1 tsp. lemon juice
- 2 Tbsp. butter
- ½ cup sliced sweet onion
- 4 medium red potatoes, thinly sliced (about 1 lb.)
- ¾ cup plus 2 Tbsp. shredded Parmesan cheese, divided
- ½ cup heavy whipping cream
- ½ tsp. minced fresh thyme or ¼ tsp. dried thyme
- ¼ tsp. salt
- ¼ tsp. pepper
- 4 bacon strips, cooked and crumbled Chopped fresh parsley, optional

1. Preheat the oven to 350°. In a small bowl, combine apple slices, sugar and lemon juice; toss to coat. Set aside. In an 8- or 9-in. cast-iron or other ovenproof skillet, heat the butter over medium heat. Add the onion; cook and stir until crisp-tender, about 3 minutes. Remove from the heat.

2. Alternately arrange potato and apple slices in a single layer in same skillet. Combine ¾ cup Parmesan cheese, cream, thyme, salt and pepper; pour over top.

3. Bake, uncovered, 50 minutes. Top with bacon and remaining 2 Tbsp. Parmesan cheese. Bake until potatoes are tender and top is lightly browned, 5-10 minutes longer. Let stand 10 minutes before serving. If desired, sprinkle with parsley.

1 serving: 376 cal., 25g fat (15g sat. fat), 70mg chol., 651mg sod., 27g carb. (7g sugars, 3g fiber), 13g pro.

Granny's Apple
Scalloped Potatoes

DOLLOPED SWEET POTATOES

A little microwave magic transforms sweet potatoes into a speedy and special side dish for hectic holiday feasts. Brown sugar and pumpkin pie spice flavor the simple but rich cream-cheese topping.
—Taste of Home *Test Kitchen*

TAKES: 15 min. • **MAKES:** 4 servings

- 4 small sweet potatoes
- 3 oz. cream cheese, softened
- 1 Tbsp. butter, softened
- 2 Tbsp. brown sugar
- ¼ tsp. pumpkin pie spice

1. Scrub and pierce sweet potatoes; place on a microwave-safe plate. Microwave, uncovered, on high until tender, 10-13 minutes, turning twice. Meanwhile, in a small bowl, beat the cream cheese, butter, brown sugar and pumpkin pie spice.
2. Cut an X in the top of each potato; fluff pulp with a fork. Dollop with the cream cheese mixture.
Note: This sweet potato recipe was tested in a 1,100-watt microwave.
1 serving: 166 cal., 7g fat (5g sat. fat), 23mg chol., 128mg sod., 22g carb. (13g sugars, 2g fiber), 3g pro. **Diabetic exchanges:** 1½ starch, 1½ fat.

Test Kitchen Tip

To make these tasty tubers even more indulgent, sprinkle the cooked sweet potatoes with mini marshmallows, chopped pecans or sweetened shredded coconut.

Jalapeno & Cotija Cheese Potato Stack Pie

JALAPENO & COTIJA CHEESE POTATO STACK PIE

Pie isn't just for dessert anymore. Stacking thinly sliced potatoes with layers of minced jalapenos and crumbled Cotija cheese turns ordinary spuds into something spectacular, especially when served with zesty salsa and sour cream.
—Colleen Delawder, Herndon, VA

PREP: 20 min. • **BAKE:** 50 min.
MAKES: 8 servings

- 2½ lbs. red potatoes, peeled and thinly sliced
- ¼ cup butter, melted
- ½ tsp. salt
- ¼ tsp. pepper
- 2 jalapeno peppers, seeded and minced
- 1¼ cups crumbled Cotija or feta cheese
  Salsa and sour cream, optional

1. Preheat the oven to 375°. Line a 15x10x1-in. sheet pan with parchment paper. Remove the bottom of a 9-in. springform pan and place the round outer edge in the middle of parchment.
2. Place the potatoes, butter, salt and pepper in a large bowl; toss to coat. Layer a third of the potatoes evenly within the springform ring. Sprinkle with a third of the jalapenos and a third of the cheese. Repeat layers. Top with remaining potatoes and jalapenos.
3. Bake for 35 minutes. Top with the remaining cheese. Bake 15-20 minutes longer or until the potatoes are tender. Let stand 5 minutes before removing ring. If desired, serve pie with salsa and sour cream.
Note: Wear disposable gloves when cutting hot peppers; the oils can burn skin. Avoid touching your face.
1 serving: 223 cal., 12g fat (7g sat. fat), 34mg chol., 477mg sod., 23g carb. (2g sugars, 3g fiber), 7g pro.

Make-Ahead
Creamy Potatoes

MAKE-AHEAD CREAMY POTATOES

On holidays, I serve the classic dishes plus a new spin or two on old family favorites. I put these creamy potatoes together the night before and bake the next day to save time on the day of the party.
—Wendy Ball, Battle Creek, MI

PREP: 1 hour + chilling • **BAKE:** 55 min.
MAKES: 16 servings (¾ cup each)

- 5 lbs. potatoes (about 6 large)
- ½ cup butter, divided
- ½ cup chopped fresh mushrooms
- 2 Tbsp. all-purpose flour
- 1 cup 2% milk or half-and-half cream
- 1 tsp. salt
- ½ tsp. pepper
- ½ tsp. dried thyme
- 2 cups shredded sharp cheddar cheese
- 2 cups sour cream
- 1 medium onion, chopped
- ½ cup dry bread crumbs
- ¼ cup grated Parmesan cheese

1. Place whole potatoes in a large stockpot; add water to cover. Bring to a boil. Reduce heat; cook, uncovered, until tender, 20-25 minutes. Drain.
2. Meanwhile, in a large saucepan, heat ¼ cup butter over medium-high heat. Add mushrooms; cook and stir until tender, 2-4 minutes. Stir in flour until blended; gradually whisk in the milk, salt, pepper and thyme. Bring to a boil, stirring constantly; cook and stir until thickened, 1-2 minutes.
3. Peel and cube potatoes when cool enough to handle. Press through a potato ricer or strainer into a large bowl; stir in cheddar cheese, sour cream, mushroom mixture, onion and remaining butter. Transfer potato mixture to a greased 13x9-in. baking dish. Refrigerate, covered, overnight.
4. Preheat oven to 375°. Remove the potatoes from refrigerator; uncover and let stand while oven heats. Sprinkle with bread crumbs and Parmesan cheese.

Bake, uncovered, until heated through, 55-65 minutes.
¾ cup: 283 cal., 16g fat (11g sat. fat), 52mg chol., 345mg sod., 25g carb. (4g sugars, 2g fiber), 8g pro.

CARAMEL SWEET POTATOES

The caramel sauce, which boasts a sweet butterscotch flavor, is the star of this recipe. Pair this side dish with poultry or ham.
—Mary Jo Patrick, Napoleon, OH

PREP: 35 min. • **BAKE:** 25 min.
MAKES: 10 servings

- 6 medium sweet potatoes, peeled and cut into 1-in. chunks
- ½ cup packed brown sugar
- ½ cup corn syrup
- ¼ cup whole milk
- 2 Tbsp. butter
- ½ to 1 tsp. salt
- ½ tsp. ground cinnamon

1. Place sweet potatoes in a Dutch oven; cover with water. Bring to a boil. Reduce heat; cover and simmer for 20 minutes.
2. Drain and transfer to a greased 13x9-in. baking dish. Bake, uncovered, at 325° for 15 minutes.
3. Meanwhile, in a small saucepan, combine the remaining ingredients. Bring to a boil; pour over the sweet potatoes. Bake 10-15 minutes longer or until glazed, basting frequently.
¾ cup: 182 cal., 3g fat (2g sat. fat), 7mg chol., 158mg sod., 40g carb. (22g sugars, 2g fiber), 1g pro.

Did You Know?

Corn syrup contains glucose (which won't crystallize), so adding it to the mix builds in a little insurance to protect against grainy caramel.

Caramel Sweet Potatoes

SWEET POTATO MERINGUE BAKE

Here's a slightly sweeter variation of a sweet potato casserole, minus the extra sugar. It's simple enough to throw together even after the holidays. For more sauce, you can add extra water, butter, brown sugar or maple syrup to the filling before baking. Rum, brandy or lemon zest can be added to change up the flavor.
—Kathy Kinomoto, Bothell, WA

PREP: 15 min. • **BAKE:** 40 min.
MAKES: 9 servings

- 5 medium sweet potatoes, peeled and cut into ¼-in. slices
- ½ cup packed brown sugar
- ½ cup chopped pecans
- ⅓ cup water
- 3 Tbsp. unsalted butter or ghee, melted
- 3 large egg whites, room temperature
- ½ tsp. vanilla extract
- ⅓ cup sugar

1. Preheat oven to 375°. Place potatoes in a greased 8-in. square baking pan. Combine brown sugar, pecans, water and butter; pour over potatoes. Bake, mixture uncovered, just until tender, 30-35 minutes.
2. Meanwhile, for meringue, in a small bowl, beat egg whites and vanilla on medium speed until foamy. Gradually add sugar, 1 Tbsp. at a time, beating on high after each addition, until sugar is dissolved. Continue beating until stiff glossy peaks form. Spread over hot potatoes. Bake until golden brown, 8-10 minutes longer.
1 serving: 265 cal., 8g fat (3g sat. fat), 10mg chol., 33mg sod., 46g carb. (30g sugars, 4g fiber), 4g pro.

Sweet Potato Meringue Bake

Rosemary Potatoes with
Caramelized Onions

ROSEMARY POTATOES WITH CARAMELIZED ONIONS

Roasted potatoes are amazing. Add some rosemary and caramelized onions and they are over-the-top delicious!
—Mary Jones, Athens, OH

PREP: 15 min. • **BAKE:** 45 min.
MAKES: 6 servings

- 2 lbs. small red potatoes, quartered
- 2 garlic cloves, minced
- 1 Tbsp. olive oil
- 2 tsp. minced fresh rosemary or ½ tsp. dried rosemary, crushed
- ½ tsp. minced fresh thyme or ⅛ tsp. dried thyme
- ¼ tsp. salt
- ¼ tsp. pepper

CARAMELIZED ONIONS
- 2 large sweet onions, chopped
- 2 Tbsp. olive oil
- 1 Tbsp. sugar
- 2 tsp. balsamic vinegar

1. In a large bowl, combine the first 7 ingredients; toss to coat. Transfer to a greased 15x10x1-in. baking pan.
2. Bake at 425° for 45-50 minutes or until potatoes are tender, stirring once.
3. Meanwhile, in a large skillet, saute onions in oil until softened. Stir in sugar. Reduce heat to medium-low; cook for 30-40 minutes or until deep golden brown, stirring occasionally. Stir in the vinegar.
4. Transfer roasted potatoes to a large bowl; stir in caramelized onions.
¾ cup: 215 cal., 7g fat (1g sat. fat), 0 chol., 117mg sod., 35g carb., 4g fiber, 4g pro.

Spiced Mashed
Sweet Potatoes

SPICED MASHED SWEET POTATOES

I created these mashed sweet potatoes shortly after my firstborn began eating solid food. She loved them then and still does today, as does her sister. The recipe is a staple in our home year-round, but especially around the holidays.
—Jenn Tidwell, Fair Oaks, CA

PREP: 10 min. • **COOK:** 20 min.
MAKES: 8 servings

 10 cups peeled and cubed sweet
    potatoes (about 6 potatoes)
 ½ cup heavy whipping cream
 ½ cup orange juice
 1 Tbsp. brown sugar
 1 tsp. grated orange zest
 ½ tsp. ground cinnamon
 ¼ tsp. salt
 ¼ tsp. ground nutmeg

1. Place sweet potatoes in a large Dutch oven; add water to cover. Bring to a boil. Reduce the heat; cook, uncovered, until tender, 15-20 minutes. Meanwhile, in a small saucepan, heat the remaining ingredients until bubbles form around the side of pan; remove from heat.
2. Drain potatoes; return to pan. Mash the potatoes, gradually adding the cream mixture.
¾ cup: 208 cal., 6g fat (4g sat. fat), 17mg chol., 170mg sod., 37g carb. (10g sugars, 5g fiber), 3g pro.

ROASTED TATER ROUNDS WITH GREEN ONIONS & TARRAGON

I'm crazy for potatoes, especially when they're toasted to crispy perfection. Toss them with fresh herbs and green onions for a bold finish.
—Ally Phillips, Murrells Inlet, SC

PREP: 25 min. • **BROIL:** 10 min.
MAKES: 8 servings

 4 lbs. potatoes (about 8 medium),
    sliced ¼ in. thick
    Cooking spray
 2 tsp. sea salt
 1 tsp. coarsely ground pepper
 6 green onions, thinly sliced
    (about ¾ cup)
 3 Tbsp. minced fresh parsley
 2 Tbsp. minced fresh tarragon
    Olive oil, optional

1. Preheat broiler. Place the potatoes in a large microwave-safe bowl; spritz with cooking spray and toss to coat. Microwave, covered, on high until almost tender, 10-12 minutes, stirring halfway through cooking.
2. Spread the potatoes into greased 15x10x1-in. baking pans. Spritz with additional cooking spray; sprinkle with salt and pepper.
3. Broil 4-6 in. from heat until golden brown, 10-12 minutes, stirring halfway through cooking. In a small bowl, mix the green onions, parsley and tarragon. Sprinkle over potatoes; toss to coat. If desired, drizzle with olive oil.
¾ cup: 185 cal., 1g fat (0 sat. fat), 0 chol., 497mg sod., 41g carb. (2g sugars, 5g fiber), 5g pro.

Roasted Tater Rounds with
Green Onions & Tarragon

SWEET POTATO SOUFFLE WITH PECANS

My grandmother makes this sweet potato souffle recipe every Thanksgiving. It's one of those heirloom recipes that stirs up so much love and memories—it must be shared!
—Natalie Gray, Moreland, GA

PREP: 30 min. • **COOK:** 30 min.
MAKES: 1 serving

- 2 large eggs, beaten
- 1 cup butter, melted
- ½ cup light corn syrup
- ½ cup sugar
- 4 cups mashed sweet potatoes
- 1 (14 oz.) evaporated milk

TOPPING

- 1 cup packed brown sugar
- ⅓ cup all-purpose flour
- ⅓ cup butter, melted
- 1 cup chopped pecans

Preheat oven to 350°. Combine eggs, butter, corn syrup and sugar in large bowl until creamy. Add the mashed potatoes and milk. Spoon mixture into a greased 2-qt. baking dish. Combine brown sugar, flour, butter and pecans. Sprinkle evenly on top of sweet potato mixture. Bake until puffy and golden brown, about 30 minutes.

½ cup: 406 cal., 23g fat (12g sat. fat), 73mg chol., 190mg sod., 48g carb. (36g sugars, 3g fiber), 5g pro.

Air-Fryer Red Potatoes

AIR-FRYER RED POTATOES

Fragrant rosemary, fresh or dried, gives these red potatoes a distinctive but subtle taste. The dish is simple to prepare in the air fryer, yet elegant in color and flavor. It's a stellar addition to any menu.
—Margie Wampler, Butler, PA

TAKES: 20 min. • **MAKES:** 8 servings

- 2 lbs. small unpeeled red potatoes, cut into wedges
- 2 Tbsp. olive oil
- 1 Tbsp. minced fresh rosemary or 1 tsp. dried rosemary, crushed
- 2 garlic cloves, minced
- ½ tsp. salt
- ¼ tsp. pepper

1. Preheat air fryer to 400°. Drizzle potatoes with oil. Sprinkle with the rosemary, garlic, salt and pepper; toss gently to coat.
2. Place on ungreased tray in air-fryer basket. Cook until potatoes are golden brown and tender, 10-12 minutes, stirring once.

1 cup: 113 cal., 4g fat (0 sat. fat), 0 chol., 155mg sod., 18g carb. (1g sugars, 2g fiber), 2g pro. **Diabetic exchanges:** 1 starch, 1 fat.

Health Tip

Air-fried foods aren't necessarily "healthy," but since little to no oil is used, they typically have fewer calories from fat that would otherwise come from deep-frying.

HASSELBACK SWEET POTATOES

My family and friends love the warm inviting flavors of the luscious citrus butter, smooth cream cheese, sweet dates, fresh sage and toasted pecans that surround and capture the deliciousness of sweet potatoes in every forkworthy bite.
—Brenda Watts, Gaffney, SC

PREP: 45 min. • **BAKE:** 1 hour 10 min.
MAKES: 6 servings

6 medium sweet potatoes
½ cup unsalted butter, melted
2 Tbsp. brown sugar
2 Tbsp. orange juice
2 tsp. grated orange zest
½ tsp. kosher salt
½ tsp. coarsely ground pepper
6 oz. cream cheese, softened
12 pitted dates, chopped
12 fresh sage leaves, chopped
½ cup chopped pecans
 Additional fresh sage, chopped, optional

1. Preheat the oven to 425°. Cut thin slices lengthwise from the bottoms of sweet potatoes to allow them to lie flat; discard slices. Place potatoes flat side down; cut crosswise into ⅛-in. slices, leaving them intact at bottom. Arrange the sweet potatoes in a greased 13x9-in. baking pan.

2. In a small bowl, whisk together butter, brown sugar, orange juice and orange zest. Spoon half of the butter mixture evenly over the sweet potatoes; sprinkle with salt and pepper. Combine cream cheese, dates and sage; spread between potato slices.

3. Bake, covered, until the potatoes are just becoming tender, 45-50 minutes. Remove pan from oven and uncover; spoon the remaining butter mixture over potatoes and top with pecans. Return to oven and bake until potatoes are completely tender and topping is golden brown, 25-30 minutes longer. If desired, serve with additional chopped fresh sage.

1 sweet potato: 552 cal., 32g fat (16g sat. fat), 69mg chol., 271mg sod., 64g carb. (34g sugars, 8g fiber), 6g pro.

WHY YOU'LL LOVE IT...

"This is a meal in itself. Unbelievably delicious, such a delightful combo of flavors. And makes an impressive presentation for guests. So worth the slight effort to make this dish. It's amazing!"
—SUSAN WALSH, TASTEOFHOME.COM

Hasselback Sweet Potatoes

Rosemary Roasted
Sweet Potatoes

⑤🍎 ROSEMARY ROASTED SWEET POTATOES

We love sweet potatoes, and these are the best. This is our go-to recipe. Roasting them brings out all the wonderful sweetness!
—Kristin Stone, Little Elm, TX

PREP: 10 min. • **BAKE:** 30 min.
MAKES: 4 servings

2	large sweet potatoes, peeled and cut into ¾-in. rounds
1	Tbsp. olive oil
1	tsp. dried rosemary, crushed
½	tsp. salt
½	tsp. chili powder
½	tsp. pepper
⅛	tsp. cayenne pepper

Preheat the oven to 425°. Place all the ingredients in a large bowl; toss to coat. Line a 15x10x1-in. baking pan with foil; grease foil. Place sweet potatoes in a single layer in the prepared pan. Bake, covered, for 20 minutes. Uncover and bake until golden brown, 10-12 minutes longer, turning once.
1 serving: 209 cal., 4g fat (1g sat. fat), 0 chol., 322mg sod., 42g carb. (17g sugars, 5g fiber), 3g pro.

Test Kitchen Tip

When shopping for sweet potatoes, it's best to pick them up and give them a once-over. They should feel heavy for their size and have a firm texture when you squeeze them lightly. Skip any with bruises, sprouts or deep gashes.

Butternut Squash & Potato Mash

🍎 BUTTERNUT SQUASH & POTATO MASH

Some people like squash, some people like potatoes. Mash the two ingredients together, and you've got a dish everyone will love! This is a smart way to get kids to eat their veggies.
—Jasmine Rose, Crystal Lake, IL

PREP: 25 min. • **COOK:** 20 min.
MAKES: 10 servings

8	cups cubed peeled butternut squash (about 4 lbs.)
4	cups cubed peeled potatoes (about 4 medium)
16	garlic cloves, peeled
2	Tbsp. sesame seeds
1	tsp. ground cumin
1	cup shredded Colby-Monterey Jack cheese
2	Tbsp. butter
1½	tsp. salt
½	tsp. pepper

1. Place squash, potatoes and garlic in a Dutch oven; add water to cover. Bring to a boil. Reduce the heat; cook, uncovered, 10-15 minutes or until tender.
2. Meanwhile, in a dry small skillet, toast sesame seeds and cumin over medium-low heat 3-4 minutes or until aromatic, stirring frequently. Remove from heat.
3. Drain the squash mixture. Mash the vegetables, adding cheese, butter, salt and pepper. Sprinkle with the sesame seed mixture.
¾ cup: 193 cal., 7g fat (4g sat. fat), 16mg chol., 450mg sod., 31g carb. (4g sugars, 4g fiber), 6g pro. **Diabetic exchanges:** 2 starch, 1½ fat.

BACON & BLUE STUFFED SWEET POTATOES

Liven up sweet potatoes with pears, bacon, honey and fresh tarragon. If Gorgonzola isn't your thing, use plain or smoked Gouda.
—Jeanne Holt, St. Paul, MN

PREP: 20 min. • **BAKE:** 65 min.
MAKES: 4 servings

- 4 medium sweet potatoes (about 10 oz. each)
- 3 Tbsp. butter, softened
- 2 tsp. honey
- ½ tsp. salt
- ⅛ tsp. cayenne pepper
- ⅛ tsp. pepper
- 1 small ripe pear, peeled and chopped
- 4 bacon strips, cooked and chopped, divided
- ¼ cup plus 3 Tbsp. crumbled Gorgonzola cheese, divided
- 2 green onions, thinly sliced
- 2 tsp. minced fresh tarragon or ¼ tsp. dried tarragon

1. Preheat oven to 375°. Scrub sweet potatoes; pierce several times with a fork. Bake on a foil-lined baking sheet until tender, 45-60 minutes. Cool slightly.
2. Cut a thin slice from the top of each potato. Scoop out the pulp, leaving ¼-in.-thick shells. Mash pulp with butter, honey and seasonings. Stir in the pear, ⅓ cup chopped bacon, ¼ cup cheese, green onions and tarragon. Spoon into shells; return to baking sheet. Top with remaining cheese.
3. Bake until heated through, roughly 20-25 minutes. Sprinkle with remaining chopped bacon.
1 stuffed potato: 388 cal., 16g fat (9g sat. fat), 42mg chol., 696mg sod., 55g carb. (25g sugars, 7g fiber), 9g pro.

SWEET CORN & POTATO GRATIN

Two popular vegetables are paired together in this old-fashioned, down-home side. The garlic and onion flavors appeal to adults, and the crispy breadcrumb topping has kids asking for seconds.
—Jennifer Olson, Pleasanton, CA

PREP: 30 min. • **BAKE:** 45 min. + standing
MAKES: 8 servings

- 1 medium onion, thinly sliced
- 2 Tbsp. butter
- 2 Tbsp. all-purpose flour
- 2 garlic cloves, minced
- 1 tsp. salt
- ½ tsp. pepper
- 1 cup whole milk
- 2 lbs. medium Yukon Gold potatoes, peeled and cut into ⅛-in. slices
- 2 cups fresh or frozen corn
- 1 can (8¼ oz.) cream-style corn
- ¾ cup panko bread crumbs
- 1 Tbsp. butter, melted

1. Preheat oven to 350°. In a large saucepan, saute onion in butter until tender. Stir in flour, garlic, salt and pepper until blended; gradually add milk. Stir in potatoes. Bring to a boil. Reduce the heat; cook and stir until potatoes are crisp-tender, 8-10 minutes.
2. Stir in corn and cream-style corn. Transfer to an 8-in. square baking dish coated with cooking spray.
3. In a small bowl, combine the bread crumbs and butter; sprinkle over the potatoes. Bake until golden brown and potatoes are tender, 45-50 minutes. Let stand 10 minutes before serving.
¾ cup: 213 cal., 6g fat (3g sat. fat), 14mg chol., 452mg sod., 37g carb. (6g sugars, 3g fiber), 5g pro.

Sweet Corn & Potato Gratin

Sweet Potato Kale Pilaf

SWEET POTATO KALE PILAF

The combination of sweet potatoes, bacon, asparagus and kale makes this simple side dish taste amazing! To save time and dishes, cook the rice in an electric pressure cooker. You can also use this appliance to saute the other ingredients.
—Courtney Stultz, Weir, KS

PREP: 15 min. • **COOK:** 1 hour
MAKES: 8 cups

1   cup uncooked wild rice
2¼ cups vegetable broth or water
1   tsp. olive oil
4   bacon strips, chopped
1   lb. fresh asparagus, trimmed and cut into 2-in. pieces
1   large sweet potato, peeled and chopped
½   cup chopped red onion
1   cup chopped fresh kale
1   garlic clove, minced
½   tsp. salt
½   tsp. pepper
    Chopped fresh parsley

1. Rinse wild rice thoroughly; drain. In a large saucepan, combine broth, rice and oil; bring to a boil. Reduce heat; simmer, covered, until rice is fluffy and tender, 50-55 minutes. Drain if necessary.
2. Meanwhile, in a large skillet, cook bacon over medium heat until crisp. Remove to paper towels to drain. Add asparagus, sweet potato and onion to drippings; cook and stir over medium-high heat until the potatoes are crisp-tender, 8-10 minutes.
3. Stir in kale, garlic, salt and pepper. Cook and stir until the vegetables are tender, 8-10 minutes. Stir in rice and reserved bacon. Sprinkle with parsley.
¾ cup: 156 cal., 5g fat (2g sat. fat), 7mg chol., 350mg sod., 23g carb. (5g sugars, 3g fiber), 5g pro. **Diabetic exchanges:** 1½ starch, 1 fat.

Cheesy Chili Fries

GRAM'S CHEESY POTATOES

For my family, comfort food often comes in the form of a potato with gooey, cheesy goodness. No gathering or special occasion is the same without it. It's a tradition in our family that once a recipe is bestowed upon you, you add one new ingredient to make it yours. My grandmother added paprika to this recipe and passed it on to my mom. My mom added the bacon, and when she passed it to me, I added the green chilies. What will you add to make it yours?
—Erin Puariea, Milwaukee, WI

PREP: 40 min. • **COOK:** 30 min.
MAKES: 8-10 servings

- 3½ to 4 lbs. baking potatoes
- ½ cup butter
- 2½ cups shredded cheddar cheese, divided
- 2 cups sour cream
- 2 Tbsp. green onions or chives
- 1 small can chopped green chilies
- 8 to 10 slices bacon, cooked and crumbled
  Salt and pepper, to taste
- ¼ tsp. paprika

1. Scrub unpeeled potatoes and bake at 400° for 40 minutes or until slightly firm. Cool overnight or few hours in the refrigerator. Peel and grate potatoes.
2. In a large pan, heat the butter and 2 cups cheese over low heat, stirring constantly, until cheese is barely melted. Remove from heat. Stir in the sour cream, green onions, chilies, bacon, salt and pepper.
3. Fold mixture into potatoes. Pour into a lightly greased 2½-qt. casserole dish; sprinkle with the remaining cheese and paprika. Bake at 350° for 30-40 minutes until lightly browned.
1 serving: 460 cal., 32g fat (18g sat. fat), 95mg chol., 483mg sod., 31g carb. (3g sugars, 4g fiber), 15g pro.

5i

CHEESY CHILI FRIES

My family is all about chili fries, but restaurant versions pile on the calories. For a healthier approach, bake them and serve with green onions and avocado.
—Beverly Nowling, Bristol, FL

TAKES: 30 min. • **MAKES:** 4 servings

- 5 cups frozen seasoned curly fries
- 1 Tbsp. olive oil
- 1 can (15 oz.) vegetarian chili with beans
- 1 cup shredded cheddar cheese
  Optional toppings: Sour cream, thinly sliced green onions and cubed avocado

1. Preheat oven to 450°. Place fries on an ungreased 15x10x1-in. baking pan; drizzle with oil and toss to coat. Bake according to package directions.
2. Divide fries among four 2-cup baking dishes; top each with chili and cheese. Bake until the cheese is melted, roughly 5-7 minutes. Serve fries with toppings as desired.
Note: You may use an 8-in. square baking dish instead of four 2-cup baking dishes. Bake as directed.
1 serving: 435 cal., 22g fat (8g sat. fat), 47mg chol., 1001mg sod., 44g carb. (4g sugars, 5g fiber), 17g pro.

Gram's Cheesy
Potatoes

⑤ GRILLED HASH BROWNS

Since my husband and I love to grill meats, we're always looking for easy side dishes that cook on the grill, too. So I came up with this simple recipe for hash browns.
—Kelly Chastain, Bedford, IN

TAKES: 20 min. • **MAKES:** 4 servings

- 3½ cups frozen cubed hash brown potatoes, thawed
- 1 small onion, chopped
- 1 Tbsp. beef bouillon granules
  Dash seasoned salt
  Dash pepper
- 1 Tbsp. butter, melted

1. Place potatoes on a piece of heavy-duty foil (about 20 in. x 18 in.) coated with cooking spray. Sprinkle with onion, bouillon, seasoned salt and pepper; drizzle with butter.
2. Fold foil around potatoes and seal tightly. Grill, covered, over indirect medium heat for 10-15 minutes or until potatoes are tender, turning once.
¾ cup: 89 cal., 3g fat (2g sat. fat), 8mg chol., 652mg sod., 14g carb. (2g sugars, 1g fiber), 2g pro.

Bourbon-Infused Fingerling Potatoes

BOURBON-INFUSED FINGERLING POTATOES

The combination of bourbon, Worcestershire sauce and garlic gives these saucy potatoes a burst of flavor. They're easy to make, too!
—JoAnn Mathias, Hoschton, GA

PREP: 15 min. • **COOK:** 30 min.
MAKES: 10 servings

- 2 lbs. assorted fingerling or other small potatoes
- 5 Tbsp. butter, divided
- 2 medium red onions, finely chopped
- 2 medium green peppers, finely chopped
- ½ cup bourbon
- ¼ cup reduced-sodium soy sauce
- 2 Tbsp. brown sugar
- 2 Tbsp. canola oil
- 2 Tbsp. Worcestershire sauce
- 2 garlic cloves, minced
- ½ tsp. salt
- ½ tsp. pepper

1. Place potatoes in a large saucepan; add water to cover. Bring to a boil. Reduce the heat; cook, uncovered, 10-15 minutes or until tender. Drain.
2. In a 12-in. skillet, heat 2 Tbsp. butter over medium-high heat; add the onions and green peppers. Cook and stir until tender; remove from pan.
3. In same pan, heat remaining butter over medium-high heat; add potatoes. Using a fork or potato masher, flatten potatoes slightly. Cook for 3-4 minutes on each side or until lightly browned. Return onion mixture to pan.
4. In a small bowl, whisk the remaining ingredients until blended; add to pan. Bring to a boil; cook 1-2 minutes or until liquid is absorbed.
¾ cup: 175 cal., 9g fat (4g sat. fat), 15mg chol., 439mg sod., 19g carb. (5g sugars, 2g fiber), 3g pro.

TWICE-BAKED CHEDDAR POTATO CASSEROLE

Bacon, cheddar and sour cream turn ordinary potatoes into an extraordinary casserole. It's one of our family's favorite standbys for the holidays.
—Kyle Cox, Scottsdale, AZ

PREP: 70 min. • **BAKE:** 15 min.
MAKES: 12 servings

- 8 medium baking potatoes (about 8 oz. each)
- ½ cup butter, cubed
- ⅔ cup sour cream
- ⅔ cup 2% milk
- 1 tsp. salt
- ¾ tsp. pepper
- 10 bacon strips, cooked and crumbled, divided
- 2 cups shredded cheddar cheese, divided
- 4 green onions, chopped, divided

1. Preheat oven to 425°. Scrub potatoes; pierce several times with a fork. Bake until tender, 45-60 minutes. Remove from oven; reduce oven setting to 350°.
2. When potatoes are cool enough to handle, cut each potato lengthwise in half. Scoop out pulp and place in a large bowl; discard shells. Mash pulp with butter; stir in sour cream, milk, salt and pepper.
3. Reserve ¼ cup crumbled bacon for topping. Gently fold remaining bacon, 1 cup cheese and half the green onions into potato mixture (do not overmix).
4. Transfer to a greased 11x7-in. baking dish. Top with remaining cheese and green onions; sprinkle with reserved bacon. Bake until heated through and cheese is melted, 15-20 minutes.
⅔ cup: 301 cal., 19g fat (11g sat. fat), 57mg chol., 517mg sod., 22g carb. (3g sugars, 2g fiber), 10g pro.

Twice-Baked Cheddar Potato Casserole

Beet & Sweet
Potato Fries, Page 184

Page 187

Page 188

Favorite Root Vegetables

Earthy, hearty and endlessly versatile, root vegetables make a distinct and satisfying addition to any dinner plate. Whether mashed, sauteed, roasted or fried, in a cool salad or a heartwarming casserole, this family of veggies always has something new to offer.

Page 182

Page 176

ROSEMARY ROOT VEGETABLES

This heartwarming side dish is sure to get rave reviews! Although the ingredient list may look long, you'll soon see that this colorful fall medley is a snap to prepare.
—Taste of Home *Test Kitchen*

PREP: 20 min. • **BAKE:** 20 min.
MAKES: 10 servings

- 1 small rutabaga, peeled and chopped
- 1 medium sweet potato, peeled and chopped
- 2 medium parsnips, peeled and chopped
- 1 medium turnip, peeled and chopped
- ¼ lb. fresh Brussels sprouts, halved
- 2 Tbsp. olive oil
- 2 Tbsp. minced fresh rosemary or 2 tsp. dried rosemary, crushed
- 1 tsp. minced garlic
- ½ tsp. salt
- ½ tsp. pepper

Preheat oven to 425°. Place vegetables in a large bowl. In a small bowl, combine oil, rosemary, garlic, salt and pepper. Pour oil mixture over vegetables; toss to coat. Arrange the vegetables in a single layer in two 15x10x1-in. baking pans coated with cooking spray. Bake, uncovered, stirring once, until tender, 20-25 minutes.

¾ cup: 78 cal., 3g fat (0 sat. fat), 0 chol., 137mg sod., 13g carb. (5g sugars, 3g fiber), 1g pro. **Diabetic exchanges:** 1 starch, ½ fat.

Rosemary
Root Vegetables

CLASSIC VEGGIE SIDE DISH

Equally good with pork or beef roast—or with a Thanksgiving turkey—this dish is one my husband of 36 years requests at least once a month.
—Marilyn Smudzinski, Peru, IL

PREP: 25 min. • **COOK:** 20 min.
MAKES: 8 servings

- 6 small red potatoes, quartered
- 1 medium rutabaga, peeled and cut into 1-in. cubes
- ½ tsp. salt
- 3 medium carrots, cut into ½-in. slices
- 1 medium turnip, peeled and cut into 1-in. cubes
- 1 to 2 medium parsnips, peeled and cut into ½-in. slices
- 1 medium onion, cut into eighths

GLAZE
- 1 Tbsp. butter
- 3 Tbsp. brown sugar
- 1 tsp. cornstarch
- ¼ cup water
- 3 Tbsp. lemon juice
- ½ tsp. dill weed
- ⅛ tsp. pepper
- ½ tsp. salt

1. Place potatoes and rutabaga in a large saucepan; cover with water. Add salt. Bring to a boil. Reduce heat; cover and simmer for 8 minutes.
2. Add remaining vegetables; return to a boil. Reduce heat; cover and simmer for 10 minutes or until the vegetables are tender; drain.
3. For glaze, melt butter in a small saucepan; stir in brown sugar and cornstarch. Stir in water, lemon juice, dill, pepper and salt. Bring to a boil; cook and stir for 2 minutes or until thickened. Pour glaze over vegetables; toss to coat.
1 cup: 85 cal., 2g fat (0 sat. fat), 0 chol., 41mg sod., 17g carb. (0 sugars, 0 fiber), 1g pro. **Diabetic exchanges:** 1 starch.

Mashed Peppery Turnips

MASHED PEPPERY TURNIPS

This recipe was created as an attempt to use up a huge turnip crop from our garden as well as lighten up one of our favorite dishes. By using turnips in place of potatoes, I made a low-carb side. Now we rarely serve plain mashed potatoes!
—Courtney Stultz, Weir, KS

TAKES: 30 min. • **MAKES:** 4 servings

- 4 medium turnips (about 1 lb.), peeled and cut into 1¼-in. pieces
- 1 large potato (about ¾ lb.), peeled and cut into 1¼-in. pieces
- 2 Tbsp. reduced-fat cream cheese
- 1 Tbsp. butter
- 1 Tbsp. minced fresh parsley
- 1 tsp. sea salt
- ½ tsp. garlic powder
- ¼ tsp. pepper
- ⅛ tsp. chili powder
- ⅛ tsp. ground chipotle pepper

1. Place turnips, potato and enough water to cover in a large saucepan; bring to a boil. Reduce the heat; cook, uncovered, until tender, 15-20 minutes. Drain; return to pan.
2. Mash the vegetables to desired consistency. Stir in the remaining ingredients.
¾ cup: 140 cal., 5g fat (3g sat. fat), 13mg chol., 608mg sod., 23g carb. (5g sugars, 3g fiber), 3g pro. **Diabetic exchanges:** 1½ starch, 1 fat.

Test Kitchen Tip
If you don't have ground chipotle powder, the best substitute is smoked paprika, which has a similar smoky, earthy flavor.

COLORFUL ROASTED ROOTS

Baking root vegetables in the oven instead of steaming them in the microwave makes them especially tender. Plus, they give my house a wonderful aroma.
—Rebecca Dornfeld, Grass Lake, MI

PREP: 15 min. • **BAKE:** 1 hour
MAKES: 15 servings

- 3 large red potatoes, cut into 1-in. cubes
- 1 large red onion, cut into wedges
- 5 medium carrots, halved and quartered
- 2 medium turnips, peeled and quartered
- 2 medium parsnips, peeled and cut into ¼-in. strips
- 1 small rutabaga, peeled and cut into ¾-in. cubes
- 2 Tbsp. canola oil
- 1 tsp. dried thyme
- ⅛ tsp. pepper

1. Toss all of the ingredients in a large bowl. Transfer to a 15x10x1-in. baking pan coated with cooking spray.
2. Bake, uncovered, at 425° until the vegetables are tender, 40-50 minutes, stirring occasionally.
1 cup: 69 cal., 2g fat (0 sat. fat), 0 chol., 31mg sod., 12g carb. (4g sugars, 3g fiber), 1g pro. **Diabetic exchanges:** 1 vegetable, ½ starch.

BEST BEETS

I enjoy preparing this recipe because it gives me a chance to use the tender, fresh beets from our garden. It's so good, and very colorful!
—Lucille Terry, Frankfort, KY

TAKES: 20 min. • **MAKES:** 8 servings

- ¾ cup sugar
- 2 tsp. cornstarch
- ⅓ cup vinegar
- ⅓ cup water or beet liquid
- 1 tsp. ground mustard
- 1 tsp. onion powder
- 4 cups cooked, sliced beets
- 3 Tbsp. butter
- ¼ tsp. salt
  Dash white pepper

In a saucepan, combine the sugar and cornstarch. Add vinegar and water or beet juice; bring to a boil. Add all the remaining ingredients; reduce heat to simmer. Heat through.
¾ cup: 142 cal., 4g fat (3g sat. fat), 11mg chol., 282mg sod., 26g carb. (23g sugars, 2g fiber), 1g pro.

WHY YOU'LL LOVE IT...

"I had always turned my nose up at beets when they were served at family gatherings. Our neighbor brought a few over from his garden. I tried this recipe, and it was wonderful! I never knew I liked beets."
—NANCYPHUDSON, TASTEOFHOME.COM

MAPLE-GINGERROOT VEGETABLES

My family loves the drizzling of golden maple syrup on these roasted vegetables. I prefer to use dark maple syrup. Either way, it's an easy way to get kids (and adults) to eat their veggies.
—Kelli Ritz, Innisfail, AB

PREP: 35 min. • **BAKE:** 45 min.
MAKES: 24 servings

- 5 medium parsnips, peeled and sliced
- 5 small carrots, sliced
- 3 medium turnips, peeled and cubed
- 1 large sweet potato, peeled and cubed
- 1 small rutabaga, peeled and cubed
- 1 large sweet onion, cut into wedges
- 1 small red onion, cut into wedges
- 2 Tbsp. olive oil
- 1 Tbsp. minced fresh gingerroot
- 1 tsp. salt
- ½ tsp. pepper
- 1 cup maple syrup

1. Preheat oven to 425°. Place the first 7 ingredients in a large bowl; add oil, ginger, salt and pepper. Toss to coat. Arrange vegetables in a single layer in two 15x10x1-in. baking pans coated with cooking spray.
2. Bake, uncovered, for 25 minutes, stirring once. Drizzle with syrup. Bake until the vegetables are tender, 20-25 minutes longer, stirring once more.
¾ cup: 92 cal., 1g fat (0 sat. fat), 0 chol., 119mg sod., 20g carb. (13g sugars, 2g fiber), 1g pro. **Diabetic exchanges:** 1 starch.

Maple-Gingerroot
Vegetables

5i

BRANDY-GLAZED CARROTS

I found this recipe about 10 years ago in an old cookbook I got at a thrift store. I changed the sugar in the original recipe to honey. These carrots aren't just delicious, they look pretty, too!
—Tammy Landry, Saucier, MS

TAKES: 30 min. • **MAKES:** 12 servings

- 3 lbs. fresh baby carrots
- ½ cup butter, cubed
- ½ cup honey
- ¼ cup brandy
- ¼ cup minced fresh parsley
- ½ tsp. salt
- ¼ tsp. pepper

1. In a large skillet, bring ½ in. of water to a boil. Add carrots. Cook, covered, for 5-9 minutes or until crisp-tender. Drain and set aside.
2. In the same skillet, warm butter and honey over medium heat until butter is melted. Remove from heat; stir in the brandy. Bring to a boil; cook until liquid is reduced to about ½ cup.
3. Add carrots, parsley, salt and pepper; heat through.
¾ cup: 153 cal., 8g fat (5g sat. fat), 20mg chol., 242mg sod., 21g carb. (17g sugars, 2g fiber), 1g pro.

Test Kitchen Tip

If you're looking for a substitute for brandy, try using rum, sherry or white wine. Or, if you want to skip the alcohol altogether, try apple juice, white grape juice or apple cider vinegar instead.

Brandy-Glazed
Carrots

Root for Winter
Vegetables

ROOT FOR WINTER VEGETABLES

This medley is an updated version of a recipe my mom grew up with. It's my favorite way to prepare veggies and is marvelous with a batch of hot rolls.
—Julie Butler, Tacoma, WA

PREP: 30 min. • **BAKE:** 55 min.
MAKES: 13 servings

- 1 whole garlic bulb
- 3 Tbsp. olive oil, divided
- 1 lb. fresh beets
- 3 medium parsnips
- 2 small rutabagas
- 2 medium turnips
- 4 medium carrots
- 2 large red onions, cut into wedges
- 1 tsp. salt
- 15 whole peppercorns
- 3 bay leaves
- ½ cup white wine or vegetable broth
- ½ cup vegetable broth
- 2 Tbsp. butter

1. Remove papery outer skin from garlic (do not peel or separate cloves). Cut top off garlic bulb. Brush with ½ tsp. oil. Wrap bulb in heavy-duty foil.
2. Peel the beets, parsnips, rutabagas, turnips and carrots; cut into 2-in. pieces. Place in a large bowl; add onions, salt, peppercorns, bay leaves and remaining 2½ tsp. oil. Toss to coat.
3. Divide the mixture between 3 greased 15x10x1-in. baking pans. Place wrapped garlic on 1 of the pans.
4. Bake at 400° for 35 minutes or until garlic is softened, stirring once. Remove garlic; set aside to cool.
5. Drizzle wine and broth over the vegetables. Bake for 20-30 minutes longer or until vegetables are tender.
6. Squeeze the softened garlic over vegetables; dot with butter. Transfer to a serving platter.

¾ cup: 117 cal., 5g fat (2g sat. fat), 5mg chol., 279mg sod., 17g carb. (7g sugars, 4g fiber), 2g pro. **Diabetic exchanges:** 1 starch, 1 fat.

Hearty
Veggie Medley

5i
HEARTY VEGGIE MEDLEY

Pleasantly seasoned with rosemary and garlic, this appealing side dish showcases good-for-you turnips, carrots and potatoes. It's a nice homey addition to our family's holiday meal.
—Kerry Sullivan, Longwood, FL

PREP: 15 min. • **BAKE:** 45 min.
MAKES: 12 servings

- 5 medium red potatoes, cubed
- 4 medium carrots, cut into ½-in. slices
- 2 small turnips, peeled and cubed
- 1 garlic clove, minced
- 2 to 4 Tbsp. olive oil
- 1 Tbsp. minced fresh rosemary or 1 tsp. dried rosemary, crushed
- ½ tsp. salt
- ¼ tsp. pepper

1. Place the potatoes, carrots, turnips and garlic in a greased 13x9-in. baking dish. Drizzle with oil; sprinkle with rosemary, salt and pepper. Stir to coat.
2. Bake, uncovered, at 350° for 35 minutes. Increase temperature to 450°; bake until vegetables are tender, 10-15 minutes longer.
¾ cup: 55 cal., 3g fat (0 sat. fat), 0 chol., 144mg sod., 7g carb. (0 sugars, 2g fiber), 1g pro. **Diabetic exchanges:** 1 vegetable, ½ fat.

Garlic Roasted Winter Vegetables

GARLIC ROASTED WINTER VEGETABLES

Roasted to perfection, these colorful, herby vegetables are guaranteed to become a popular harvest dish at your house.
—Donna Lamano, Olathe, KS

PREP: 20 min. • **BAKE:** 45 min.
MAKES: 6 servings

- 2 medium carrots
- 1 medium turnip
- 1 medium parsnip
- 1 cup cubed red potatoes
- 1 cup cubed peeled butternut squash
- 3 whole garlic bulbs, cloves separated and peeled
- 3 shallots, quartered
- 4½ tsp. olive oil
- ¼ tsp. salt
- ¼ tsp. dried thyme
- ¼ tsp. pepper

1. Preheat oven to 400°. Peel the carrots, turnip and parsnip; cut into 1-in. pieces. Place in a large bowl; add the potatoes, squash, garlic, shallots, oil, salt, thyme and pepper. Toss to coat. Transfer to a greased 15x10x1-in. baking pan.
2. Bake, uncovered, for 45-50 minutes or until tender, stirring once.
⅔ cup: 135 cal., 4g fat (1g sat. fat), 0 chol., 137mg sod., 24g carb. (5g sugars, 3g fiber), 3g pro. **Diabetic exchanges:** 1½ starch, ½ fat.

Sauteed
Tarragon Radishes

Curried Carrots with
Crunchy Peanut Topping

SAUTEED
TARRAGON RADISHES

Who says radishes only belong in salads? Saute them in wine and tarragon—it may just change the way you look at radishes forever. These can be served on their own, or added to your favorite au gratin recipe.
—Taste of Home *Test Kitchen*

TAKES: 25 min. • **MAKES:** 12 servings

- ½ cup unsalted butter, cubed
- 6 lbs. radishes, quartered (about 9 cups)
- ¼ cup white wine or water
- 2 tsp. minced fresh tarragon or ½ tsp. dried tarragon
- ½ tsp. salt
- ¼ tsp. pepper

In a Dutch oven, heat butter over medium heat. Add radishes; cook and stir 2 minutes. Stir in wine; increase heat to medium-high. Cook, uncovered, until the radishes are crisp-tender, 8-10 minutes. Stir in tarragon, salt and pepper.

¾ cup: 108 cal., 8g fat (5g sat. fat), 20mg chol., 188mg sod., 8g carb. (4g sugars, 4g fiber), 2g pro.

CURRIED CARROTS WITH CRUNCHY PEANUT TOPPING

My homegrown carrots are sweet and tender. When I have a bumper crop, I use this recipe to make the most of them. Warm curry spice and crunchy peanutty topping make this a no-leftovers dish. If you want to add a burst of green, use half carrots and half broccoli florets.
—Trisha Kruse, Eagle, ID

PREP: 20 min. • **BAKE:** 20 min.
MAKES: 6 servings

 2 lbs. fresh carrots, cut into ½-in. slices
 2 medium onions, halved and sliced ¼ in. thick
 ¾ cup mayonnaise
 ⅓ cup half-and-half cream
 1 to 2 Tbsp. curry powder
 1 tsp. salt
 ¼ tsp. pepper
 20 Ritz crackers, crushed (about 1 cup)
 ½ cup chopped salted peanuts
 2 Tbsp. butter, melted

1. Preheat oven to 350°. In a large saucepan, bring 2 in. of water to a boil. Add carrots; return to a boil. Reduce heat; simmer 4 minutes. Add onions; return to a boil. Reduce heat; simmer until carrots are tender, 4-5 minutes. Drain vegetables; return to pan.
2. Whisk together mayonnaise, cream, curry powder, salt and pepper. Pour over vegetables; toss to coat. Transfer to a greased 11x7-in. or 8-in. square baking dish.
3. Combine crushed crackers and peanuts; sprinkle over carrots. Drizzle melted butter over top. Bake, uncovered, until bubbly, 20-25 minutes.
⅔ cup: 438 cal., 35g fat (8g sat. fat), 19mg chol., 820mg sod., 28g carb. (10g sugars, 6g fiber), 6g pro.

Herb-Roasted Root Vegetables

HERB-ROASTED ROOT VEGETABLES

Here's a simple-to-fix side that is perfect for a festive dinner. It looks beautiful with any entree. Roasting brings out the vegetables' natural sweetness.
—*Deirdre Cox, Kansas City, MO*

PREP: 30 min. • **BAKE:** 20 min.
MAKES: 10 servings

- 1 large potato, peeled and cut into 1-in. cubes
- 1 medium sweet potato, peeled and cut into 1-in. cubes
- 2 medium carrots, halved lengthwise and cut into 2-in. pieces
- 1 medium parsnip, peeled, halved lengthwise and cut into 2-in. pieces
- 1 small turnip, peeled and cut into 1-in. cubes
- ½ lb. kohlrabi, peeled and cut into 1-in. cubes
- 6 large shallots, halved
- 3 Tbsp. olive oil
- 2 tsp. coarsely ground pepper
- 1 tsp. salt
- 6 fresh thyme sprigs
- 6 fresh rosemary sprigs

1. Preheat oven to 425°. Place the first 7 ingredients in a Dutch oven and cover with water. Bring to a boil. Cover and cook for 6-8 minutes or until crisp-tender; drain.
2. Transfer vegetables to a large bowl. Combine oil, pepper and salt; drizzle over vegetables and toss to coat. Divide between 2 greased 15x10x1-in. baking pans; arrange herb sprigs over top.
3. Bake, uncovered, 20-25 minutes or until tender, stirring occasionally.
¾ cup: 130 cal., 4g fat (1g sat. fat), 0 chol., 263mg sod., 22g carb. (5g sugars, 4g fiber), 3g pro.

RAVISHING RADISH SALAD

Showcase radishes in all their glory with a fresh, crunchy salad. Herbs and fennel take it up another notch.
—*Maggie Ruddy, Altoona, IA*

PREP: 30 min. + chilling
MAKES: 6 servings

- 24 radishes, quartered
- 1 tsp. salt
- 1 tsp. pepper
- 6 green onions, chopped
- ½ cup thinly sliced fennel bulb
- 6 fresh basil leaves, thinly sliced
- ¼ cup snipped fresh dill
- ¼ cup olive oil
- 2 Tbsp. champagne vinegar
- 2 Tbsp. honey
- 2 garlic cloves, minced
- ½ cup chopped walnuts, toasted

1. Place radishes in a large bowl. Sprinkle with salt and pepper; toss to coat. Add the onions, fennel, basil and dill. In a small bowl, whisk the oil, vinegar, honey and garlic. Pour over salad and toss to coat.
2. Cover and refrigerate for at least 1 hour. Sprinkle with walnuts just before serving.
⅔ cup: 177 cal., 15g fat (2g sat. fat), 0 chol., 408mg sod., 10g carb. (7g sugars, 2g fiber), 2g pro. **Diabetic exchanges:** 3 fat, 1 vegetable.

Ravishing
Radish Salad

BEET & SWEET POTATO FRIES

Instead of offering traditional french fries, try these oven-baked root vegetables as a flavorful side dish.
—Marie Rizzio, Interlochen, MI

PREP: 15 min. • **BAKE:** 20 min.
MAKES: 5 servings (½ cup sauce)

- ½ cup reduced-fat mayonnaise
- 1 tsp. pink peppercorns, crushed
- ½ tsp. green peppercorns, crushed
- ½ tsp. coarsely ground pepper, divided
- 1 large sweet potato (about 1 lb.)
- 2 Tbsp. olive oil, divided
- ½ tsp. sea salt, divided
- 2 large fresh beets (about 1 lb.)

1. Preheat oven to 425°. In a small bowl, combine the mayonnaise, peppercorns and ¼ tsp. ground pepper. Cover and refrigerate until serving.

2. Peel and cut the sweet potato in half widthwise; cut each half into ½-in. strips. Place in a small bowl. Add 1 Tbsp. oil, ¼ tsp. salt and ⅛ tsp. pepper; toss to coat. Spread onto a parchment-lined baking sheet.

3. Peel and cut beets in half; cut each half into ½-in. strips. Transfer to the same bowl used for the sweet potatoes; add the remaining 1 Tbsp. oil, ¼ tsp. salt and ⅛ tsp. ground pepper. Toss to coat. Spread onto a second parchment-lined baking sheet.

4. Bake the vegetables, uncovered, for 20-30 minutes or until tender, turning once. Serve with the peppercorn mayonnaise.

1 serving: 226 cal., 14g fat (2g sat. fat), 8mg chol., 455mg sod., 25g carb. (14g sugars, 4g fiber), 3g pro. **Diabetic exchanges:** 2 starch, 2 fat.

Beet & Sweet Potato Fries

HEALTHY ROASTED VEGGIES

After experimenting with several combinations of fresh, aromatic herbs and a touch of olive oil, we came up with a sensational blend to coat a batch of naturally sweet root vegetables.
—Taste of Home *Test Kitchen*

PREP: 20 min. • **BAKE:** 25 min.
MAKES: 4 servings

  2 cups cubed peeled rutabaga
  ¾ cup chopped peeled turnip
  1 small onion, cut into wedges
  1 small carrot, chopped
  ½ cup chopped peeled parsnip
1½ tsp. olive oil
  ½ tsp. minced fresh thyme or
     ¼ tsp. dried thyme
  ½ tsp. minced fresh oregano or
     ¼ tsp. dried oregano
  ½ tsp. minced fresh rosemary or
     ¼ tsp. dried rosemary, crushed
  ¼ tsp. pepper
  ⅛ tsp. salt

1. Preheat oven to 425°. In a large bowl, combine all the ingredients; toss to coat. Transfer to a 15x10x1-in. baking pan coated with cooking spray.
2. Bake, uncovered, until vegetables are tender, 25-30 minutes stirring occasionally.
¾ cup: 72 cal., 2g fat (0 sat. fat), 0 chol., 115mg sod., 13g carb. (7g sugars, 4g fiber), 2g pro. **Diabetic exchanges:** 2 vegetable.

CIDER VEGETABLES

Christmas dinner wouldn't be the same without this colorful side dish. We love the interesting combination of vegetables including red potatoes, Brussels sprouts and parsnips covered with a zippy sauce.
—Mary Jane Jones, Williamstown, WV

TAKES: 30 min. • **MAKES:** 12 servings

  2 lbs. small red potatoes, quartered
  1 lb. Brussels sprouts, halved
  ½ lb. parsnips, peeled and julienned
  ½ lb. carrots, cut into chunks
  ½ lb. turnips, peeled and cut
     into chunks
  ½ cup butter, cubed
  2 Tbsp. prepared horseradish
  2 Tbsp. cider vinegar
  2 Tbsp. snipped fresh dill or
     2 tsp. dill weed
  ½ tsp. salt, optional
  ¼ tsp. pepper

Cook vegetables separately in water until tender; drain. Melt butter; stir in remaining ingredients. Combine the vegetables and butter mixture; toss to coat.
¾ cup: 97 cal., 5g fat (0 sat. fat), 0 chol., 72mg sod., 12g carb. (0 sugars, 0 fiber), 2g pro. **Diabetic exchanges:** 1 vegetable, 1 fat, ½ starch.

Health Tip

Despite common misconceptions, potatoes can be healthy—they have no fat, no added sugar and are low in sodium. Red potatoes have more vitamins and minerals than other potatoes, and are a good source of vitamin B6, niacin and potassium.

Roasted Beets with Orange
Gremolata & Goat Cheese

ROASTED BEETS WITH ORANGE GREMOLATA & GOAT CHEESE

My grandma always grew her own beets and then pickled or canned them. I have fond memories of her cooking, but I prefer to prepare them differently.
—Courtney Archibeque, Greeley, CO

PREP: 25 min. • **BAKE:** 55 min. + cooling
MAKES: 12 servings

- 3 medium fresh golden beets (about 1 lb.)
- 3 medium fresh beets (about 1 lb.)
- 2 Tbsp. lime juice
- 2 Tbsp. orange juice
- ½ tsp. fine sea salt
- 1 Tbsp. minced fresh parsley
- 1 Tbsp. minced fresh sage
- 1 garlic clove, minced
- 1 tsp. grated orange zest
- 3 Tbsp. crumbled goat cheese
- 2 Tbsp. sunflower kernels

1. Preheat oven to 400°. Scrub beets and trim tops by 1 in. Place beets on a double thickness of heavy-duty foil (about 24x12 in.). Fold foil around beets, sealing tightly. Place on a baking sheet. Roast until tender, 55-65 minutes. Open foil carefully to allow steam to escape.
2. When cool enough to handle, peel, halve and slice beets; place in a serving bowl. Add lime juice, orange juice and salt; toss to coat. Combine parsley, sage, garlic and orange zest; sprinkle over beets. Top with goat cheese and sunflower kernels. Serve either warm or chilled.
¾ cup: 49 cal., 1g fat (0 sat. fat), 2mg chol., 157mg sod., 9g carb. (6g sugars, 2g fiber), 2g pro. **Diabetic exchanges:** 1 vegetable.

GOLDEN BEET CURRY RISOTTO WITH CRISPY BEET GREENS

I was delighted to find golden beets at the farmers market and knew they'd be perfect in a risotto recipe I was working on. And please, don't forget the baked crispy beet greens...amazing! Move over, main dish! This vibrant side will steal the show.
—Merry Graham, Newhall, CA

PREP: 30 min. • **COOK:** 50 min.
MAKES: 6 servings

- 3 medium fresh golden beets and beet greens
- 3 Tbsp. melted coconut oil, divided
- ¾ tsp. sea salt, divided
- 5 cups reduced-sodium chicken broth
- 1 cup chopped leeks (white portion only)
- 1 tsp. curry powder
- 1 tsp. garlic salt
- 1 cup medium pearl barley
- ½ cup white wine or unsweetened apple juice
- 1 cup grated Manchego cheese
- 3 Tbsp. lemon juice (Meyer lemons preferred)
- 4 tsp. grated lemon zest, divided
- ¼ tsp. coarsely ground pepper
- ¼ cup chopped fresh parsley
  Lemon slices

1. Preheat oven to 350°. Wash and trim beet greens, removing the stems; dry with paper towels. Place greens in a single layer on parchment-lined baking sheets. Brush with 1 Tbsp. coconut oil; sprinkle with ¼ tsp. sea salt. Bake until dry and crisp, 15-18 minutes. Set aside.
2. Meanwhile, peel and dice the beets. In a large saucepan, bring the chicken broth to a boil. Add beets. Reduce heat; simmer, covered, until beets are tender, 15-18 minutes. Remove beets with a slotted spoon. Keep broth hot.
3. In another large saucepan, heat remaining 2 Tbsp. coconut oil over medium heat. Add leeks; cook and stir 2-3 minutes. Add curry powder, garlic salt and remaining ½ tsp. sea salt; cook, stirring, until the leeks are tender, 2-3 minutes. Increase heat to medium-high. Add barley; stir constantly until lightly toasted, 2-3 minutes. Add wine; stir until liquid has evaporated.
4. Add enough broth, about 1 cup, to cover barley. Reduce heat to medium; cook and stir until broth is absorbed. Add remaining broth, ½ cup at a time, cooking and stirring until the broth is absorbed after each addition. Stir in beets with last addition of broth. Cook until barley is tender but firm to the bite and risotto is creamy, 25-30 minutes.
5. Remove from heat. Stir in cheese, lemon juice, 2½ tsp. grated lemon zest and pepper. Transfer to a serving dish. Sprinkle with parsley and remaining 1½ tsp. lemon zest. Serve with crispy beet greens and lemon slices.
⅔ cup: 314 cal., 14g fat (11g sat. fat), 19mg chol., 1238mg sod., 37g carb. (7g sugars, 8g fiber), 12g pro.

ROOT VEGETABLE PAVE

This is a stunning side dish to serve company. The robust blend features earthy root vegetables in a lightly herbed cream sauce. It's a perfect make-ahead dish for special occasions.
—Carla Mendres, Winnipeg, MB

PREP: 40 min. • **BAKE:** 1¾ hours + standing
MAKES: 8 servings

- 3 medium russet potatoes, peeled
- 2 large carrots
- 2 medium turnips, peeled
- 1 large onion, halved
- 1 medium fennel bulb, fronds reserved
- ½ cup all-purpose flour
- 1 cup heavy whipping cream
- 1 Tbsp. minced fresh thyme, plus more for topping
- 1 Tbsp. minced fresh rosemary
- ½ tsp. salt
- ½ tsp. pepper, plus more for topping
- 1 cup shredded Asiago cheese, divided

1. Preheat the oven to 350°. With a mandoline or vegetable peeler, cut first 5 ingredients into very thin slices. Transfer to a large bowl; toss with flour. Stir in the cream, 1 Tbsp. thyme, the rosemary, salt and pepper.

2. Place half vegetable mixture into a greased 9-in. springform pan. Sprinkle with ½ cup cheese. Top with remaining vegetable mixture. Place the pan on a baking sheet and cover with a double thickness of foil.

3. Bake until vegetables are tender and easily pierced with a knife, 1¾ to 2 hours. Remove from oven and top foil with large canned goods as weights. Let stand 1 hour. Remove cans, foil and rim from pan before cutting. Top with the remaining ½ cup cheese. Add fennel fronds and, as desired, additional fresh thyme and pepper. Refrigerate leftovers.

1 piece: 248 cal., 15g fat (9g sat. fat), 46mg chol., 216mg sod., 23g carb. (4g sugars, 2g fiber), 7g pro.

PARSNIP-ASPARAGUS AU GRATIN

We pair parsnips with spring asparagus to create a terrific spring side dish. The cheesy and buttery crumb topping will entice everyone to eat their veggies!
—Taste of Home *Test Kitchen*

PREP: 30 min. • **BAKE:** 40 min.
MAKES: 16 servings

- 10 medium parsnips, peeled and cut into 1-in. slices
- ½ tsp. salt
- ⅛ tsp. pepper
- ½ cup butter, divided
- 2 lbs. fresh asparagus, trimmed and cut into 2-in. pieces
- 2 medium onions, chopped
- 4 garlic cloves, minced
- 2 cups soft bread crumbs
- ½ cup grated Parmesan cheese

1. Preheat oven to 400°. In a large bowl, combine the parsnips, salt and pepper. In a microwave, melt 2 Tbsp. butter. Drizzle over parsnips; toss to coat. Transfer to a greased 15x10x1-in. baking pan. Bake for 20 minutes.

2. Meanwhile, in a microwave, melt another 2 Tbsp. butter. Combine the asparagus and melted butter; add to parsnips. Bake until the vegetables are tender, 20-25 minutes longer.

3. In a large saucepan, saute onions in remaining 4 Tbsp. butter until tender. Add garlic; saute 1 minute longer. Add bread crumbs; cook and stir until lightly toasted. Stir in cheese. Transfer parsnip mixture to a serving platter; sprinkle with crumb mixture.

⅔ cup: 162 cal., 7g fat (4g sat. fat), 17mg chol., 204mg sod., 23g carb. (7g sugars, 5g fiber), 4g pro. **Diabetic exchanges:** 1½ starch, 1 fat.

Root Vegetable Pave

Triple Mash with Horseradish Bread Crumbs

TRIPLE MASH WITH HORSERADISH BREAD CRUMBS

Rutabagas have a subtle sweetness we love to pair with Yukon Gold potatoes and parsnips. Add a zip of horseradish, and you've got a creamy treat.
—Lily Julow, Lawrenceville, GA

TAKES: 30 min. • **MAKES:** 12 servings

- 1¾ lbs. Yukon Gold potatoes, peeled and cubed
- 4 medium parsnips (about 1¼ lbs.), peeled and cubed
- 2½ cups cubed peeled rutabaga
- 2 tsp. salt
- ½ cup butter, divided
- 1 cup soft bread crumbs
- 2 Tbsp. prepared horseradish
- 1 cup whole milk
- ¼ tsp. pepper

1. Place potatoes, parsnips, rutabaga and salt in a Dutch oven; add water to cover. Bring to a boil. Reduce heat; cook, uncovered, 15-20 minutes or until tender.
2. Meanwhile, in a skillet, heat ¼ cup butter over medium heat. Add bread crumbs; cook and stir until toasted, 3-5 minutes. Stir in the horseradish; remove from heat.
3. Drain vegetables; return to pot. Mash over low heat, gradually adding milk, pepper and remaining ¼ cup butter. Transfer to a serving dish; sprinkle with bread crumbs.
⅔ cup: 199 cal., 9g fat (5g sat. fat), 22mg chol., 240mg sod., 28g carb. (6g sugars, 4g fiber), 4g pro.

Twice-Baked
Rutabagas

PRESSURE-COOKER TRULY TASTY TURNIP GREENS

These savory greens are a hit at every church dinner. Adjust the seasonings as you please to make the recipe your own. .
—Amy Inman, Hiddenite, NC

PREP: 20 min. • **COOK:** 5 min. + releasing
MAKES: 14 servings

- 2 lbs. peeled turnips, cut into ½-in. cubes
- 12 oz. fresh turnip greens
- 8 oz. fully cooked country ham or 2 smoked ham hocks
- 1 medium onion, chopped
- 3 Tbsp. sugar
- 1½ tsp. coarsely ground pepper
- ¾ tsp. salt
- 2 cartons (32 oz. each) chicken broth

1. In a 6-qt. electric pressure cooker, combine all the ingredients. Lock lid; close pressure-release valve. Adjust to pressure-cook on high for 5 minutes. Allow pressure to naturally release for 10 minutes, then quick-release any remaining pressure.
2. If using ham hocks, remove meat from bones when cool enough to handle; cut ham into small pieces and return to pressure cooker. Serve with a slotted spoon.

¾ cup: 63 cal., 1g fat (0 sat. fat), 11mg chol., 903mg sod., 9g carb. (6g sugars, 2g fiber), 5g pro.

Test Kitchen Tip
Sugar is added to many recipes for turnip greens to offset their somewhat bitter flavor. If you like, you can substitute Swiss chard in place of the turnip greens.

TWICE-BAKED RUTABAGAS

Mix it up for dinner by swapping your go-to spuds dish with these rutabagas combined with bacon, cheese and cream. Even the skeptics won't be able to resist a bite!
—Lisa L. Bynum, Brandon, MS

PREP: 30 min. • **BAKE:** 20 min.
MAKES: 8 servings

- 4 small rutabagas, peeled and cut into 1-in. cubes
- 3 Tbsp. water
- 8 cooked bacon strips, chopped
- 1 cup heavy whipping cream
- ¼ cup butter, cubed
- 2 tsp. garlic powder
- ½ tsp. salt
- ¼ tsp. pepper
- 2 cups shredded cheddar cheese, divided
- 3 green onions, sliced, divided

1. Preheat oven to 350°. In a microwave-safe bowl, combine rutabagas and water. Microwave, covered, on high until tender, 16-20 minutes, stirring halfway.
2. Mash rutabagas; add bacon, cream, butter, garlic powder, salt and pepper. Stir in 1 cup of cheese and ¼ cup of green onions.
3. Spoon mixture into 8 greased 6-oz. ramekins or custard cups. Sprinkle with remaining 1 cup cheese. Place ramekins on a baking sheet. Bake until rutabagas are bubbly and the cheese is melted, 18-22 minutes. Sprinkle with remaining green onions.
1 serving: 361 cal., 30g fat (17g sat. fat), 89mg chol., 592mg sod., 11g carb. (5g sugars, 2g fiber), 13g pro.

Pressure-Cooker
Truly Tasty Turnip Greens

Vegetable Couscous
Salad, Page 219

Page 211

Page 218

Rice & Grains

From couscous and quinoa to lentils and barley, there's a dinner addition here for any menu. Featuring color and comfort, these rice and grain specialties always get thumbs-up approval.

Page 195

Page 221

RICE WITH COLLARD GREENS RELISH

This is a staple in my country of origin, Zimbabwe. It is served with sadza; a cornmeal-based stiff porridge that is used like rice or potatoes in other cultures.
—Loveness Murinda, Upland, CA

PREP: 15 min. • **COOK:** 20 min.
MAKES: 6 servings

- 1 large bunch collard greens (about 2 lbs.)
- ¼ cup finely chopped onion
- 1 garlic clove, minced
- 2 Tbsp. olive oil
- ¾ cup water
- ¾ cup crushed tomatoes
- 1 tsp. curry powder
- ½ tsp. salt
- ⅛ tsp. pepper
- 2 pkg. (8.8 oz. each) ready-to-serve long grain rice

1. Remove and discard center ribs and stems from collard greens. Cut leaves into 1-in. pieces. In a Dutch oven, cook onion and garlic in oil over medium heat until crisp-tender, about 2 minutes.
2. Stir in water, tomatoes, curry powder, salt and pepper. Bring to a boil. Add collard greens in batches; cook and stir until they begin to wilt. Reduce heat; cover and simmer, stirring occasionally, until greens are tender, 10-15 minutes. Prepare rice according to package directions. Serve with collard greens.
⅔ cup collards with ⅔ cup rice: 239 cal., 7g fat (1g sat. fat), 0 chol., 279mg sod., 38g carb. (2g sugars, 8g fiber), 8g pro.

Test Kitchen Tip
If you're making the rice from scratch, start with about ¾ cup uncooked long grain rice.

Rice with Collard Greens Relish

BACON APPLE RISOTTO

A bit of savory, a touch of sweet and the perfect creaminess of risotto make it a game-changer. Feel free to replace the consomme with chicken broth if desired. You can also use white wine instead of red.
—Evan Young, Studio City, CA

PREP: 15 min. • **COOK:** 40 min.
MAKES: 8 servings

- 3 medium Fuji apples, peeled and cut into ½-in. dice
- 3 Tbsp. lemon juice, divided
- 2½ cups unsweetened apple juice
- 2 cups condensed beef consomme, undiluted
- 2 Tbsp. butter
- 2 large yellow onions, cut into ½-in. dice
- 2 cups uncooked arborio rice
- ¾ cup dry red wine
- ½ tsp. salt
- ¼ tsp. coarsely ground pepper
- 8 bacon strips, cooked and roughly chopped
     Optional: Grated Parmesan cheese and soft-boiled eggs

1. Toss apples in 1 Tbsp. lemon juice; set aside. In a large saucepan, heat apple juice and consomme over medium-low heat.
2. In a Dutch oven, melt the butter over medium heat. Add the onions; saute until softened and translucent, about 10 minutes. Stir in rice. Cook, stirring occasionally, until rice and onions begin to brown, 4-6 minutes.
3. Add wine; cook, stirring, until liquid is almost evaporated, 1-2 minutes. Stir in the hot apple juice mixture. Bring to a boil. Reduce heat; simmer, stirring occasionally, until liquid is absorbed, about 20 minutes. Stir in apples, salt, pepper and remaining lemon juice; cook until apples are crisp-tender, about 5 minutes.
4. Sprinkle with bacon. If desired, sprinkle with Parmesan cheese and top with egg.

1¼ cups: 365 cal., 7g fat (3g sat. fat), 19mg chol., 775mg sod., 61g carb. (16g sugars, 3g fiber), 10g pro.

CILANTRO-LIME RICE

I love this no-fuss side dish, particularly with salmon and Asian entrees. Best of all, it's a fat-free side!
—Robin Baskette, Lexington, KY

TAKES: 20 min. • **MAKES:** 3 cups

- 1 cup uncooked jasmine rice
- 2 cups reduced-sodium chicken broth
- 2 Tbsp. lime juice
- 2 Tbsp. minced fresh cilantro
- ⅛ tsp. ground nutmeg

In a small saucepan, combine rice and broth; bring to a boil. Reduce heat; simmer, covered, until liquid is absorbed and rice is tender, 12-15 minutes. Add lime juice, cilantro and nutmeg; fluff with a fork.

½ cup: 130 cal., 0 fat (0 sat. fat), 0 chol., 191mg sod., 28g carb. (0 sugars, 0 fiber), 4g pro. **Diabetic exchanges:** 2 starch.

WHY YOU'LL LOVE IT...

"I love these flavors together, and it's pretty versatile as a filler for enchiladas, tacos, burritos. Will make again!"
—TKUEL, TASTEOFHOME.COM

Cilantro-Lime Rice

Slow-Cooker
Mushroom Rice Pilaf

HAWAIIAN FRIED RICE

Growing up in the South Pacific, rice was the mainstay of our diet. When my husband and I moved stateside, we created this recipe. We bring this dish to every potluck, and it's always the hit of the party.
—Janice Edwards, Plainville, IL

PREP: 25 min. • **COOK:** 20 min.
MAKES: 8 servings

- 3 cups uncooked long grain rice
- 10 Tbsp. margarine or butter, divided
- 8 large eggs
- 1 can (12 oz.) lite SPAM, cut into
   ¼-in. cubes
- ⅓ cup chopped onion
- 4 cups frozen mixed vegetables (about
   16 oz.), thawed and drained
- 2 garlic cloves, minced
- ½ tsp. pepper
- ⅓ cup soy sauce
   Sliced green onions, optional

1. Cook rice according to package directions. Meanwhile, in a Dutch oven, heat 1 Tbsp. margarine over medium-high heat. Whisk eggs until blended; pour into pan. The mixture should set immediately at edge. As eggs set, push cooked portions toward center, letting uncooked portions flow underneath. When eggs are thickened and no liquid egg remains, remove to a cutting board and chop.

2. In same pan, heat 1 Tbsp. margarine over medium-high heat. Add Spam and onion; cook and stir until Spam is lightly browned, 6-8 minutes. Add the mixed vegetables, garlic and pepper; cook until heated through. Stir in cooked rice, soy sauce and remaining ½ cup margarine; cook and stir until margarine is melted. Gently stir in eggs. If desired, top with sliced green onion.

1¾ cups: 621 cal., 24g fat (6g sat. fat), 220mg chol., 1191mg sod., 74g carb. (4g sugars, 5g fiber), 24g pro.

🥔🍲 SLOW-COOKER MUSHROOM RICE PILAF

A few modifications to our dear great-aunt Bernice's easy mushroom rice pilaf recipe have made this an always-requested dish for potlucks, barbecues and family get-togethers. It'll become a slow-cooker favorite in your house, too!
—Amy Williams, Rialto, CA

PREP: 20 min. • **COOK:** 3 hours
MAKES: 6 servings

- 1 cup medium grain rice
- ¼ cup butter
- 6 green onions, chopped
- 2 garlic cloves, minced
- ½ lb. sliced baby portobello
   mushrooms
- 2 cups warm water
- 4 tsp. beef base
   Thinly sliced green onions, optional

1. In a large skillet, saute rice in butter until lightly browned. Add green onions and garlic; cook and stir until tender. Stir in mushrooms.

2. Transfer to a 1½-qt. slow cooker. In a small bowl, whisk water and beef base; pour over rice mixture. Cover and cook on low for 3-3½ hours or until rice is tender and liquid is absorbed. Fluff with a fork. If desired, add sliced green onions.

Note: Look for beef base near the broth and bouillon.

⅔ cup: 210 cal., 8g fat (5g sat. fat), 20mg chol., 512mg sod., 30g carb. (2g sugars, 1g fiber), 4g pro. **Diabetic exchanges:** 2 starch, 2 fat.

Hawaiian Fried
Rice

BUTTERNUT SQUASH WITH WHOLE GRAINS

Fresh ingredients shine in this scrumptious slow-cooked side. This is how you spread a little cheer.
—Taste of Home *Test Kitchen*

PREP: 15 min. • **COOK:** 4 hours
MAKES: 12 servings

- 1   medium butternut squash (about 3 lbs.), cut into ½-in. cubes
- 1   cup uncooked whole grain brown and red rice blend
- 1   medium onion, chopped
- ½   cup water
- 3   garlic cloves, minced
- 2   tsp. minced fresh thyme or ½ tsp. dried thyme
- ½   tsp. salt
- ¼   tsp. pepper
- 1   can (14½ oz.) vegetable broth
- 1   pkg. (6 oz.) fresh baby spinach

1. In a 4-qt. slow cooker, combine first 8 ingredients. Stir in broth.

2. Cook, covered, on low 4-5 hours or until grains are tender. Stir in spinach before serving.

Note: This recipe was tested with RiceSelect Royal Blend Whole Grain Texmati Brown & Red Rice with Barley and Rye. Look for it in the rice aisle.

¾ cup: 97 cal., 1g fat (0 sat. fat), 0 chol., 252mg sod., 22g carb. (3g sugars, 4g fiber), 3g pro. **Diabetic exchanges:** 1½ starch.

Butternut Squash
with Whole Grains

Quinoa
Tabbouleh

QUINOA TABBOULEH

When my mom and sister developed food allergies, we had to modify several recipes. I substituted quinoa for couscous in this tabbouleh, and now we make it all the time.
—Jennifer Klann, Corbett, OR

PREP: 35 min. + chilling
MAKES: 8 servings

- 2 cups water
- 1 cup quinoa, rinsed
- 1 can (15 oz.) black beans, rinsed and drained
- 1 small cucumber, peeled and chopped
- 1 small sweet red pepper, chopped
- ⅓ cup minced fresh parsley
- ¼ cup lemon juice
- 2 Tbsp. olive oil
- ½ tsp. salt
- ½ tsp. pepper

1. In a large saucepan, bring the water to a boil. Add quinoa. Reduce heat; cover and simmer until liquid is absorbed, 12-15 minutes. Remove from heat; fluff with a fork. Transfer to a bowl; cool completely.

2. Add beans, cucumber, red pepper and parsley. In a small bowl, whisk remaining ingredients; drizzle over salad and toss to coat. Refrigerate until chilled.

¾ cup: 159 cal., 5g fat (1g sat. fat), 0 chol., 255mg sod., 24g carb. (1g sugars, 4g fiber), 6g pro. **Diabetic exchanges:** 1½ starch, 1 fat.

Vegetable
Barley Saute

VEGETABLE BARLEY SAUTE

Here's a wonderful side dish you can easily adjust to suit your tastes. Use broccoli instead of green beans, sweet potato ribbons instead of carrots, and switch up the nuts.
—Taste of Home *Test Kitchen*

TAKES: 30 min. • **MAKES:** 4 servings

- ½ cup quick-cooking barley
- ⅓ cup water
- 3 Tbsp. reduced-sodium soy sauce
- 2 tsp. cornstarch
- 1 garlic clove, minced
- 1 Tbsp. canola oil
- 2 carrots, thinly sliced
- 1 cup cut fresh green beans (2-in. pieces)
- 2 green onions, sliced
- ½ cup unsalted cashews, optional

1. Prepare barley according to package directions. In a small bowl, combine water, soy sauce and cornstarch until smooth; set aside.

2. In a large skillet or wok, saute garlic in oil for 15 seconds. Add the carrots and beans; stir-fry for 2 minutes. Add onions; stir-fry 1 minute longer. Stir soy sauce mixture; stir into skillet. Bring to a boil; cook and stir until thickened, about 1 minute. Add barley; heat through. If desired, stir in cashews.

⅔ cup: 148 cal., 4g fat (1g sat. fat), 0 chol., 458mg sod., 24g carb. (3g sugars, 6g fiber), 5g pro. **Diabetic exchanges:** 1½ starch, 1 fat.

Brown Rice with Almonds & Cranberries

BROWN RICE WITH ALMONDS & CRANBERRIES

I'm always looking to switch things up during the holiday season. This rice salad fits the bill, as its on the lighter side and it uses ingredients I always have on hand.
—Joan Hallford, North Richland Hills, TX

PREP: 35 min. • **BAKE:** 1¼ hours
MAKES: 10 servings

- 3 cans (14½ oz. each) beef broth
- ¼ cup butter, cubed
- 1 large onion, chopped
- 1 cup uncooked long grain brown rice
- ½ cup bulgur
- ½ cup slivered almonds
- ½ cup dried cranberries
- ¾ cup minced fresh parsley, divided
- ¼ cup chopped green onions
- ¼ tsp. salt
- ¼ tsp. pepper

1. Preheat oven to 375°. In a large saucepan, bring broth to a simmer; reduce heat to low and keep hot. In a large skillet, heat butter over medium heat. Add onion; cook and stir until tender, 3-4 minutes. Add rice, bulgur and almonds; cook and stir until rice is lightly browned and has a nutty aroma, 2-3 minutes.

2. Transfer to a greased 13x9-in. baking dish. Stir in cranberries, ½ cup parsley, green onions, salt and pepper. Stir in hot broth. Bake, covered, 45 minutes. Uncover and continue to cook until liquid is absorbed and rice is tender, 30-35 minutes longer. Remove from oven and fluff with a fork. Cover; let stand 5-10 minutes. Sprinkle with remaining parsley before serving.

¾ cup: 207 cal., 8g fat (3g sat. fat), 12mg chol., 658mg sod., 29g carb. (7g sugars, 4g fiber), 5g pro. **Diabetic exchanges:** 2 starch, 1½ fat.

Health Tip

Brown rice is considered a whole grain because it contains the bran, germ and endosperm of the grain, unlike white rice which just contains the endosperm. It's a smart choice because brown rice is higher in fiber, magnesium and other nutrients than white rice.

ARROZ CON GANDULES (RICE WITH PIGEON PEAS)

Feed a crowd with this authentic Puerto Rican rice dish, which was handed down to me from my mom. It's a staple with the familia at all our gatherings.
—Evelyn Robles, Oak Creek, WI

PREP: 15 min. • **COOK:** 30 min.
MAKES: 18 servings

- ½ cup sofrito
- 2 Tbsp. canola oil
- 4 cups uncooked long grain rice
- 1 envelope Goya sazon with coriander and annatto
- 7 cups water
- 1 can (15 oz.) pigeon peas, drained
- 2 cans (5 oz. each) Vienna sausage, drained and chopped
- ½ cup tomato sauce
- 1¼ tsp. salt
- 1 envelope Goya ham-flavored concentrate
- ½ tsp. chicken bouillon granules
- ¼ tsp. pepper

In a Dutch oven, cook sofrito in oil over medium-low heat, stirring occasionally, about 5 minutes. Add rice and sazon; cook and stir until rice is lightly toasted, 3-4 minutes. Add remaining ingredients. Bring to a boil. Reduce the heat; cover and simmer until the rice is tender, 15-20 minutes. Fluff with a fork.

Note: Look for Goya sazon, a seasoning blend, in the international foods section.

¾ cup: 220 cal., 5g fat (1g sat. fat), 14mg chol., 537mg sod., 38g carb. (1g sugars, 2g fiber), 6g pro.

Test Kitchen Tip

Although this dish could be a meal in itself, you can pair it with other Puerto Rican-inspired dishes like juicy, crispy chicken or pork picadillo lettuce wraps.

Arroz con Gandules
(Rice with Pigeon Peas)

APPLE & SAUSAGE WILD RICE

Chunks of apples and summer sausage bring a delicious, sweet-and-savory contrast to wild rice. My husband absolutely loves it, and the prep work takes only 15 minutes.
—Rebecca McIntire, Manitou Springs, CO

PREP: 15 min. • **COOK:** 1 hour
MAKES: 4 servings

- 2 Tbsp. olive oil
- 5 oz. summer sausage, cut into ¼-in. cubes
- 2 celery ribs, chopped
- 1 small onion, finely chopped
- ½ cup uncooked long grain brown rice
- ½ cup uncooked wild rice
- 2 medium apples, coarsely chopped
- 2 garlic cloves, minced
- 1½ cups apple cider or juice
- 1 cup beef broth
- ⅛ tsp. pepper

1. In a large saucepan, heat oil over medium-high heat. Add sausage, celery and onion; cook and stir 4-6 minutes or until tender.
2. Add rice, apples and garlic; cook and stir 1-2 minutes or until rice is lightly browned. Add cider, broth and pepper; bring to a boil. Reduce heat; simmer, covered, 1-1¼ hours or until the liquid is absorbed and rice is tender. Fluff with a fork.
1 cup: 424 cal., 17g fat (4g sat. fat), 22mg chol., 690mg sod., 59g carb. (20g sugars, 5g fiber), 11g pro.

Multigrain & Veggie Side Dish

MULTIGRAIN & VEGGIE SIDE DISH

Packed with all the good things we are supposed to eat, this dish is delicious and so pretty. It's fun to make, too. Most of the fiber in this healthy side comes from spinach, pinto beans and barley.
—Marian Platt, Sequim, WA

TAKES: 30 min. • **MAKES:** 8 servings

- 2⅔ cups water
- ⅔ cup uncooked long grain rice
- ⅔ cup quick-cooking barley
- ½ tsp. salt
- 1 large onion, chopped
- 2 medium carrots, chopped
- 1 medium sweet red pepper, chopped
- 1 small turnip, chopped
- ½ cup chopped celery or celery root
- 1 Tbsp. minced fresh gingerroot
- 2 Tbsp. olive oil
- 1 pkg. (10 oz.) fresh spinach, torn
- 1 cup canned pinto beans, rinsed and drained
- 2 Tbsp. reduced-sodium soy sauce

1. In a small saucepan, bring water to a boil. Stir in the rice, barley and salt. Reduce heat; cover and simmer for 12-18 minutes or until grains are tender. Remove from the heat; let stand for 5 minutes.
2. In a Dutch oven, saute the onion, carrots, red pepper, turnip, celery and ginger in oil until crisp-tender. Stir in the spinach, beans, soy sauce and rice mixture; cook and stir until heated through and spinach is wilted.
1¼ cups: 199 cal., 4g fat (1g sat. fat), 0 chol., 387mg sod., 35g carb. (4g sugars, 6g fiber), 6g pro. **Diabetic exchanges:** 2 starch, 1 vegetable, ½ fat.

WILD RICE-STUFFED ACORN SQUASH

I tried many variations of ingredients for the stuffing in my acorn squash. Here's the version I liked best.
—Michelle Springer, Spring, TX

PREP: 1 hour • **BAKE:** 35 min.
MAKES: 8 servings

- 4 small acorn squash
- 3 Tbsp. olive oil, divided
- ¾ tsp. salt, divided
- 2 tsp. ground coriander, divided
- ½ tsp. ground nutmeg, divided
- 1 lb. fresh carrots, peeled and cut into ½-in. cubes
- ¾ cup pecan halves, coarsely chopped
- ¾ cup dried cherries, coarsely chopped
- 10 fresh sage leaves, chopped
- 2 garlic cloves, minced
- 2 Tbsp. maple syrup

FILLING
- 1 cup uncooked wild rice
- 1 Tbsp. olive oil
- ¾ cup finely chopped sweet onion
- ¼ tsp. ground cinnamon
- 2 cups vegetable broth

1. Preheat oven to 375°. Cut squash lengthwise in half; remove and discard seeds. Brush with 2 Tbsp. oil; sprinkle with ¼ tsp. salt, ½ tsp. coriander and ¼ tsp. nutmeg. Place squash in a 15x10x1-in. baking pan, cut sides up. Bake 35-45 minutes or until easily pierced with a fork.

2. In an 8-in. square dish, combine carrots and remaining 1 Tbsp. oil, ½ tsp. salt, 1½ tsp. coriander and ¼ tsp. nutmeg. Bake just until tender, 15-20 minutes, stirring occasionally. Stir in pecans, cherries, sage, garlic and syrup. Bake 10 minutes longer.

3. Rinse the wild rice thoroughly; drain. In a small saucepan, heat the oil over medium heat. Add the onion; cook and stir 2-3 minutes or until softened. Stir in rice and cinnamon, then add broth. Bring to a boil. Reduce heat; cover and simmer for 40-50 minutes or until rice is fluffy and tender. Drain if necessary.

4. Combine the rice and carrot mixtures. Arrange the squash on a serving platter, cut sides up. Fill with the rice mixture. Serve warm.

1 stuffed squash half: 409 cal., 14g fat (2g sat. fat), 0 chol., 441mg sod., 70g carb. (24g sugars, 9g fiber), 7g pro.

CREAMY CAULIFLOWER RICE

What began as a quick fix dish has become a staple in our house. It's an ideal way to add veggies to a meal, and it's a nice change from traditional cauliflower.
—Caresse Caton, Mobile, AL

TAKES: 30 min. • **MAKES:** 10 servings

- 3 cups uncooked long grain rice
- 3 cups frozen cauliflower, thawed
- 6 cups reduced-sodium chicken broth
- 6 oz. cream cheese, cubed
- ¾ tsp. salt
- ¼ tsp. pepper

In a large saucepan, combine rice, cauliflower and broth; bring to a boil. Reduce heat; simmer, covered, until liquid is absorbed and rice is tender, 15-20 minutes. Remove from heat. Add cream cheese, salt and pepper; stir until melted.

¾ cup: 301 cal., 6g fat (4g sat. fat), 17mg chol., 584mg sod., 52g carb. (2g sugars, 2g fiber), 8g pro.

Wild Rice-Stuffed Acorn Squash

Creamy
Cauliflower Rice

Veggie-Topped
Polenta Slices

VEGGIE-TOPPED
POLENTA SLICES

*Even though we didn't have too many
ingredients in the kitchen at the time,
this amazing side came from a stroke
of genius I had one day.*
—Jenn Tidwell, Fair Oaks, CA

PREP: 20 min. • **COOK:** 20 min.
2MAKES: 4 servings

1	tube (1 lb.) polenta, cut into 12 slices
2	Tbsp. olive oil, divided
1	medium zucchini, chopped
2	shallots, minced
2	garlic cloves, minced
3	Tbsp. reduced-sodium chicken broth
½	tsp. pepper
⅛	tsp. salt
4	plum tomatoes, seeded and chopped
2	Tbsp. minced fresh basil or 2 tsp. dried basil
1	Tbsp. minced fresh parsley
½	cup shredded part-skim mozzarella cheese

1. In a large nonstick skillet, cook polenta in 1 Tbsp. oil over medium heat for 9-11 minutes on each side or until golden brown.

2. Meanwhile, in another large skillet, saute zucchini in remaining oil until tender. Add shallots and garlic; cook 1 minute longer. Add the broth, pepper and salt. Bring to a boil; cook until liquid is almost evaporated.

3. Stir in tomatoes, basil and parsley; heat through. Serve with polenta; sprinkle with cheese.

3 polenta slices with 1 cup vegetable mixture: 222 cal., 9g fat (2g sat. fat), 8mg chol., 558mg sod., 28g carb. (5g sugars, 2g fiber), 7g pro. **Diabetic exchanges:** 1½ starch, 1½ fat, 1 vegetable.

Lentil White Bean Pilaf

LENTIL WHITE BEAN PILAF

Vegetarians will be happy to see this hearty meatless grain pilaf on the buffet table. I like to make this when I have extra cooked lentils, barley, quinoa and rice on hand.
—Juli Meyers, Hinesville, GA

PREP: 35 min. • **COOK:** 15 min.
MAKES: 10 servings

- 1 cup dried lentils, rinsed
- ½ cup quick-cooking barley
- ½ cup quinoa, rinsed
- ⅓ cup uncooked long grain rice
- ½ lb. sliced baby portobello mushrooms
- 3 medium carrots, finely chopped
- 3 celery ribs, finely chopped
- 1 large onion, finely chopped
- ¼ cup butter, cubed
- 3 garlic cloves, minced
- 2 tsp. minced fresh rosemary or ½ tsp. dried rosemary, crushed
- ½ cup vegetable broth
- ½ tsp. salt
- ½ tsp. pepper
- 2 cups canned cannellini beans, rinsed and drained

1. Cook the lentils, barley, quinoa and rice according to package directions; set aside.
2. In a Dutch oven, saute mushrooms, carrots, celery and onion in butter until tender. Add the garlic and rosemary; cook 1 minute longer. Add broth, salt and pepper, stirring to loosen browned bits from pan. Stir in beans and the cooked lentils, barley, quinoa and rice; heat through.

¾ cup: 259 cal., 6g fat (3g sat. fat), 12mg chol., 290mg sod., 41g carb. (3g sugars, 11g fiber), 11g pro.

Pressure-Cooker
Bulgur & Beans

PRESSURE-COOKER BULGUR & BEANS

A rich blend of treasured spices turn bulgur and chickpeas into a tangy stew with just the right amount of heat. And the hint of sweetness from golden raisins makes the perfect accent.
—*Faith Cromwell, San Francisco, CA*

PREP: 30 min. • **COOK:** 15 min.
MAKES: 10 servings

- 3 Tbsp. canola oil, divided
- 1½ cups bulgur
- 2 medium onions, chopped
- 1 medium sweet red pepper, chopped
- 5 garlic cloves, minced
- 1 Tbsp. ground cumin
- 1 Tbsp. paprika
- 2 tsp. ground ginger
- 1 tsp. pepper
- ½ tsp. ground cinnamon
- ½ tsp. cayenne pepper
- 1 carton (32 oz.) vegetable broth
- 2 Tbsp. soy sauce
- 1 can (28 oz.) crushed tomatoes
- 1 can (14½ oz.) diced tomatoes, undrained
- 1 can (15 oz.) garbanzo beans or chickpeas, rinsed and drained
- ½ cup golden raisins
- 2 Tbsp. brown sugar
  Minced fresh cilantro, optional

1. Select saute setting on a 6-qt. electric pressure cooker. Adjust for medium heat; add 1 Tbsp. oil. When oil is hot, cook and stir bulgur until lightly browned, 2-3 minutes. Remove from pressure cooker.
2. Heat remaining 2 Tbsp. oil in pressure cooker. Cook and stir onions and red pepper until crisp-tender, 2-3 minutes. Add garlic and seasonings; cook 1 minute longer. Press cancel. Add the broth, soy sauce and bulgur to pressure cooker.
3. Lock lid; close pressure-release valve. Adjust to pressure-cook on low for 12 minutes. Quick-release pressure. Select saute setting and adjust for low heat. Add tomatoes, beans, raisins and brown sugar; simmer, uncovered, until mixture is slightly thickened and heated through, about 10 minutes, stirring occasionally. If desired, sprinkle with cilantro.
1¼ cups: 245 cal., 6g fat (0 sat. fat), 0 chol., 752mg sod., 45g carb. (15g sugars, 8g fiber), 8g pro.

BUTTERNUT SQUASH OVEN RISOTTO

Squash and beer make my risotto taste different and delicious. Plus, cooking it in the oven cuts down on the hands-on time typically spent preparing risotto.
—*Katie Ferrier, Houston, TX*

PREP: 20 min. • **BAKE:** 30 min.
MAKES: 10 servings

- 6 cups cubed peeled butternut squash (1 in.)
- 4 Tbsp. olive oil, divided
- ½ tsp. salt
- ¼ tsp. pepper
- 1 carton (32 oz.) chicken broth
- 1 cup water
- 1 small onion, chopped
- 2 cups uncooked arborio rice
- 2 garlic cloves, minced
- 1 cup beer
- 2 Tbsp. butter
- ½ tsp. chili powder
- ¼ tsp. ground nutmeg
- 1 cup grated Parmesan cheese

1. Preheat oven to 375°. Place squash in a greased 15x10x1-in. baking pan. Drizzle with 2 Tbsp. oil; sprinkle with salt and pepper. Toss to coat. Roast on a lower oven rack 30-35 minutes or until tender, stirring occasionally.
2. Meanwhile, in a large saucepan, bring broth and water to a simmer; keep hot. In an ovenproof Dutch oven, heat the remaining oil over medium heat. Add onion; cook and stir 4-6 minutes or until tender. Add rice and garlic; cook and stir until rice is coated, 1-2 minutes longer.
3. Stir in beer. Reduce heat to maintain a simmer; cook and stir until beer is absorbed. Stir in 4 cups hot broth mixture. Place Dutch oven on an oven rack above squash; bake, covered, until rice is tender but firm to the bite, risotto is creamy and liquid is almost absorbed, 20-25 minutes.
4. Remove Dutch oven from oven. Add the butter, chili powder, nutmeg and remaining broth mixture. Stir vigorously until blended and the liquid is almost absorbed. Stir in roasted squash and cheese. Serve immediately.
¾ cup: 311 cal., 11g fat (4g sat. fat), 15mg chol., 662mg sod., 46g carb. (4g sugars, 3g fiber), 7g pro.

MUSHROOMS & PEAS RICE PILAF

Anything can be in a rice pilaf. Adding peas and baby portobello mushrooms gives this version a springlike burst of color and a variety of textures.
—*Stacy Mullens, Gresham, OR*

TAKES: 25 min. • **MAKES:** 6 servings

- 1 pkg. (6.6 oz.) rice pilaf mix with toasted almonds
- 1 Tbsp. butter
- 1½ cups fresh or frozen peas
- 1 cup sliced baby portobello mushrooms

1. Prepare pilaf according to the package directions.
2. In a large skillet, heat butter over medium heat. Add the peas and mushrooms; cook and stir until tender, 6-8 minutes. Stir in rice.
⅔ cup: 177 cal., 6g fat (2g sat. fat), 10mg chol., 352mg sod., 28g carb. (3g sugars, 3g fiber), 5g pro. **Diabetic exchanges:** 2 starch, ½ fat.

GRILLED POLENTA WITH MUSHROOM SAUCE

Wild mushrooms are abundant in our area in spring. That's when I turn to this recipe. Guests enjoy the distinctive flavors of the homemade sauce infused with Marsala wine and served over polenta.
—Barbara Sidway, Baker City, OR

PREP: 45 min. + cooling • **GRILL:** 10 min.
MAKES: 9 servings

- 1 Tbsp. chopped shallot
- ¼ cup olive oil
- 2 Tbsp. minced fresh basil or 2 tsp. dried basil
- 3 garlic cloves, minced
- ½ tsp. dried oregano
- ½ cup white wine or chicken broth
- 3 cups chicken broth
- ⅓ cup chopped seeded tomatoes
- ½ tsp. salt
- 1 cup cornmeal

MUSHROOM SAUCE
- 1 lb. sliced assorted fresh mushrooms
- 1 Tbsp. chopped shallot
- 2 Tbsp. olive oil
- 1 garlic clove, minced
- ½ tsp. salt
- ¼ tsp. pepper
- ¼ cup Marsala wine or chicken broth
- 1 cup heavy whipping cream

1. In a large heavy saucepan, saute shallot in oil until tender. Add basil, garlic and oregano; cook 1 minute longer. Stir in wine. Bring to a boil. Reduce heat; simmer, uncovered, for 5 minutes.
2. Add broth, tomatoes and salt; bring to a boil. Reduce to heat to a gentle boil; slowly whisk in cornmeal. Cook and stir with a wooden spoon until polenta is thickened and pulls away cleanly from side of the pan, 15-20 minutes. Spread into a 9-in. square baking pan coated with cooking spray. Cool to room temperature, about 30 minutes.
3. Meanwhile, in a large skillet, saute mushrooms and shallot in oil until tender. Add the garlic, salt and pepper; cook 1 minute longer. Add wine, stirring to loosen browned bits from pan. Gradually stir in cream. Bring to a boil. Reduce heat; cook and stir until slightly thickened, 5-10 minutes.
4. Cut polenta into 9 squares. Grill, covered, over medium heat for 5-7 minutes on each side or until crisp and golden brown. Serve with mushroom sauce.

1 serving: 258 cal., 19g fat (7g sat. fat), 38mg chol., 603mg sod., 17g carb. (2g sugars, 2g fiber), 4g pro.

DEEP-FRIED RICE BALLS

My mother moved in with us about eight years ago and started making this side dish. Now that she is her nineties, I've taken over the duty of making these unique rice balls. Everyone in our family is thrilled to see them when they are placed on the table.
—Elizabeth Blake, Chesapeake, VA

PREP: 35 min. + chilling
COOK: 5 min./batch • **MAKES:** 12 servings

- 4½ cups water
- 2 cups uncooked long grain rice
- 2 Tbsp. butter
- 1 tsp. salt
- ½ tsp. pepper
- 4 eggs, beaten
- ⅓ cup grated Parmesan cheese
- 2 Tbsp. dried parsley flakes
- 1¾ cups seasoned bread crumbs
  Oil for deep-fat frying

1. In a large saucepan, bring water, rice, butter, salt and pepper to a boil. Reduce heat; cover and simmer 15-18 minutes or until the liquid is absorbed and rice is tender. Cool slightly.
2. In a large bowl, combine eggs, cheese, parsley and rice. Cover and refrigerate for 20 minutes. Place bread crumbs in a shallow bowl. Shape ½ cupfuls of rice mixture into balls; roll in bread crumbs.
3. In a deep-fat fryer or electric skillet, heat oil to 375°. Fry rice balls, a few at a time until golden brown, 2-3 minutes. Drain on paper towels.

1 rice ball: 343 cal., 20g fat (3g sat. fat), 77mg chol., 461mg sod., 34g carb. (1g sugars, 1g fiber), 7g pro.

CURRY RICE PILAF

Salted cashews add wonderful crunch to this simple rice dish nicely flavored with curry and turmeric.
—Katie Rose, Pewaukee, WI

TAKES: 10 min. • **MAKES:** 5 servings

- 2 pkg. (8½ oz. each) ready-to-serve jasmine rice
- 2 Tbsp. butter
- 1 cup salted whole cashews
- 2 green onions, sliced
- ½ tsp. curry powder
- ¼ tsp. salt
- ¼ tsp. ground turmeric
- ¼ tsp. pepper

Heat the rice according to package directions. Meanwhile, in a small skillet, melt butter over medium heat. Add the cashews, onions and seasonings; cook and stir until onions are tender, about 2-3 minutes. Add rice; toss to coat.

¾ cup: 436 cal., 23g fat (6g sat. fat), 12mg chol., 362mg sod., 50g carb. (2g sugars, 2g fiber), 10g pro.

Test Kitchen Tip

Curry powder imparts a distinctive flavor and rich golden color to recipes and can be found in both mild and hot versions. Most cooks season dishes lightly with curry powder and add more as desired to reach an acceptable spice level.

Quinoa with
Peas & Onion

QUINOA WITH PEAS & ONION

Even picky eaters will love this protein-packed dish. If you have freshly shelled peas on hand, substitute them for the frozen.
—Lori Panarella, Phoenixville, PA

PREP: 30 min. • **COOK:** 10 min.
MAKES: 6 servings

- 2 cups water
- 1 cup quinoa, rinsed
- 1 small onion, chopped
- 1 Tbsp. olive oil
- 1½ cups frozen peas
- ½ tsp. salt
- ¼ tsp. pepper
- 2 Tbsp. chopped walnuts

1. In a large saucepan, bring water to a boil. Add quinoa. Reduce heat; cover and simmer until water is absorbed, 12-15 minutes. Remove from the heat; fluff with a fork.

2. Meanwhile, in a large cast-iron or other heavy skillet, saute onion in oil until tender, 2-3 minutes. Add peas; cook and stir until heated through. Stir in the cooked quinoa, salt and pepper. Sprinkle with walnuts.

⅔ cup: 174 cal., 6g fat (1g sat. fat), 0 chol., 244mg sod., 26g carb. (2g sugars, 4g fiber), 6g pro. **Diabetic exchanges:** 1½ starch, 1 fat.

HOT AND ZESTY QUINOA: Omit peas, salt, pepper and walnuts. Prepare the quinoa as directed. Saute the onion in oil until tender. Add 3 minced garlic cloves; cook 1 minute. Stir in 2 cans (10 oz. each) tomatoes and green chiles. Bring to a boil over medium heat. Reduce heat; simmer, uncovered, 10 minutes. Stir in quinoa and ¼ cup chopped marinated quartered artichoke hearts; heat through. Sprinkle with 2 Tbsp. grated Parmesan.

Creamy
Pumpkin Polenta

CREAMY PUMPKIN POLENTA

*Sometimes I like to hollow out a pumpkin
and serve this creamy, hearty polenta inside
it. The crunchy pumpkin seeds add fantastic
texture and a fun flair.*
—*Debi George, Mansfield, TX*

TAKES: 25 min. • **MAKES:** 6 servings

5⅓ cups water
1 tsp. salt
1⅓ cups yellow cornmeal
½ tsp. ground nutmeg
¾ cup canned pumpkin
½ cup cream cheese, cubed
   Salted pumpkin seeds or pepitas,
   optional

1. In a large heavy saucepan, bring
water and salt to a boil.
2. Reduce heat to a gentle boil; slowly
whisk in the cornmeal and nutmeg.
Cook and stir with a wooden spoon for
15-20 minutes or until the polenta is
thickened and pulls away cleanly from
the sides of the pan. Stir in the pumpkin
and cream cheese until smooth.
Sprinkle each serving with pumpkin
seeds if desired.
¾ cup: 191 cal., 7g fat (4g sat. fat), 21mg
chol., 453mg sod., 27g carb. (1g sugars,
4g fiber), 5g pro. **Diabetic exchanges:**
2 starch, 1 fat.

QUINOA WITH ROASTED VEGETABLES

*Grab all of your garden-fresh produce for
this quinoa with roasted vegetables. The
tangy dressing and fresh herbs really make
the flavors shine in this wholesome quinoa
side dish.*
—*Sonali Ruder, New York, NY*

PREP: 25 min. • **BAKE:** 35 min.
MAKES: 8 servings

1 small eggplant, chopped
1 medium zucchini, chopped
1 medium sweet yellow pepper,
   chopped
1 medium red onion, chopped
1 cup grape tomatoes, halved
2 garlic cloves, diced
4 Tbsp. olive oil, divided
½ tsp. salt
¼ tsp. pepper
3 cups reduced-sodium chicken broth
1½ cups quinoa, rinsed
3 Tbsp. balsamic vinegar
¾ tsp. Dijon mustard
¼ cup each minced fresh basil,
   parsley and chives

1. Place vegetables and garlic in an
ungreased 15x10x1-in. baking pan.
Drizzle with 2 Tbsp. oil; sprinkle with
salt and pepper. Bake, uncovered, at
425° for 35-40 minutes or until tender,
stirring once.
2. Meanwhile, in a large saucepan, bring
broth to a boil. Add quinoa. Reduce heat;
cover and simmer for 12-15 minutes or
until liquid is absorbed. Remove from
the heat; fluff with a fork.
3. Transfer vegetables and quinoa to a
large bowl. Whisk the vinegar, mustard
and remaining oil; drizzle over vegetable
mixture. Sprinkle with fresh herbs; toss
to combine.
¾ cup: 222 cal., 9g fat (1g sat. fat), 0 chol.,
388mg sod., 31g carb. (4g sugars, 5g
fiber), 7g pro. **Diabetic exchanges:**
1½ starch, 1½ fat, 1 vegetable.

Quinoa with Roasted
Vegetables

CARROT RAISIN COUSCOUS

Golden raisins add a slightly sweet flavor to this unique side dish featuring couscous and carrots. The recipe will brighten any table.
—*Jordan Sucher, Brooklyn, NY*

PREP: 15 min. • **COOK:** 20 min.
MAKES: 10 servings

- ⅓ cup port wine or chicken broth
- ⅓ cup golden raisins
- 1 medium onion, chopped
- 3 Tbsp. olive oil, divided
- 1 pkg. (10 oz.) couscous
- 2 cups chicken broth
- ¼ tsp. salt, divided
- ¼ tsp. pepper, divided
- 4 medium carrots, julienned
- 1 Tbsp. sugar
- 1 tsp. molasses

1. In a small saucepan, heat wine until hot. In a small bowl, soak raisins in wine for 5 minutes. Drain raisins, reserving the wine.

2. In a large saucepan, saute onion in 1 Tbsp. oil until tender. Stir in couscous. Cook and stir until lightly browned. Stir in the broth, raisins and half each of the salt and pepper. Bring to a boil. Cover and remove from the heat. Let stand for 5 minutes; fluff with a fork.

3. In a small skillet, saute the carrots in remaining oil until crisp-tender. Combine sugar, molasses, reserved wine and tremaining salt and pepper. Stir into carrots; heat through.

4. In a large bowl, combine couscous mixture and carrots; toss to combine.

¾ cup: 188 cal., 5g fat (1g sat. fat), 1mg chol., 277mg sod., 32g carb. (8g sugars, 2g fiber), 5g pro. **Diabetic exchanges:** 1½ starch, 1 vegetable, 1 fat.

Vegetable & Barley Pilaf

Carrot Raisin Couscous

VEGETABLE & BARLEY PILAF

Hearty, colorful, easy and fast were the reviews we gave this good-for-you dish. Barley has a healthy amount of soluble fiber, which aids digestion. And it can help to lower cholesterol, too! You can easily substitute other fresh veggies you have on hand.
—Jesse Klausmeier, Burbank, CA

TAKES: 30 min. • **MAKES:** 4 servings

- 1 large zucchini, quartered and sliced
- 1 large carrot, chopped
- 1 Tbsp. butter
- 2 cups reduced-sodium chicken broth
- 1 cup quick-cooking barley
- 2 green onions, chopped
- ½ tsp. dried marjoram
- ¼ tsp. salt
- ⅛ tsp. pepper

1. In a large saucepan, saute zucchini and carrot in butter until crisp-tender. Add broth; bring to a boil. Stir in barley. Reduce heat; cover and simmer until barley is tender, 10-12 minutes.

2. Stir in the onions, marjoram, salt and pepper. Remove from the heat; cover and let stand for 5 minutes.

¾ cup: 219 cal., 4g fat (2g sat. fat), 8mg chol., 480mg sod., 39g carb. (3g sugars, 10g fiber), 9g pro.

Jasmine Rice with Coconut & Cherries

TEXAS PECAN RICE

For a special holiday side dish, I dressed up an old recipe to give it a little more Texas character. Everyone loved the savory flavor and crunchy pecans.
—Joan Hallford, North Richland Hills, TX

PREP: 30 min. • **BAKE:** 1 hour
MAKES: 10 servings

- ½ cup unsalted butter, cubed
- 1½ cups sliced fresh mushrooms
- 3 green onions, sliced
- 2 cups uncooked long grain brown rice
- 1 garlic clove, minced
- 1½ cups chopped pecans, toasted
- ½ tsp. salt
- ½ tsp. dried thyme
- ½ tsp. pepper
- ¼ tsp. ground cumin
- 3 cans (10½ oz. each) condensed beef consomme, undiluted
- 2¼ cups water
- 5 bacon strips, cooked and crumbled
  Toasted pecan halves, optional

1. Preheat oven to 400°. In a Dutch oven, heat butter over medium-high heat. Add mushrooms and green onions; cook and stir until tender, 3-5 minutes. Add rice and garlic; cook and stir 3 minutes. Stir in the pecans, salt, thyme, pepper and cumin. Add consomme and water; bring to a boil.

2. Bake, covered, until liquid is absorbed and rice is tender, 1-1¼ hours. Transfer to a serving bowl. Top with bacon and, if desired, pecan halves.

¾ cup: 372 cal., 24g fat (8g sat. fat), 29mg chol., 783mg sod., 32g carb. (2g sugars, 4g fiber), 10g pro.

JASMINE RICE WITH COCONUT & CHERRIES

Our favorite rice deserves a bit of color and sweetness. We add dried cherries, peanuts, orange zest and coconut. That does the trick.
—Joy Zacharia, Clearwater, FL

PREP: 10 min. • **COOK:** 20 min. + standing
MAKES: 6 servings

- 2½ cups water
- 1 Tbsp. olive oil
- ¾ tsp. salt
- 1½ cups uncooked jasmine rice
- ⅓ cup dried cherries
- ¼ cup chopped salted peanuts
- 1 tsp. grated orange zest
- ¼ cup sweetened shredded coconut, toasted

1. In a large saucepan, bring water, oil and salt to a boil. Stir in rice; return to a boil, stirring once. Reduce heat; simmer, covered, until water is absorbed, about 15-17 minutes.

2. Stir in cherries, peanuts and orange zest; let stand, covered, 10 minutes. Sprinkle with coconut.

Note: To toast coconut, bake in a shallow pan in a 350° oven for 5-10 minutes or cook in a skillet over low heat until golden brown, stirring occasionally.

¾ cup: 291 cal., 7g fat (2g sat. fat), 0 chol., 332mg sod., 50g carb. (8g sugars, 1g fiber), 6g pro.

Health Tip

The berries and nuts in this recipe add extra vitamins and protein. To make the dish even healthier, try brown rice, which is a whole grain.

Texas Pecan Rice

GO FOR THE GRAINS CASSEROLE

This casserole is hearty and delicious. A friend gave me the recipe when I was compiling healthier recipes. This colorful medley has "good for you" written all over it.
—Melanie Blair, Warsaw, IN

PREP: 25 min. • **BAKE:** 55 min.
MAKES: 10 servings

- 5 medium carrots, thinly sliced
- 2 cups frozen corn, thawed
- 1 medium onion, diced
- 1 cup quick-cooking barley
- ½ cup bulgur
- ⅓ cup minced fresh parsley
- 1 tsp. salt
- ½ tsp. pepper
- 3 cups vegetable broth
- 1 can (15 oz.) black beans, rinsed and drained
- 1½ cups shredded reduced-fat cheddar cheese

1. Preheat oven to 350°. In a large bowl, combine carrots, corn, onion, barley, bulgur, parsley, salt and pepper. Stir in broth and beans. Transfer to a 13x9-in. baking dish coated with cooking spray.
2. Cover and bake 50-55 minutes or until grains are tender, stirring once. Sprinkle with cheese. Bake, uncovered, 3-5 minutes longer or until the cheese is melted.
¾ cup: 226 cal., 5g fat (3g sat. fat), 12mg chol., 741mg sod., 38g carb. (6g sugars, 8g fiber), 12g pro. **Diabetic exchanges:** 2 starch, 1 lean meat, 1 vegetable.

Portobello Polenta Bake

PORTOBELLO POLENTA BAKE

Any recipe with melted cheese in it is a favorite of mine. That's just one reason I love this polenta bake. It even has enough protein to make it a meatless meal!
—Margee Berry, White Salmon, WA

PREP: 25 min. • **BAKE:** 25 min. + standing
MAKES: 6 servings

- 1 can (14½ oz.) reduced-sodium chicken broth
- 1¼ cups water
- 1 cup cornmeal
- 2 tsp. olive oil
- 1 large onion, chopped
- ½ lb. sliced baby portobello mushrooms
- ¼ cup julienned soft sun-dried tomatoes (not packed in oil)
- 2 garlic cloves, minced
- 2 large eggs, lightly beaten
- 1 cup shredded Gruyere or fontina cheese
- ½ tsp. salt
- 1 cup part-skim ricotta cheese
  Minced fresh parsley

1. Preheat oven to 350°. In a large heavy saucepan, bring broth and water to a boil. Reduce heat to a gentle boil; slowly whisk in cornmeal. Cook and stir until thickened and cornmeal is tender, 8-10 minutes.
2. Meanwhile, in a large nonstick skillet, heat oil over medium-high heat; saute onion and mushrooms until tender, about 4-5 minutes. Stir in tomatoes and garlic; cook 1 minute.
3. Mix eggs, Gruyere cheese and salt; stir into polenta. Spread half the mixture into a greased 11x7-in. baking dish. Top with vegetable mixture. Drop ricotta cheese by tablespoonfuls over top. Spread with remaining polenta.
4. Bake, uncovered, until edges are lightly browned, 25-30 minutes. Let stand 10 minutes before serving. Sprinkle with parsley.
1¼ cups: 304 cal., 13g fat (6g sat. fat), 96mg chol., 605mg sod., 29g carb. (4g sugars, 3g fiber), 17g pro. **Diabetic exchanges:** 2 starch, 2 medium-fat meat, ½ fat.

VEGETABLE COUSCOUS SALAD

*This healthy salad is a welcome partner for
any grilled meat or fish. Feel free to add a
little crumbled goat cheese or tangy feta.*
—Patricia Levenson, Santa Ana, CA

PREP: 35 min. • **GRILL:** 10 min.
MAKES: 10 servings

- ½ cup olive oil
- ⅓ cup balsamic vinegar
- 4 tsp. capers, drained
- 4 tsp. lemon juice
- 2 garlic cloves, minced
- ¾ tsp. Dijon mustard
- 1¼ tsp. minced fresh rosemary or
  ½ tsp. dried rosemary, crushed
- 1¼ tsp. minced fresh thyme or
  ½ tsp. dried thyme
- ⅛ tsp. salt
- ⅛ tsp. pepper

SALAD

- 1 pkg. (10 oz.) uncooked couscous
- 2 medium zucchini or yellow summer
  squash, halved lengthwise
- 2 medium sweet yellow or red
  peppers, quartered
- 1 Japanese eggplant, halved
  lengthwise
- 2 Tbsp. olive oil
- ¼ tsp. salt
- ¼ tsp. pepper
- 1 cup grape tomatoes, halved
- ½ cup Greek olives, pitted and sliced
- 1 Tbsp. minced fresh parsley or
  1 tsp. dried parsley flakes
- 1 Tbsp. minced fresh basil or
  1 tsp. dried basil

1. In a small bowl, whisk the first 10
ingredients. Refrigerate until serving.
2. Cook couscous according to package
directions. Meanwhile, brush zucchini,
yellow peppers and eggplant with oil;
sprinkle with salt and pepper. Grill,
covered, over medium heat until
crisp-tender, 10-12 minutes, turning
vegetables once.
3. Chop grilled vegetables; place in a
large bowl. Add the tomatoes, olives,
parsley, basil and couscous. Pour
dressing over salad and toss to coat.
Serve warm or chilled.
¾ cup: 272 cal., 16g fat (2g sat. fat),
0 chol., 244mg sod., 29g carb. (5g sugars,
3g fiber), 5g pro. **Diabetic exchanges:**
2 fat, 1½ starch, 1 vegetable.

Test Kitchen Tip

Since this can be served warm or
chilled, it's a smart make-and-take
for potlucks and picnics.

Vegetable
Couscous Salad

Vegetable
Barley Bake

VEGETABLE BARLEY BAKE

Forget the potatoes and rice, and consider this change-of-pace dinner accompaniment. Wholesome barley makes for a heart-smart dish that complements just about any main course and other sides, too.
—Shirley Doyle, Mount Prospect, IL

PREP: 25 min. • **BAKE:** 55 min.
MAKES: 10 servings

- 3 medium sweet red or green peppers, chopped
- 4 cups sliced fresh mushrooms
- 2 medium onions, chopped
- 2 Tbsp. butter
- 2 cups reduced-sodium chicken broth or vegetable broth
- 1½ cups medium pearl barley
- ⅛ tsp. pepper

1. Preheat oven to 350°. In a large nonstick skillet, saute the peppers, mushrooms and onions in butter for 8-10 minutes or until tender. Transfer to a 13x9-in. baking dish coated with cooking spray. Stir in the broth, barley and pepper.

2. Cover and bake 50 minutes. Uncover; bake 5-10 minutes longer or until barley is tender and liquid is absorbed.

¾ cup: 157 cal., 3g fat (2g sat. fat), 6mg chol., 153mg sod., 30g carb. (4g sugars, 6g fiber), 5g pro. **Diabetic exchanges:** 1½ starch, 1 vegetable, ½ fat.

Mango Barley Salad

MANGO BARLEY SALAD

I made this fresh, colorful mango salad on the fly and it was a big hit! The bright flavor is perfect for a spring or summer picnic, served right away or chilled.
—Dan Wellberg, Elk River, MN

TAKES: 25 min. • **MAKES:** 6 servings

- 1¾ cups water
- 1 cup quick-cooking barley
- 2 medium limes
- ¼ cup olive oil
- 1 Tbsp. Dijon mustard
- 1 Tbsp. honey
- ½ tsp. salt
- ¼ tsp. ground cumin
- ¼ tsp. pepper
- ½ cup chopped sweet red pepper
- ½ cup chopped green pepper
- ¼ cup chopped red onion
- 1 medium mango, peeled and chopped
- ¼ cup minced fresh cilantro

1. In a small saucepan, bring the water to a boil. Stir in the barley. Reduce heat; simmer, covered, until barley is tender, 10-12 minutes. Remove from heat; let stand 5 minutes.

2. Finely grate enough zest from limes to measure 1 teaspoon. Cut limes crosswise in half; squeeze juice from limes. In a small bowl, whisk lime juice, lime zest, oil, mustard, honey, salt, cumin and pepper until blended.

3. In a large bowl, combine the barley, peppers, onion, mango and cilantro. Add dressing; toss to coat. Refrigerate until serving.

¾ cup: 185 cal., 10g fat (1g sat. fat), 0 chol., 261mg sod., 25g carb. (9g sugars, 5g fiber), 2g pro. **Diabetic exchanges:** 2 fat, 1½ starch.

Test Kitchen Tip

Just because we call for barley doesn't mean you can't try this tangy side dish with quinoa, farro or whatever other grains your family might enjoy most.

Tex-Mex Bean Bake
with Cornbread Topping,
Page 233

Page 235

Page 226

Beans, Lentils & Legumes

When you need a stick-to-your-ribs dish, these recipes always fit the bill. From summer-time favorites to winter warmer-uppers, the hearty sides in this chapter offer all the flavor you crave. Best of all, many simmer on their own in the slow cooker.

Page 225

Page 240

BEANS, BACON & TOMATO BAKE

On cold winter days, I pull out the bacon, tomatoes and lima beans for a veggie-packed side that satisfies everyone.
—Karen Kumpulainen, Forest City, NC

PREP: 10 min. • **BAKE:** 35 min.
MAKES: 12 servings

- 8 bacon strips, cut into 1-in. pieces
- 1 cup finely chopped onion
- ⅔ cup finely chopped celery
- ½ cup finely chopped green pepper
- 2 garlic cloves, minced
- 2 tsp. all-purpose flour
- 2 tsp. sugar
- 2 tsp. salt
- ¼ tsp. pepper
- 2 cans (14½ oz. each) diced tomatoes, undrained
- 8 cups frozen lima beans (about 42 oz.), thawed

1. Preheat oven to 325°. In a 6-qt. stockpot, cook bacon, onion, celery and green pepper over medium heat until bacon is crisp and the vegetables are tender. Add garlic; cook 1 minute longer. Stir in flour, sugar, salt and pepper. Add the tomatoes. Bring to a boil, stirring constantly; cook and stir 1-2 minutes or until thickened. Stir in beans.
2. Transfer to a greased 3-qt. baking dish or a 13x9-in. baking pan. Bake, covered, 35-40 minutes or until beans are tender.

⅔ cup: 230 cal., 8g fat (3g sat. fat), 12mg chol., 666mg sod., 30g carb. (6g sugars, 9g fiber), 11g pro. **Diabetic exchanges:** 2 starch, 1½ fat.

Beans, Bacon & Tomato Bake

SWEET & SPICY BEANS

My husband and I love this sweet and savory bean dish. It can be used as a side or even as a dip. When you fill up a corn scoop chip, the party starts in your mouth!
—Sondra Pope, Mooresville, NC

PREP: 10 min. • **COOK:** 5 hours
MAKES: 12 servings (⅔ cup each)

- 1 can (16 oz.) kidney beans, rinsed and drained
- 1 can (15¼ oz.) whole kernel corn, drained
- 1 can (15 oz.) garbanzo beans or chickpeas, rinsed and drained
- 1 can (15 oz.) black beans, rinsed and drained
- 1 can (15 oz.) chili with beans
- 1 cup barbecue sauce
- 1 cup salsa
- ⅓ cup packed brown sugar
- ¼ tsp. hot pepper sauce
  Chopped green onions, optional

In a 4- or 5-qt. slow cooker, combine the first 9 ingredients. Cover and cook on low for 5-6 hours. Top with green onions if desired.

⅔ cup: 201 cal., 2g fat (0 sat. fat), 4mg chol., 712mg sod., 36g carb. (13g sugars, 7g fiber), 9g pro.

Slow-Simmered
Kidney Beans

SLOW-SIMMERED KIDNEY BEANS

My husband always puts us down for a side dish when we're invited to a potluck. Canned beans cut down on prep time, yet you get plenty of zip from bacon, apple, red pepper and onion. I like how the slow cooker blends the flavors for me, and I don't have to stand over the stove.
—Sheila Vail, Long Beach, CA

PREP: 15 min. • **COOK:** 6 hours
MAKES: 16 servings (¾ cup each)

- 6 bacon strips, diced
- ½ lb. smoked Polish sausage or kielbasa, sliced
- 4 cans (16 oz. each) kidney beans, rinsed and drained
- 1 can (28 oz.) diced tomatoes, drained
- 2 medium sweet red peppers, chopped
- 1 large onion, chopped
- 1 cup ketchup
- ½ cup packed brown sugar
- ¼ cup honey
- ¼ cup molasses
- 1 Tbsp. Worcestershire sauce
- 1 tsp. salt
- 1 tsp. ground mustard
- 2 medium unpeeled red apples, cubed

1. In a large skillet, cook bacon until crisp. Remove with a slotted spoon to paper towels. Add sausage to drippings; cook and stir for 5 minutes. Drain and set aside.

2. In a 6-qt. slow cooker, combine the beans, tomatoes, red peppers, onion, ketchup, brown sugar, honey, molasses, Worcestershire sauce, salt and mustard. Stir in the bacon and sausage. Cover and cook on low for 4-6 hours. Stir in apples. Cover and cook 2 hours longer or until bubbly.

¾ cup: 216 cal., 9g fat (3g sat. fat), 15mg chol., 664mg sod., 30g carb. (21g sugars, 3g fiber), 5g pro.

Pressure-Cooker Smoky
White Beans & Ham

TOMATO-GARLIC LENTIL BOWLS

An Ethiopian recipe inspired this feel-good dinner that's tangy, creamy and packed with hearty comfort.
—Rachael Cushing, Portland, OR

TAKES: 30 min. • **MAKES:** 6 servings

- 1 Tbsp. olive oil
- 2 medium onions, chopped
- 4 garlic cloves, minced
- 2 cups dried brown lentils, rinsed
- 1 tsp. salt
- ½ tsp. ground ginger
- ½ tsp. paprika
- ¼ tsp. pepper
- 3 cups water
- ¼ cup lemon juice
- 3 Tbsp. tomato paste
- ¾ cup fat-free plain Greek yogurt
  Optional: Chopped tomatoes and minced fresh cilantro

1. In a saucepan, heat oil over medium-high heat; saute the onions 2 minutes. Add garlic; cook 1 minute. Stir in lentils, seasonings and water; bring to a boil. Reduce heat; simmer, covered, until lentils are tender, 25-30 minutes.
2. Stir in lemon juice and tomato paste; heat through. Serve with yogurt and, if desired, tomatoes and cilantro.
¾ cup: 294 cal., 3g fat (0 sat. fat), 0 chol., 419mg sod., 49g carb. (5g sugars, 8g fiber), 21g pro. **Diabetic exchanges:** 3 starch, 2 lean meat, ½ fat.

Health Tip
Cup for cup, lentils have twice as much protein and iron as quinoa.

PRESSURE-COOKER SMOKY WHITE BEANS & HAM

I had never made or even eaten this dish before meeting my husband. Now I make it at least once a week. I serve it with some homemade sweet cornbread. Delicious!
—Christine Duffy, Sturgis, KY

PREP: 15 min. • **COOK:** 30 min. + releasing
MAKES: 10 servings

- 1 lb. dried great northern beans
- 3 smoked ham hocks (about 1½ lbs.)
- 3 cans (14½ oz. each) reduced-sodium chicken or beef broth
- 2 cups water
- 1 large onion, chopped
- 1 Tbsp. onion powder
- 1 Tbsp. garlic powder
- 2 tsp. pepper
  Thinly sliced green onions, optional

1. Rinse and sort beans. Transfer to a 6-qt. electric pressure cooker. Add ham hocks. Stir in broth, water, onion and seasonings. Lock lid; close pressure-release valve. Adjust to pressure-cook on high for 30 minutes. Let pressure release naturally for 10 minutes; quick-release any remaining pressure.
2. When cool enough to handle, remove meat from bones; cut ham into small pieces and return to pressure cooker. Serve with a slotted spoon. Sprinkle with green onions if desired.
⅔ cup: 196 cal., 2g fat (0 sat. fat), 8mg chol., 594mg sod., 32g carb. (2g sugars, 10g fiber), 15g pro. **Diabetic exchanges:** 2 starch, 2 lean meat.

Tomato-Garlic
Lentil Bowls

DAD'S CREAMED PEAS & PEARL ONIONS

When I was growing up, it was a family tradition to make creamed peas with pearl onions for Thanksgiving and Christmas dinner. My dad would not be a happy camper if he didn't see this dish on the table. It was his favorite! I made it for my own family while our kids were growing up; my daughter now makes this dish for her family.
—Nancy Heishman, Las Vegas, NV

TAKES: 25 min. • **MAKES:** 6 servings

- 5 cups frozen peas (about 20 oz.), thawed and drained
- 2 cups frozen pearl onions (about 9 oz.), thawed and drained
- 2 celery ribs, finely chopped
- ¾ cup chicken broth
- ½ tsp. salt
- ½ tsp. pepper
- ½ tsp. dried thyme
- ½ cup sour cream
- 10 bacon strips, cooked and crumbled
- ¾ cup salted cashews

In a large skillet, combine the first 7 ingredients; bring to a boil. Reduce heat to medium; cook, uncovered, until onions are tender and most of liquid is evaporated, 8-10 minutes, stirring occasionally. Remove from heat; stir in the sour cream. Top with the bacon and cashews.

¾ cup: 322 cal., 18g fat (6g sat. fat), 19mg chol., 783mg sod., 26g carb. (10g sugars, 7g fiber), 14g pro.

WHY YOU'LL LOVE IT...

"This recipe is so delicious! I made this for a Memorial Day cookout, and there was almost nothing left of it after everyone ate their fill."
—APRIL F, TASTEOFHOME.COM

Dad's Creamed
Peas & Pearl Onions

Frijoles y
Chorizo

FRIJOLES Y CHORIZO

Chorizo (pork sausage) and frijoles (beans)
make a tasty and authentic side dish. The
flavorful meat combined with the zippy
mixture of beans, peppers and seasonings
are unforgettable.
—Taste of Home *Test Kitchen*

PREP: 40 min. + soaking • **COOK:** 2 hours
MAKES: 16 servings (2 qt.)

    1   lb. dried pinto beans
    2   poblano peppers
    2   serrano peppers
    6   cups water
    1   bay leaf
    ½   lb. uncooked chorizo, casing removed
    2   Tbsp. lard
    1   cup chopped onion
    2   tsp. salt
    ¼   cup chopped fresh cilantro

1. Place beans in a Dutch oven; add
water to cover by 2 in. Bring to a boil;
boil for 2 minutes. Remove from the
heat; cover and let stand for 1 hour.
2. Place peppers on a baking sheet;
broil 4 in. from heat until skins blister,
about 4 minutes. With tongs, rotate
the peppers a quarter turn. Broil and
rotate until all sides are blistered and
blackened. Immediately place the
peppers in a bowl; cover and let stand
for 15 minutes. Peel off and discard
charred skin. Remove the stems and
seeds. Chop peppers.
3. Drain and rinse the pinto beans,
discarding liquid. Return the beans to
the Dutch oven. Add 6 cups water and
bay leaf; bring to a boil. Reduce heat;
simmer, uncovered, for 1½-2 hours
or until beans are tender.
4. Meanwhile, crumble chorizo into
a skillet; cook over medium heat until
fully cooked, 6-8 minutes. Drain and set
aside. In the same skillet, melt lard. Add
onion and reserved peppers; cook and
stir until tender, about 5 minutes.
5. Add the chorizo, pepper mixture and
salt to beans. Simmer, uncovered, for
30 minutes. Discard bay leaf. Just before
serving, stir in cilantro.
Note: Wear disposable gloves when
cutting hot peppers; the oils can burn
skin. Avoid touching your face.
½ cup: 173 cal., 6g fat (2g sat. fat), 14mg
chol., 472mg sod., 20g carb. (2g sugars,
5g fiber), 9g pro.

Lemon-Garlic
Lima Beans

SLOW-COOKED BEAN MEDLEY

I often change the variety of beans in this classic recipe, using whatever I have on hand to total the five cans called for. The sauce makes any combination delicious! It's a gluten-free side dish that's popular with just about everyone.
—*Peggy Gwillim, Strasbourg, , SK*

PREP: 25 min. • **COOK:** 5 hours
MAKES: 12 servings

- 1½ cups ketchup
- 2 celery ribs, chopped
- 1 medium onion, chopped
- 1 medium green pepper, chopped
- 1 medium sweet red pepper, chopped
- ½ cup packed brown sugar
- ½ cup water
- ½ cup Italian salad dressing
- 2 bay leaves
- 1 Tbsp. cider vinegar
- 1 tsp. ground mustard
- ⅛ tsp. pepper
- 1 can (16 oz.) kidney beans, rinsed and drained
- 1 can (15½ oz.) black-eyed peas, rinsed and drained
- 1 can (15½ oz.) great northern beans, rinsed and drained
- 1 can (15¼ oz.) whole kernel corn, drained
- 1 can (15¼ oz.) lima beans, rinsed and drained
- 1 can (15 oz.) black beans, rinsed and drained

In a 5-qt. slow cooker, combine the first 12 ingredients. Stir in the remaining ingredients. Cover and cook on low for 5-6 hours or until onion and peppers are tender. Discard bay leaves.
¾ cup: 255 cal., 4g fat (0 sat. fat), 0 chol., 942mg sod., 45g carb. (21g sugars, 7g fiber), 9g pro. **Diabetic exchanges:** 1½ starch, ½ fat.

LEMON-GARLIC LIMA BEANS

When I was growing up on Cyprus, my mother would often make this side dish to have with roast lamb. Although I hated lima beans when I was a kid (who didn't?), I love them now. They always remind me of home.
—*Paris Paraskeva, San Francisco, CA*

PREP: 15 min. + soaking • **COOK:** 1¼ hours
MAKES: 6 servings

- 1 lb. dried lima beans
- 2 bay leaves
- 3 Tbsp. extra virgin olive oil, divided
- 1 medium onion, chopped
- 4 garlic cloves, thinly sliced
- ¼ cup chopped fresh parsley
- 2 Tbsp. lemon juice
- 1 Tbsp. chopped fresh oregano
- 2 tsp. grated lemon zest
- ½ tsp. salt
- ¼ tsp. pepper
  Additional chopped fresh parsley

1. Rinse and sort beans; soak according to package directions. Drain and rinse beans, discarding liquid.
2. Place beans in a large saucepan; add bay leaves and water to cover by 2 in. Bring to a boil. Reduce heat; simmer, covered, until the beans are tender, 1¼-1½ hours. Drain.
3. In a large skillet, heat 1 Tbsp. oil over medium heat. Add onion; cook and stir until tender, 3-4 minutes. Add sliced garlic; cook 1 minute longer. Add next 6 ingredients. Stir in drained beans and remaining oil; toss to combine. Sprinkle with additional fresh parsley.
½ cup: 326 cal., 8g fat (1g sat. fat), 0 chol., 209mg sod., 51g carb. (7g sugars, 16g fiber), 16g pro.

Slow-Cooked
Bean Medley

BAKED BEANS MOLE

We love this side dish that is quick and easy to prepare but so flavorful. Chocolate, chili and honey mingle to create a rich, savory flavor that's not too spicy and not too sweet.
—Roxanne Chan, Albany, CA

PREP: 25 min. • **BAKE:** 40 minutes
MAKES: 8 servings

- ¼ lb. fresh chorizo, crumbled
- ½ cup chopped onion
- ½ cup chopped sweet red pepper
- 1 large garlic clove, minced
- 1 can (15 oz.) black beans, rinsed and drained
- 1 can (15 oz.) pinto beans, rinsed and drained
- 1 can (15 oz.) black-eyed peas, rinsed and drained
- 1 cup salsa (medium or hot)
- 1 cup chili sauce
- 2 Tbsp. honey
- 1 Tbsp. instant coffee granules
- ½ tsp. ground cinnamon
- 2 oz. chopped bittersweet or semisweet chocolate
  Minced fresh cilantro

Preheat oven to 375°. In a large, ovenproof skillet with a lid, cook the chorizo, onion, red pepper and garlic over medium heat until sausage is browned, 4-6 minutes. Add the next 9 ingredients; mix well. Bake, covered, until mixture is thickened and flavors are blended, about 40 minutes. Sprinkle with cilantro.

⅔ cup: 284 cal., 7g fat (3g sat. fat), 13mg chol., 989mg sod., 40g carb. (14g sugars, 6g fiber), 11g pro.

Test Kitchen Tip

Although this dish is fantastic with several different types of beans, it would be equally good with just one. You could also add 2 to 3 cups of broth to make a festive mole chili.

Baked Beans Mole

TEX-MEX BEAN BAKE WITH CORNBREAD TOPPING

I frequently cooked this dish when I was on the cross-country team in college. We loved this veggie-packed bake so much I would have to make two! For an entree, substitute shredded chicken for half of the potato.
—Samantha Westveer, Kentwood, MI

PREP: 35 min. • **BAKE:** 25 min.
MAKES: 8 servings

- 1 Tbsp. olive oil
- 1 large sweet potato, peeled and finely chopped
- 1 medium onion, coarsely chopped
- 1 small green pepper, coarsely chopped
- 1 small sweet red pepper, coarsely chopped
- 1 can (15 oz.) black beans, rinsed and drained
- 1 can (15 oz.) pinto beans, rinsed and drained
- 1 cup frozen corn
- 1 can (4 oz.) chopped green chiles
- ½ tsp. salt
- ½ tsp. ground cumin
- ½ cup vegetable broth
- 3 oz. cream cheese, softened

TOPPING
- 1 pkg. (8½ oz.) cornbread/muffin mix
- 1 large egg
- ⅓ cup low-fat milk
- ⅓ cup solid-pack pumpkin

1. Preheat oven to 400°. In a large skillet, heat oil over medium-high heat. Add sweet potato, onion and peppers; cook and stir until potato is cooked halfway through, 5-7 minutes.
2. Stir in beans, corn, chiles, salt and cumin; heat through. Stir in broth and cream cheese until blended. Transfer to a greased 13x9-in. baking dish.
3. In a large bowl, combine cornbread mix, egg, milk and pumpkin. Spoon over bean mixture. Bake, uncovered, until a toothpick inserted in the topping portion comes out clean, 25-30 minutes.

MAKE AHEAD: Can be made a day in advance. Prepare as directed, omitting topping. Cover and refrigerate overnight. Remove from refrigerator 30 minutes before baking. Prepare topping and bake as directed.
1 serving: 310 cal., 10g fat (4g sat. fat), 35mg chol., 645mg sod., 47g carb. (14g sugars, 7g fiber), 8g pro.

SLOW-COOKER CHICKPEA TAGINE

While traveling through Morocco, my wife and I fell in love with the complex flavors of the many tagines we tried. Resist the urge to stir, as it will break down the veggies. We like it alongside grilled fish, but if you add cooked chicken in the last 10 minutes it becomes a main course.
—Raymond Wyatt, West St. Paul, MN

PREP: 20 min. • **COOK:** 4 hours
MAKES: 12 servings

- 1 small butternut squash (about 2 lbs.), peeled and cut into ½-in. cubes
- 2 medium zucchini, cut into ½-in. pieces
- 1 medium sweet red pepper, coarsely chopped
- 1 medium onion, coarsely chopped
- 1 can (15 oz.) chickpeas or garbanzo beans, rinsed and drained
- 12 dried apricots, halved
- 2 Tbsp. olive oil
- 2 garlic cloves, minced
- 2 tsp. paprika
- 1 tsp. ground ginger
- 1 tsp. ground cumin
- ½ tsp. salt
- ¼ tsp. pepper
- ¼ tsp. ground cinnamon
- 1 can (14.5 oz.) crushed tomatoes
- 2 to 3 tsp. harissa chili paste
- 2 tsp. honey
- ¼ cup chopped fresh mint leaves
  Optional: Plain Greek yogurt and additional olive oil, honey and fresh mint

1. Place the first 6 ingredients in a 5- or 6-qt. slow cooker.
2. In a skillet, heat oil over medium heat. Add garlic, paprika, ginger, cumin, salt, pepper and cinnamon; cook and stir until fragrant, about 1 minute. Add tomatoes, harissa and honey; bring to a boil. Pour the tomato mixture over vegetables; stir to combine. Cook, covered, on low until the vegetables are tender and sauce has thickened, 4-5 hours. Stir in mint.
3. If desired, top with yogurt, and additional mint, olive oil and honey to serve.
¾ cup: 127 cal., 3g fat (0 sat. fat), 0 chol., 224mg sod., 23g carb. (9g sugars, 6g fiber), 4g pro. **Diabetic exchanges:** 1½ starch, ½ fat.

PEAS WITH SHALLOTS

I first served this at an Easter dinner. My guests suggested I use even more shallots. It's easy, nutritious and always a hit.
—Rosemary Schirm, Avondale, PA

TAKES: 15 min. • **MAKES:** 4 servings

- 1 Tbsp. butter
- ½ lb. fresh sugar snap peas, trimmed
- 1 cup frozen peas
- 2 shallots, thinly sliced
- ½ tsp. salt
- ¼ tsp. pepper

In a large cast-iron or other heavy skillet, heat butter over medium-high heat. Add snap peas, frozen peas and shallots; cook and stir until crisp-tender, 5-6 minutes. Stir in salt and pepper.
¾ cup: 91 cal., 3g fat (2g sat. fat), 8mg chol., 360mg sod., 12g carb. (4g sugars, 3g fiber), 4g pro. **Diabetic exchanges:** 1 vegetable, 1 fat, ½ starch.

Coconut Lentils
with Rice

COCONUT LENTILS WITH RICE

Years ago I made this recipe for my kids and they loved it. One of my daughter's friends would always request this dish when she came over to visit. We like making it with basmati rice.
—Diane Donato, Columbus, OH

PREP: 20 min. • **COOK:** 35 min.
MAKES: 6 servings

1	**Tbsp. canola oil**
6	**green onions, chopped**
1	**Tbsp. minced fresh gingerroot**
2	**garlic cloves, minced**
¼	**tsp. crushed red pepper flakes**
1½	**cups dried lentils, rinsed**
1	**tsp. ground turmeric**
½	**tsp. salt**
5½	**cups vegetable stock**
2	**large tomatoes, chopped**
½	**cup flaked coconut**
2	**Tbsp. minced fresh mint**
3	**cups hot cooked rice**
⅓	**cup plain Greek yogurt**

1. In a large saucepan, heat oil over medium heat; saute green onions, ginger, garlic and pepper flakes until onions are tender, 2-4 minutes. Stir in lentils, turmeric, salt and stock; bring to a boil. Reduce heat; simmer, covered, until lentils are tender, 25-30 minutes, stirring occasionally.
2. Stir in tomatoes, coconut and mint. Serve with rice; top with yogurt.
1 serving: 374 cal., 7g fat (4g sat. fat), 3mg chol., 757mg sod., 63g carb. (7g sugars, 7g fiber), 16g pro.

Baked Beans with Bacon

BAKED BEANS WITH BACON

This recipe came from my mother and was always a hit. The chopped jalapeno pepper spices it up a bit. And the recipe is easy to remember—it's a half-cup of this and a half-cup of that!
—Nadine Brissey, Jenks, OK

PREP: 15 min. • **COOK:** 6 hours
MAKES: 8 servings

3	**cans (15 oz. each) pork and beans**
½	**cup finely chopped onion**
½	**cup chopped green pepper**
½	**cup ketchup**
½	**cup maple syrup**
2	**Tbsp. finely chopped seeded jalapeno pepper**
½	**cup crumbled cooked bacon**

In a 3-qt. slow cooker, combine the first 6 ingredients. Cover and cook on low for 6-8 hours or until vegetables are tender. Just before serving, stir in bacon.
Note: Wear disposable gloves when cutting hot peppers; the oils can burn skin. Avoid touching your face.
⅔ cup: 232 cal., 3g fat (0 sat. fat), 5mg chol., 932mg sod., 47g carb. (25g sugars, 8g fiber), 10g pro.

Hearty
Maple Beans

Fiesta Corn
& Beans

HEARTY MAPLE BEANS

I modified this recipe to suit my family's taste. It's a great side dish for a backyard barbecue with hamburgers and hot dogs. Best of all, it can be made in advance and kept warm in a slow cooker for hours without losing any flavor.
—Margaret Glassic, Easton, PA

PREP: 15 min. • **BAKE:** 25 min.
MAKES: 10 servings

- 6 bacon strips, diced
- ½ lb. smoked kielbasa or Polish sausage, sliced
- 1 small onion, chopped
- 1 can (15¾ oz.) pork and beans
- 1 can (16 oz.) kidney beans, rinsed and drained
- 1 can (16 oz.) butter beans, rinsed and drained
- ½ cup maple syrup
- 3 Tbsp. white vinegar
- 3 Tbsp. ketchup
- 3 Tbsp. prepared mustard

1. Preheat oven to 350°. In a large skillet, cook bacon over medium heat until crisp. Using a slotted spoon, remove to paper towels. Drain, reserving 1 Tbsp. drippings. In drippings, cook sausage and onion over medium-high heat until sausage is lightly browned. Stir in bacon and remaining ingredients.

2. Transfer to an ungreased 2-qt. baking dish. Bake, uncovered, 25-30 minutes or until bubbly.

¾ cup: 294 cal., 13g fat (4g sat. fat), 26mg chol., 673mg sod., 35g carb. (15g sugars, 6g fiber), 12g pro.

FIESTA CORN & BEANS

Bursting with southwestern flavors, the zesty veggie medley here can be served as a side dish or a meatless meal-in-one. A dollop of yogurt offers a cool, creamy finishing touch.
—Gerald Hetrick, Erie, PA

PREP: 25 min. • **COOK:** 3 hours
MAKES: 10 servings

1 large onion, chopped
1 medium green pepper, cut into 1-in. pieces
1 to 2 jalapeno peppers, seeded and sliced
1 Tbsp. olive oil
1 garlic clove, minced
2 cans (16 oz. each) kidney beans, rinsed and drained
1 pkg. (16 oz.) frozen corn
1 can (14½ oz.) diced tomatoes, undrained
1 tsp. chili powder
¾ tsp. salt
½ tsp. ground cumin
½ tsp. pepper
   Optional toppings: Plain yogurt and sliced ripe olives

1. In a large skillet, saute onion and peppers in oil until tender. Add garlic; cook 1 minute longer. Transfer to a 4-qt. slow cooker. Stir in the beans, corn, tomatoes and seasonings.
2. Cover and cook on low until heated through, 3-4 hours. Serve with yogurt and olives if desired.
Note: Wear disposable gloves when cutting hot peppers; the oils can burn skin. Avoid touching your face.
¾ cup: 149 cal., 2g fat (0 sat. fat), 0 chol., 380mg sod., 28g carb. (5g sugars, 7g fiber), 8g pro. **Diabetic exchanges:** 1 starch, 1 lean meat, 1 vegetable.

Slow-Cooker
Calico Beans

BLACK BEAN POTATO AU GRATIN

The addition of black beans and vegetables add both protein and fiber to this otherwise one dimensional side dish. For a tasty southwestern twist, try adding a handful or two of chopped cooked ham or chorizo sausage and replace the peas with one cup of corn.
—Erin Chilcoat, Central Islip, NY

PREP: 25 min. • **COOK:** 8 hours
MAKES: 6 servings

- 2 cans (15 oz. each) black beans, rinsed and drained
- 1 can (10¾ oz.) condensed cream of mushroom soup, undiluted
- 1 medium sweet red pepper, chopped
- 1 cup frozen peas
- 1 cup chopped sweet onion
- 1 celery rib, thinly sliced
- 2 garlic cloves, minced
- 1 tsp. dried thyme
- ¼ tsp. coarsely ground pepper
- 1½ lbs. medium red potatoes, cut into ¼-in. slices
- 1 tsp. salt
- 1 cup shredded cheddar cheese

In a large bowl, combine the beans, soup, red pepper, peas, onion, celery, garlic, thyme and pepper. Spoon half of mixture into a greased 3- or 4-qt. slow cooker. Layer with half the potatoes, salt and cheese. Repeat layers. Cover and cook on low until potatoes are tender, 8-10 hours.
1 cup: 340 cal., 9g fat (5g sat. fat), 22mg chol., 1178mg sod., 50g carb. (6g sugars, 10g fiber), 15g pro.

SLOW-COOKER CALICO BEANS

With so many folks moving to meatless or healthier food choices, I decided to remove the meat from the original recipe but turn up the flavor. The savory veggie blend balances the sweetness of the baked beans.
—David Dixon, Shaker Heights, OH

PREP: 20 min. • **COOK:** 5 hours
MAKES: 15 servings (¾ cup each)

- 2 tsp. canola oil
- 1 large sweet onion, chopped
- 1 medium sweet red pepper, chopped
- 2 cans (28 oz. each) vegetarian baked beans
- 1 can (16 oz.) butter beans, rinsed and drained
- 1 can (16 oz.) kidney beans, rinsed and drained
- 1 can (14½ oz.) fire-roasted diced tomatoes, undrained
- ½ cup ketchup
- ⅓ cup packed brown sugar
- 1 Tbsp. ground mustard
- 1 Tbsp. cider vinegar
- 1 tsp. salt
- 1 tsp. Worcestershire sauce

In a large skillet, heat oil over medium-high heat. Add onion and pepper; cook and stir until tender. Transfer to a 5-qt. slow cooker; stir in the remaining ingredients. Cook, covered, on low until heated through, 5-6 hours.
¾ cup: 195 cal., 1g fat (0 sat. fat), 0 chol., 859mg sod., 42g carb. (18g sugars, 8g fiber), 9g pro.

Black Bean
Potato au Gratin

BLACK-EYED PEAS & HAM

Every New Year's Day we have these slow-cooked black-eyed peas to bring good luck for the coming year.
—Dawn Legler, Fort Morgan, CO

PREP: 20 min. + soaking • **COOK:** 5 hours
MAKES: 12 servings

- 1 pkg. (16 oz.) dried black-eyed peas, rinsed and sorted
- ½ lb. fully cooked boneless ham, finely chopped
- 1 medium onion, finely chopped
- 1 medium sweet red pepper, finely chopped
- 5 bacon strips, cooked and crumbled
- 1 large jalapeno pepper, seeded and finely chopped
- 2 garlic cloves, minced
- 1½ tsp. ground cumin
- 1 tsp. reduced-sodium chicken bouillon granules
- ½ tsp. salt
- ½ tsp. cayenne pepper
- ¼ tsp. pepper
- 6 cups water
  Minced fresh cilantro, optional
  Hot cooked rice

1. Soak peas according to the package directions.
2. Transfer peas to a 6-qt. slow cooker; add the next 12 ingredients. Cover and cook on low 5-7 hours, until peas are tender. Sprinkle with cilantro if desired. Serve with rice.
Note: Wear disposable gloves when cutting hot peppers; the oils can burn skin. Avoid touching your face.
¾ cup: 170 cal., 3g fat (1g sat. fat), 13mg chol., 386mg sod., 24g carb. (5g sugars, 7g fiber), 13g pro. **Diabetic exchanges:** 1½ starch, 1 lean meat.

Black-Eyed
Peas & Ham

Patio Pintos

PATIO PINTOS

Any time Mom had the gang over for dinner, she made these pinto beans. Once, she made a batch for my cousin's birthday and he ate the entire thing.
—Joan Hallford, North Richland Hills, TX

PREP: 25 min. • **BAKE:** 1 hour
MAKES: 10 servings

- ½ lb. bacon strips, chopped
- 1 large onion, chopped
- 2 garlic cloves, minced
- 6 cans (15 oz. each) pinto beans, rinsed and drained
- 4 cans (8 oz. each) tomato sauce
- 2 cans (4 oz. each) chopped green chiles
- ⅓ cup packed brown sugar
- 1 tsp. chili powder
- ¾ tsp. salt
- ½ tsp. dried oregano
- ¼ tsp. pepper

1. Preheat oven to 350°. In a Dutch oven, cook bacon over medium heat until crisp, stirring occasionally. Remove with a slotted spoon; drain on paper towels. Discard drippings, reserving 2 Tbsp. in pan.

2. Add onion to drippings; cook and stir over medium heat until tender, 6-8 minutes. Add garlic; cook 1 minute longer. Stir in the beans, tomato sauce, chiles, brown sugar and seasonings. Sprinkle top with bacon. Bake, covered, until heated through, 60-70 minutes.

Freeze option: Freeze cooled bean mixture in freezer containers. To use, partially thaw in refrigerator overnight. Heat through in a saucepan, stirring occasionally; add water if necessary.

¾ cup: 349 cal., 8g fat (2g sat. fat), 11mg chol., 1183mg sod., 55g carb. (13g sugars, 12g fiber), 17g pro.

Black-Eyed Peas
with Collard Greens

BLACK-EYED PEAS WITH COLLARD GREENS

This dish has special meaning on New Year's Day, when southerners eat greens for future wealth and black-eyed peas for prosperity.
—*Athena Russell, Greenville, SC*

TAKES: 25 min. • **MAKES:** 6 servings

- 2 Tbsp. olive oil
- 1 garlic clove, minced
- 8 cups chopped collard greens
- ½ tsp. salt
- ¼ tsp. cayenne pepper
- 2 cans (15½ oz. each) black-eyed peas, rinsed and drained
- 4 plum tomatoes, seeded and chopped
- ¼ cup lemon juice
- 2 Tbsp. grated Parmesan cheese

In a Dutch oven, heat oil over medium heat. Add garlic; cook and stir 1 minute. Add collard greens, salt and cayenne; cook and stir 6-8 minutes or until greens are tender. Add peas, tomatoes and lemon juice; heat through. Sprinkle servings with cheese.

¾ cup: 177 cal., 5g fat (1g sat. fat), 1mg chol., 412mg sod., 24g carb. (3g sugars, 6g fiber), 9g pro.

Lora's Red Beans & Rice

LORA'S RED BEANS & RICE

My dear mother-in-law passed this simple recipe to me. With meats, beans and savory veggies that simmer all day, it's tasty, easy and economical, too!
—*Carol Simms, Madison, MS*

PREP: 15 min. + soaking • **COOK:** 8 hours
MAKES: 10 servings

- 1 lb. dried kidney beans (about 2½ cups)
- 2 cups cubed fully cooked ham (about 1 lb.)
- 1 pkg. (12 oz.) fully cooked andouille chicken sausage links or flavor of choice, sliced
- 1 medium green pepper, chopped
- 1 medium onion, chopped
- 2 celery ribs, chopped
- 1 Tbsp. hot pepper sauce
- 2 garlic cloves, minced
- 1½ tsp. salt
   Hot cooked rice

1. Place beans in a large bowl; add cool water to cover. Soak overnight.
2. Drain beans, discarding water; rinse with cool water. Place soaked beans in a greased 6-qt. slow cooker. Stir in the ham, sausage, vegetables, pepper sauce, garlic and salt. Add water to cover by 1 in.
3. Cook, covered, on low 8-9 hours or until beans are tender. Serve with rice.

1 cup bean mixture: 249 cal., 5g fat (1g sat. fat), 43mg chol., 906mg sod., 31g carb. (2g sugars, 7g fiber), 23g pro.

Test Kitchen Tip
Try smoked turkey sausage in place of andouille if you'd like.

Fruit with
Poppy Seed Dressing,
Page 259

Page 250

Page 268

Fruits & Berries

It's easy to lighten up menus and add color to tables when you serve any of these change-of-pace sides and salads. Perfect for formal brunches and busy weeknights alike, each recipe brings a burst of flavor to any meal.

Page 260

Page 255

APRICOTS WITH HERBED GOAT CHEESE

After ending up with bunches of apricots one summer, I created this quick and simple dish. My friends were blown away with its fresh taste and uniqueness.
—Wendy Weidner, Ham Lake, MN

TAKES: 20 min. • **MAKES:** 4 servings

- 3 oz. fresh goat cheese
- 2 tsp. minced fresh basil
- 2 tsp. minced fresh chives
- 2 tsp. 2% milk
- 4 fresh apricots, sliced
- ⅛ tsp. salt
  Dash pepper
- 2 Tbsp. balsamic glaze
  Fresh basil leaves

Place goat cheese, minced basil, chives and milk in a mini food processor; process until smooth. Arrange apricot slices on a serving platter. Drop goat cheese mixture by teaspoonfuls over top. Sprinkle with salt and pepper; drizzle with balsamic glaze. Garnish with basil leaves. Serve immediately.

1 serving: 71 cal., 3g fat (2g sat. fat), 14mg chol., 163mg sod., 9g carb. (6g sugars, 1g fiber), 3g pro. **Diabetic exchanges:** ½ fruit, ½ fat.

Test Kitchen Tip

If you can't find fresh apricots, substitute 3 small peaches for the 4 apricots.

Apricots with
Herbed Goat Cheese

GRILLED MANGO & AVOCADO SALAD

A big hit with my family, this light salad is so easy to make! The healthy option of mango and avocado is simply the best combination you could serve.
—Amy Liesemeyer, Tucson, AZ

TAKES: 25 min. • **MAKES:** 8 servings

- 4 medium firm mangoes, peeled
- 1 Tbsp. canola oil
- ¼ cup lime juice
- ¼ cup olive oil
- 1 Tbsp. black sesame seeds
- ½ tsp. salt
- 2 Tbsp. minced fresh cilantro, optional
- 1 Tbsp. minced fresh mint, optional
- 2 medium cucumbers, peeled, seeded and coarsely chopped
- 2 medium ripe avocados, peeled and coarsely chopped

1. Cut a thin slice off the bottom of each mango. Standing mango upright, slice off a large section of flesh, cutting close to the pit. Rotate and repeat until all flesh is removed.

2. Brush mangoes with canola oil; place on a greased grill rack. Cook, covered, over medium heat or broil 4 in. from heat 6-8 minutes or until lightly browned, turning once. Remove from heat; cool slightly. Cut into ¾-in. cubes.

3. Meanwhile, in a large bowl, whisk lime juice, olive oil, sesame seeds, salt and, if desired, cilantro and mint. Add mangoes, cucumbers and avocados; toss to coat. Refrigerate until serving.

¾ cup: 249 cal., 15g fat (2g sat. fat), 0 chol., 152mg sod., 31g carb. (24g sugars, 6g fiber), 3g pro. **Diabetic exchanges:** 3 fat, 2 starch.

Eggnog Fruit Fluff

EGGNOG FRUIT FLUFF

I regularly fit blends of apples, blueberries and other fruit into my December menus. The eggnog in this dressing suits the sweet salad for Christmas.
—Tami Harrington, Scottsdale, AZ

PREP: 10 min. + chilling
MAKES: 12 servings

- 1 cup eggnog, chilled
- 1 envelope whipped topping mix
- ¼ tsp. ground nutmeg
- 1 can (20 oz.) pineapple tidbits, drained
- 1 can (15¼ oz.) sliced peaches, drained
- 2 medium tart apples, chopped
- 1 cup fresh blueberries
- ¾ cup halved maraschino cherries
- ¾ cup chopped walnuts

Beat eggnog, whipped topping mix and nutmeg on high speed until soft peaks form. Combine remaining ingredients; fold into eggnog mixture. Refrigerate, covered, until chilled. Gently stir before serving.

Note: This recipe was tested with commercially prepared eggnog.

¾ cup: 164 cal., 6g fat (2g sat. fat), 12mg chol., 24mg sod., 27g carb. (22g sugars, 2g fiber), 2g pro.

Quick Crunchy
Apple Salad

PLANTAIN & PUMPKIN MASH

Beautiful and simple to prepare, this plantain mash is perfectly flavored with roasted garlic and caramelized shallots.
—Donna Noel, Gray, ME

PREP: 30 min. • **BAKE:** 30 min.
MAKES: 6 servings

- 1 medium pie pumpkin, peeled and cut into 1½-in. cubes
- 1 ripe plantain, peeled and cut into 1½-in. cubes
- 4 garlic cloves, unpeeled
- 12 shallots, sliced
- 1 Tbsp. olive oil
- 2 Tbsp. white wine or chicken broth
- 1 tsp. brown sugar
- ⅛ tsp. plus ½ tsp. salt, divided
- ⅛ tsp. plus ¼ tsp. pepper, divided
- ¼ tsp. chili powder
- ⅓ cup chicken broth
- 3 Tbsp. butter

1. Place the pumpkin, plantain and garlic in a greased 15x10x1-in. baking pan. Bake at 375° for 30-35 minutes or until tender.
2. Meanwhile, in a large skillet over medium heat, cook shallots in oil until tender. Add the wine, brown sugar, ⅛ tsp. salt, ⅛ tsp. pepper and chili powder; cook and stir for 6-8 minutes or until shallots are golden brown.
3. Squeeze softened garlic into a large saucepan; add broth and bring to a boil. Remove from the heat; add pumpkin and plantain. Mash with butter and remaining salt and pepper. Top with the shallots.
⅔ cup: 216 cal., 8g fat (4g sat. fat), 15mg chol., 355mg sod., 35g carb. (7g sugars, 2g fiber), 4g pro. **Diabetic exchanges:** 2 vegetable, 1½ fat, 1 starch.

QUICK CRUNCHY APPLE SALAD

This salad pairs crunchy toppings with smooth vanilla yogurt, creating a mixture you'll love!
—Kathy Armstrong, Post Falls, ID

TAKES: 15 min. • **MAKES:** 5 servings

- 6 Tbsp. vanilla yogurt
- 6 Tbsp. reduced-fat whipped topping
- ¼ tsp. plus ⅛ tsp. ground cinnamon, divided
- 2 medium red apples, chopped
- 1 large Granny Smith apple, chopped
- ¼ cup dried cranberries
- 2 Tbsp. chopped walnuts

In a large bowl, combine the yogurt, whipped topping and ¼ tsp. cinnamon. Add apples and cranberries; toss to coat. Refrigerate until serving. Sprinkle with walnuts and remaining cinnamon before serving.

¾ cup: 116 cal., 3g fat (1g sat. fat), 1mg chol., 13mg sod., 23g carb. (17g sugars, 3g fiber), 2g pro. **Diabetic exchanges:** 1 fruit, ½ starch, ½ fat.

Test Kitchen Tip

Cinnamon comes in two basic types: Ceylon and cassia. Ceylon cinnamon's delicate, complex flavor is ideal for ice creams and simple sauces. The spicy, bolder cassia cinnamon (often labeled simply as cinnamon) is preferred for baking.

Plantain &
Pumpkin Mash

PEACH MANGO CAPRESE SALAD

Summer in the Midwest offers a bounty of fresh produce, so I wanted to come up with a new recipe for the harvested goods. This bright, flavorful salad is the refreshing end result.
—Richard Robinson, Park Forest, IL

TAKES: 25 min. • **MAKES:** about 6 servings

- 2　medium peaches, cut into ½-in. pieces
- 2　cups grape tomatoes, halved
- 1　carton (8 oz.) fresh mozzarella cheese pearls, drained
- 1　cup chopped peeled mango
- 2　Tbsp. minced fresh cilantro
- 2　Tbsp. minced fresh basil

DRESSING
- 3　Tbsp. balsamic vinegar
- 3　fresh basil leaves
- 2　tsp. honey
- ¼　tsp. salt
- ⅛　tsp. pepper
- ¼　cup olive oil

Place the first 6 ingredients in a large bowl. For the dressing, place vinegar, basil, honey, salt and pepper in a blender. While processing, gradually add oil in a steady stream. Pour over peach mixture; gently toss to coat. Refrigerate until serving. Garnish with additional basil.

¾ cup: 248 cal., 17g fat (7g sat. fat), 30mg chol., 156mg sod., 16g carb. (14g sugars, 2g fiber), 8g pro.

Peach Mango
Caprese Salad

Pineapple & Coconut
Carrot Salad

PINEAPPLE & COCONUT CARROT SALAD

I enjoyed a salad like this at a tropical-inspired restaurant. I tried to get the staff to give me the recipe but had no luck. So I went home and created my own! I will sometimes drain a can of mandarin orange slices and toss those in as well.
—Shirley Turpin, Williams, MN

TAKES: 20 min.
MAKES: 12 servings

- 1½ cups sour cream
- ⅓ cup honey
- 2 tsp. grated lime zest
- 3 Tbsp. lime juice
- 2 tsp. grated fresh gingerroot
- 1 tsp. grated orange zest
- 1½ lbs. carrots, shredded (about 5 cups)
- 1 can (20 oz.) unsweetened crushed pineapple, drained
- 1½ cups flaked coconut
- 1½ cups golden raisins

In a large bowl, mix the first 6 ingredients. Stir in the remaining ingredients. Refrigerate, covered, until serving.
⅔ cup: 254 cal., 10g fat (7g sat. fat), 7mg chol., 83mg sod., 42g carb. (34g sugars, 3g fiber), 3g pro.

Frozen
Christmas Salad

MINTED FRUIT SALAD

Filled with the season's best, freshest fruit, this salad shouts summer. The hint of mint adds a refreshing note to the colorful melon compote.
—Edie DeSpain, Logan, UT

PREP: 20 min. + cooling
MAKES: 6 servings

- 1 cup unsweetened apple juice
- 2 Tbsp. honey
- 4 tsp. finely chopped crystallized ginger
- 4 tsp. lemon juice
- 4 cups cantaloupe balls
- 1 cup sliced fresh strawberries
- 1 cup fresh blueberries
- 2 tsp. chopped fresh mint leaves

1. In a small saucepan, combine the apple juice, honey, ginger and lemon juice. Bring to a boil over medium-high heat. Cook and stir for 2 minutes or until mixture is reduced to ¾ cup. Remove from the heat. Cool.
2. In a serving bowl, combine the cantaloupe, strawberries, blueberries and mint. Drizzle with cooled apple juice mixture; gently toss to coat.
1 cup: 113 cal., 1g fat (0 sat. fat), 0 chol., 14mg sod., 28g carb. (23g sugars, 2g fiber), 1g pro. **Diabetic exchanges:** 1 fruit, ½ starch.

FROZEN CHRISTMAS SALAD

My mom's use of red and green cherries to decorate dishes at Christmastime inspired me to create this holiday gelatin mold. It's cool, creamy and fun to serve guests.
—Pat Habiger, Spearville, KS

PREP: 25 min. + freezing
MAKES: 10 servings

- 1 can (20 oz.) crushed pineapple, drained
- 2 cups miniature marshmallows
- 1 pkg. (8 oz.) cream cheese, softened
- ½ cup mayonnaise
- 12 red maraschino cherries, chopped and patted dry
- 12 green maraschino cherries, chopped and patted dry
- ½ cup chopped walnuts
- 1 cup heavy whipping cream

1. In a small bowl, combine pineapple and marshmallows. Set aside until marshmallows are softened, about 15 minutes.
2. Meanwhile, in a small bowl, beat cream cheese and mayonnaise until smooth. Stir into marshmallow mixture. Fold in cherries and walnuts.
3. In a small bowl, beat whipping cream until soft peaks form. Fold into the marshmallow mixture. Spoon into a 6-cup mold; freeze overnight. Let stand at room temperature for 15-20 minutes; unmold onto a serving plate.
1 slice: 371 cal., 28g fat (12g sat. fat), 51mg chol., 142mg sod., 29g carb. (24g sugars, 1g fiber), 3g pro.

Minted
Fruit Salad

CRANBERRY AMBROSIA SALAD

*My paternal grandmother used to make this
for Christmas dinner. I'm not sure how many
batches she made since there were nearly
50 aunts, uncles and cousins in our family.
I still make the recipe in memory of her,
and it's still as good as I remember.*
—Janet Hurley, Shell Rock, IA

PREP: 20 min. + chilling
MAKES: 9 servings

- 1 lb. fresh or frozen cranberries
- 1 can (20 oz.) crushed pineapple, drained
- 1 cup sugar
- 2 cups miniature marshmallows
- 1 cup heavy whipping cream, whipped
- ½ cup chopped pecans

1. In a food processor, cover and
process cranberries until coarsely
chopped. Transfer to a large bowl;
stir in pineapple and sugar. Cover
and refrigerate overnight.

2. Just before serving, fold in the
marshmallows, whipped cream and
pecans. If desired, top with additional
chopped pecans.

¾ cup: 331 cal., 15g fat (7g sat. fat),
36mg chol., 17mg sod., 52g carb.
(43g sugars, 3g fiber), 2g pro.

Test Kitchen Tip

Feel free to jazz up this recipe with
the ingredients you like best. Stir in
a handful of sliced grapes or some
shredded coconut. Drain a can of
mandarin oranges and add them
for even more flair.

Cranberry
Ambrosia Salad

TANGY CRANBERRY SAUCE

I serve this fruity sauce with baked or grilled poultry and pork. The molasses, cumin and allspice give the sauce a wonderful earthy flavor.
—Marlene Muckenhirn, Delano, MN

PREP: 10 min. • **COOK:** 30 min.
MAKES: 3 cups

- 1 can (14½ oz.) Italian stewed tomatoes
- ½ cup chopped onion
- 2 Tbsp. brown sugar
- 1 Tbsp. cider vinegar
- 1 Tbsp. molasses
- 2 garlic cloves, minced
- ½ tsp. ground cumin
- ½ tsp. paprika
- ¼ tsp. ground allspice
- 1 can (14 oz.) whole-berry cranberry sauce

Place the first 9 ingredients in a blender; cover and process until almost smooth. Transfer to a saucepan; add cranberry sauce. Bring to a boil; reduce heat. Simmer, uncovered, for 30 minutes or until thickened, stirring occasionally. Serve warm or cold. Refrigerate leftovers.

¼ cup: 75 cal., 0 fat (0 sat. fat), 0 chol., 92mg sod.,19g carb., (13g sugars, 1g fiber), 0 pro. **Diabetic exchanges:** 1 starch.

Avocado Fruit Salad with Tangerine Vinaigrette

AVOCADO FRUIT SALAD WITH TANGERINE VINAIGRETTE

On long summer days when we just want to relax, I make a cool salad with avocado, berries and mint. The tangerine dressing is refreshingly different.
—Carole Resnick, Cleveland, OH

TAKES: 25 min. • **MAKES:** 8 servings

- 3 medium ripe avocados, peeled and thinly sliced
- 3 medium mangoes, peeled and thinly sliced
- 1 cup fresh raspberries
- 1 cup fresh blackberries
- ¼ cup minced fresh mint
- ¼ cup sliced almonds, toasted

DRESSING
- ½ cup olive oil
- 1 tsp. grated tangerine or orange zest
- ¼ cup tangerine or orange juice
- 2 Tbsp. balsamic vinegar
- ½ tsp. salt
- ¼ tsp. freshly ground pepper

Arrange avocados and fruit on a serving plate; sprinkle with mint and almonds. In a small bowl, whisk the dressing ingredients until blended; drizzle over salad.

Note: To toast nuts, bake in a shallow pan in a 350° oven for 5-10 minutes or cook in a skillet over low heat until lightly browned, stirring occasionally.

1 cup salad with 4 tsp. dressing: 321 cal., 23g fat (3g sat. fat), 0 chol., 154mg sod., 29g carb. (20g sugars, 8g fiber), 3g pro.

Refreshing Tropical
Fruit Salad

REFRESHING TROPICAL FRUIT SALAD

Kids and adults will love this salad. It's a visually appealing way to serve up fruit.
—Sharon Ricci, Spooner, WI

TAKES: 30 min.
MAKES: 12 servings

- 2 large bananas, sliced
- 2 medium pears, cubed
- ⅓ cup fresh orange juice
- ⅓ cup unsweetened pineapple juice
- 3 cups cubed fresh pineapple
- 1½ cups sliced fresh strawberries
- 1 cup seedless red grapes, halved
- 4 medium kiwifruit, peeled and sliced
- 2 medium mangoes, peeled and cubed
- 2 star fruit, sliced

In a large bowl, combine the bananas, pears and juices. Add the pineapple, strawberries, grapes, kiwi and mangoes; stir gently to combine. Arrange star fruit over the top.

1 cup: 120 cal., 1g fat (0 sat. fat), 0 chol., 3mg sod., 31g carb. (22g sugars, 4g fiber), 1g pro. **Diabetic exchanges:** 2 fruit.

Test Kitchen Tip

If you're not going to serve this salad right away, consider adding the bananas later or tossing them in a little lemon juice first to prolong any browning.

Grapes with Lemon-Honey Yogurt

GRAPES WITH LEMON-HONEY YOGURT

We like to sweeten up Greek yogurt with honey, cinnamon and vanilla. The tasty dressing is a delightful counterpoint to plump grapes and crunchy nuts.
—Julie Sterchi, Campbellsville, KY

TAKES: 10 min. • **MAKES:** 8 servings

- 1 cup fat-free plain Greek yogurt
- 2 Tbsp. honey
- 1 tsp. vanilla extract
- ½ tsp. grated lemon zest
- ⅛ tsp. ground cinnamon
- 3 cups seedless red grapes
- 3 cups green grapes
- 3 Tbsp. sliced almonds, toasted

In a small bowl, combine the first 5 ingredients. Divide grapes among 8 serving bowls. Top with yogurt mixture; sprinkle with almonds.

Note: To toast nuts, bake in a shallow pan in a 350° oven for 5-10 minutes or cook in a skillet over low heat until lightly browned, stirring occasionally.

¾ cup grapes with 2 Tbsp. yogurt mixture and about 1 tsp. almonds: 138 cal., 2g fat (0 sat. fat), 0 chol., 20mg sod., 28g carb. (26g sugars, 2g fiber), 6g pro. **Diabetic exchanges:** 1½ fruit, ½ starch.

GORGONZOLA BAKED APPLES WITH BALSAMIC SYRUP

Gorgonzola cheese and a balsamic vinegar reduction sauce are pleasing partners to sweet apples. Serve this fruity favorite alongside any entree.
—Crystal Holsinger, Waddell, AZ

PREP: 20 min. • **BAKE:** 40 min.
MAKES: 6 servings

- ⅓ cup chopped hazelnuts
- ¼ cup butter, chopped
- 3 Tbsp. crumbled Gorgonzola cheese
- 1 Tbsp. brown sugar
- ¼ tsp. ground cinnamon
- ⅛ tsp. salt
- ⅛ tsp. onion powder
- 6 medium tart apples, cored
- 1 cup balsamic vinegar

1. In a small bowl, combine the first 7 ingredients. Stuff apples with mixture and place in a greased 11x7-in. baking dish. Bake, uncovered, at 325° for 40-45 minutes or until the apples are tender.
2. Meanwhile, in a small saucepan, bring vinegar to a boil; cook until liquid is reduced to ⅓ cup. Drizzle over apples.
1 stuffed apple with 2 tsp. balsamic syrup: 226 cal., 13g fat (6g sat. fat), 23mg chol., 163mg sod., 29g carb. (23g sugars, 4g fiber), 2g pro.

CORN & BERRY COUSCOUS

My husband wowed me with this confetti couscous the first time he cooked for me while we were dating. It's still one of my favorite dishes.
—Laurel Porterfield, Bristow, VA

TAKES: 20 min. • **MAKES:** 6 servings

- 2¼ cups chicken broth
- 1 Tbsp. butter
- ½ tsp. salt
- 1½ cups frozen corn
- ¾ cup dried cranberries
- ¼ to ½ tsp. ground cinnamon
- 1 pkg. (10 oz.) couscous

1. In a large saucepan, bring the broth, butter and salt to a boil. Stir in the corn, cranberries and cinnamon. Cover and return to a boil; cook for 2 minutes. Stir in couscous.
2. Remove from the heat; cover and let stand for 5 minutes or until broth is absorbed. Fluff with a fork.
1 cup: 270 cal., 3g fat (1g sat. fat), 5mg chol., 570mg sod., 56g carb. (12g sugars, 4g fiber), 8g pro.

Health Tip

Dried cranberries are often substituted for raisins in recipes. Commercially dried cranberries contain added sugar, making them a sweet snack by the handful or a perfect addition to salads, breads, stuffings or trail mixes.

FRUIT WITH POPPY SEED DRESSING

Cool, colorful and easy to prepare, this refreshing, good-for-you fruit salad is a springtime favorite.
—Peggy Mills, Texarkana, AR

PREP: 20 min. + standing
MAKES: 12 servings

- 3 Tbsp. honey
- 1 Tbsp. white vinegar
- 1 tsp. ground mustard
- ¼ tsp. salt
- ¼ tsp. onion powder
- ⅓ cup canola oil
- 1 tsp. poppy seeds
- 1 fresh pineapple, cut into 1½-in. cubes
- 3 medium kiwifruit, halved and sliced
- 2 cups fresh strawberries, halved

1. In a small bowl, whisk the first 5 ingredients. Gradually whisk in oil until blended. Stir in poppy seeds; let stand 1 hour.
2. In a large bowl, combine fruits. Drizzle with the dressing; toss gently to coat.
1 cup: 129 cal., 7g fat (0 sat. fat), 0 chol., 51mg sod., 19g carb. (14g sugars, 2g fiber), 1g pro. **Diabetic exchanges:** 1½ fat, 1 fruit.

Fruit with Poppy Seed Dressing

Cranberry
Roasted Squash

WARM CABBAGE, FENNEL & PEAR SALAD

This crunchy salad makes an elegant first course or side, but it's hearty enough to be an entree when paired with a crusty artisan bread. We love it served warm.
—Grace Voltolina, Westport, CT

TAKES: 25 min. • **MAKES:** 4 servings

- 2 **firm medium pears**
- ¼ **cup brandy or Cognac, optional**
- 3 **Tbsp. olive oil**
- 1 **large fennel bulb, halved, cored and thinly sliced**
- 4 **cups shredded or thinly sliced cabbage**
- ¼ **cup water**
- 3 **Tbsp. lemon juice**
- 2 **tsp. honey or agave nectar**
- 1 **tsp. kosher salt**
- ½ **tsp. pepper**
- ¾ **cup crumbled or sliced Gorgonzola cheese**
- ½ **cup chopped walnuts, toasted**

1. Peel and core pears; cut into ½-in. slices. If desired, toss with brandy. Set pears aside.
2. In a large skillet, heat the oil over medium-high heat. Add fennel; saute until crisp-tender, 2-3 minutes. Add cabbage; toss with fennel. Cook until both are tender, 2-3 minutes longer. Add pears, water, lemon juice, honey, salt and pepper to skillet, gently combining ingredients. Cook until the liquid is evaporated, 6-8 minutes.
3. Transfer to a serving bowl. Top with Gorgonzola cheese and toasted walnuts. Serve warm or at room temperature.
Note: To toast nuts, bake in a shallow pan in a 350° oven for 5-10 minutes or cook in a skillet over low heat until lightly browned, stirring occasionally.
1 cup: 391 cal., 26g fat (7g sat. fat), 19mg chol., 810mg sod., 28g carb. (14g sugars, 8g fiber), 9g pro.

🍎 CRANBERRY ROASTED SQUASH

I created this recipe one day when I wanted a warm, fragrant side dish. The aroma of the cranberries and squash cooking in the oven is just as heavenly as the flavor itself.
—Jamillah Almutawakil, Superior, CO

PREP: 15 min. • **BAKE:** 45 min.
MAKES: 12 servings

- 1 **medium butternut squash (5 to 6 lbs.), peeled and cut into 1-in. cubes**
- 1 **medium acorn squash (about 1½ lbs.), peeled and cut into 1-in. cubes**
- ⅔ **cup chopped fresh or frozen cranberries**
- ¼ **cup sugar**
- 2 **Tbsp. olive oil**
- 1 **Tbsp. butter, melted**
- 1 **Tbsp. molasses**
- 2 **garlic cloves, minced**
- 1½ **tsp. rubbed sage**
- 1 **tsp. salt**
- ½ **tsp. pepper**

Preheat oven to 400°. In a large bowl, combine all ingredients. Transfer to two 15x10x1-in. baking pans. Roast until tender, stirring and rotating pans halfway through cooking, 45-55 minutes.
¾ cup: 161 cal., 3g fat (1g sat. fat), 3mg chol., 214mg sod., 35g carb. (12g sugars, 8g fiber), 2g pro. **Diabetic exchanges:** 2 starch, ½ fat.

Warm Cabbage, Fennel
& Pear Salad

MIXED FRUIT WITH LEMON-BASIL DRESSING

A slightly savory dressing really compliments the sweet fruit in this recipe. I also use the dressing on salad greens.
—Dixie Terry, Goreville, IL

TAKES: 15 min. • **MAKES:** 8 servings

2	Tbsp. lemon juice
½	tsp. sugar
¼	tsp. salt
¼	tsp. ground mustard
⅛	tsp. onion powder
	Dash pepper
6	Tbsp. olive oil
4½	tsp. minced fresh basil
1	cup cubed fresh pineapple
1	cup sliced fresh strawberries
1	cup sliced peeled kiwifruit
1	cup seedless watermelon balls
1	cup fresh blueberries
1	cup fresh raspberries

1. Place the lemon juice, sugar, salt, mustard, onion powder and pepper in a blender; cover and pulse until blended. While processing, gradually add oil in a steady stream. Stir in basil.
2. In a large bowl, combine the fruit. Drizzle with dressing and toss to coat. Refrigerate until serving.
¾ cup: 145 cal., 11g fat (1g sat. fat), 0 chol., 76mg sod., 14g carb. (9g sugars, 3g fiber), 1g pro. **Diabetic exchanges:** 2 fat, 1 fruit.

Cranberry-Walnut
Brussels Sprouts

Mixed Fruit with
Lemon-Basil Dressing

5i

CRANBERRY-WALNUT BRUSSELS SPROUTS

Brussels sprouts are one food that picky eaters often resist, but a burst of cranberry flavor may change their minds. You can also add garlic and dried fruits.
—Jennifer Armellino, Lake Oswego, OR

TAKES: 20 min. • **MAKES:** 4 servings

- ¼ cup olive oil
- 1 lb. fresh Brussels sprouts, trimmed and halved lengthwise
- ½ cup dried cranberries
- 2 Tbsp. water
- ⅓ cup chopped walnuts
- 2 Tbsp. balsamic vinegar

1. In a large skillet, heat oil over medium heat. Place Brussels sprouts in pan, cut side down; cook 4-5 minutes or until bottoms are browned.

2. Add cranberries and water; cook, covered, until Brussels sprouts are crisp-tender, 1-2 minutes. Stir in walnuts; cook and stir until water is evaporated. Stir in vinegar.

¾ cup: 281 cal., 20g fat (3g sat. fat), 0 chol., 26mg sod., 25g carb. (14g sugars, 5g fiber), 5g pro.

Coconut Tropical
Fruit Salad

COCONUT TROPICAL FRUIT SALAD

Add a serving of fruit to breakfast with this delicious medley. Toasted coconut, mango and more bring the flavor of the tropics to any menu.
—Katie Covington, Blacksburg, SC

TAKES: 25 min. • **MAKES:** 8 servings

- 1 medium mango, peeled and cubed
- 1 medium green apple, cubed
- 1 medium red apple, cubed
- 1 medium pear, cubed
- 1 medium navel orange, peeled and chopped
- 2 medium kiwifruit, peeled and chopped
- 10 seedless red grapes, halved
- 2 Tbsp. orange juice
- 1 firm medium banana, sliced
- ¼ cup sweetened shredded coconut, toasted

In a large bowl, combine the first 7 ingredients. Drizzle with orange juice; toss gently to coat. Refrigerate until serving. Just before serving, fold in banana and sprinkle with coconut.
¾ cup: 101 cal., 1g fat (1g sat. fat), 0 chol., 10mg sod., 24g carb. (17g sugars, 3g fiber), 1g pro. **Diabetic exchanges:** 1½ fruit.

Health Tip
Looking for a flavorful fruit salad that isn't loaded with added sugar? Look no further. You can also use unsweetened coconut for a no-sugar-added version.

German Apple Salad

GERMAN APPLE SALAD

In culinary school, I had to make a salad with Granny Smith apples. I remembered my mother's German potato salad and substituted apples for the potatoes.
—Sharyn LaPointe Hill, Las Cruces, NM

PREP: 10 min. • **COOK:** 25 min.
MAKES: 6 servings

- 6 bacon strips, cut crosswise into ½-in. slices
- ½ cup chopped onion
- 2 Tbsp. all-purpose flour
- 1 tsp. salt
- ½ tsp. pepper
- 1 cup water
- ½ cup cider vinegar
- ¼ cup sugar
- 5½ cups Granny Smith apples (about 4 large), cut into ½-in. slices

1. In a large skillet, cook bacon over medium heat until crisp; drain on paper towels. Discard all but 2 Tbsp. drippings. Add onion; cook until tender, 2-3 minutes. Stir in flour, salt and pepper until blended. Add water and vinegar; cook and stir until slightly thickened, about 1 minute. Stir in sugar until dissolved.
2. Return bacon to pan; gently add apple slices. Cook, stirring constantly, until apples are wilted and slightly caramelized, 10-12 minutes. Remove from heat; serve warm.
¾ cup: 232 cal., 11g fat (4g sat. fat), 18mg chol., 582mg sod., 29g carb. (22g sugars, 3g fiber), 4g pro.

MINTY PINEAPPLE FRUIT SALAD

Fresh mint adds bright flavor to this quick and low-fat pineapple salad. Give it a berry twist by using blueberries and raspberries in place of the grapes, but don't forget to use the secret dressing ingredient—lemonade!
—Janie Colle, Hutchinson, KS

TAKES: 15 min. • **MAKES:** 8 servings

- 4 cups cubed fresh pineapple
- 2 cups sliced fresh strawberries
- 1 cup green grapes
- 3 Tbsp. thawed lemonade concentrate
- 2 Tbsp. honey
- 1 Tbsp. minced fresh mint

Place fruit in a large bowl. In another bowl, mix remaining ingredients; stir gently into fruit. Refrigerate, covered, until serving.

¾ cup: 99 cal., 0 fat (0 sat. fat), 0 chol., 4mg sod., 26g carb. (21g sugars, 2g fiber), 1g pro. **Diabetic exchanges:** 1½ fruit, ½ starch.

EASY HOMEMADE CHUNKY APPLESAUCE

Here's a comforting, home-style treat that never loses its appeal. Dish up big bowlfuls and wait for the smiles!
—Marilee Cardinal, Burlington, NJ

TAKES: 30 min. • **MAKES:** 5 cups

- 7 medium McIntosh, Empire or other apples (about 3 lbs.)
- ½ cup sugar
- ½ cup water
- 1 Tbsp. lemon juice
- ¼ tsp. almond or vanilla extract

1. Peel, core and cut each apple into 8 wedges. Cut each wedge crosswise in half; place in a large saucepan. Add remaining ingredients.
2. Bring to a boil. Reduce heat; simmer, covered, until desired consistency is reached, 15-20 minutes, stirring occasionally.
¾ cup: 139 cal., 0 fat (0 sat. fat), 0 chol., 0 sod., 36g carb. (33g sugars, 2g fiber), 0 pro.

Minty Pineapple Fruit Salad

**California
Avocado Salad**

CALIFORNIA AVOCADO SALAD

*Spread a little sunshine with this easy salad.
Just four ingredients drizzled with Orange
Yogurt Dressing and you have a light lunch
or a pretty side to serve with dinner.*
—James Schend, Pleasant Prairie, WI

TAKES: 20 min. • **MAKES:** 8 servings

- 3 medium oranges,
  peeled and sectioned
- 2 medium ripe avocados,
  peeled and sliced
- ¼ cup toasted pine nuts
- 2 tsp. minced fresh rosemary
  Orange Yogurt Dressing (see below)

Arrange oranges and avocados on
a platter; sprinkle with pine nuts and
rosemary. Drizzle dressing over salad.
Serve immediately.
½ cup: 135 cal., 11g fat (1g sat. fat), 3mg
chol., 129mg sod., 10g carb. (5g sugars,
3g fiber), 2g pro. **Diabetic exchanges:**
2 fat, ½ fruit.

ORANGE YOGURT DRESSING

*Honey brings a hint of sweetness to this
creamy citrus salad dressing.*
—Beverly Florence, Midwest City, OK

TAKES: 10 min. + chilling
MAKES: ⅔ cup

- ¼ cup reduced-fat mayonnaise
- ¼ cup fat-free plain yogurt
- 2 tablespoons orange juice
- 2 teaspoons honey
- 1 teaspoon grated orange zest
- ¼ teaspoon salt
  Dash white pepper

In a small bowl, whisk together all
ingredients; cover and refrigerate
for at least 1 hour.
2 Tbsp.: 57 cal., 4g fat (1g sat. fat), 4mg
chol., 220mg sod., 5g carb. (0 sugars,
0 fiber), 1g pro. **Diabetic exchanges:**
1 fat.

Fresh Apple &
Pear Salad

HOT SPICED FRUIT

*My baked pears, apples and cranberries
have a touch of spice and sweetness—
just like a pie without the crust. Serve the
fruit over waffles or yogurt, or alongside
pork chops.*
—Lin Koppen, Orchard Park, NY

PREP: 25 min. • **BAKE:** 30 min. + cooling
MAKES: 12 servings

- ¼ cup packed brown sugar
- 2 Tbsp. cornstarch
- ¼ tsp. ground cinnamon
- ¼ tsp. ground ginger
- ⅛ tsp. ground cloves
- 1 cup cranberry or white grape juice
- 3 medium pears, peeled and sliced
- 3 medium apples, peeled and sliced
- 1 cup fresh or frozen cranberries, thawed and chopped
- 1 can (11 oz.) mandarin oranges, drained

1. Preheat oven to 375°. In a small
bowl, mix the first 5 ingredients;
gradually whisk in cranberry juice.
2. In a greased 13x9-in. baking dish,
combine remaining ingredients. Pour
cranberry juice mixture over top.
3. Bake, uncovered, 30-35 minutes
or until pears and apples are tender,
stirring once. Let cool 10 minutes
before serving. Serve warm or cold.
½ cup: 88 cal., 0 fat (0 sat. fat), 0 chol.,
5mg sod., 23g carb. (17g sugars, 3g
fiber), 1g pro.

FRESH APPLE & PEAR SALAD

*This fun combination of ingredients comes
together beautifully in one flavor-packed
dish. Crunchy apples and ripe, juicy pears
are fantastic tossed with crisp, cool
cucumbers and a spicy dressing.*
—Jean Ecos, Hartland, WI

TAKES: 20 min. • **MAKES:** 8 servings

- 4 medium apples, thinly sliced
- 2 medium pears, thinly sliced
- 1 medium cucumber, seeded and chopped
- 1 medium red onion, halved and thinly sliced
- ¼ cup apple cider or juice
- 1 Tbsp. snipped fresh dill or minced fresh tarragon
- 1 Tbsp. olive oil
- 1 Tbsp. spicy brown mustard
- 2 tsp. brown sugar
- ½ tsp. salt
- ¼ tsp. pepper

In a large bowl, combine apples, pears,
cucumber and onion. In a small bowl,
whisk remaining ingredients until
blended. Pour over apple mixture and
toss to coat. Refrigerate until serving.
1 cup: 96 cal., 2g fat (0 sat. fat), 0 chol.,
175mg sod., 20g carb. (14g sugars,
4g fiber), 1g pro. **Diabetic exchanges:**
1 fruit, ½ fat.

Hot Spiced Fruit

NECTARINE FRUIT SALAD WITH LIME SPICE DRESSING

The lime spice dressing gives this fruit salad a little something extra to make it special. It's a crowd pleaser as a side dish or as a light and healthy way to end an outdoor meal with friends. Mix and match the fruit with what's in season.
—Paula Hudson, Cary, NC

PREP: 20 min. + chilling
MAKES: 8 servings

1½ tsp. grated lime zest
2 Tbsp. lime juice
2 Tbsp. honey
½ tsp. ground ginger
¼ tsp. cayenne pepper
6 medium nectarines,
  cut into 1-in. pieces (about 4 cups)
2 cups seedless red grapes
¼ cup chopped fresh mint
½ cup mascarpone cheese
2 Tbsp. confectioners' sugar
2 Tbsp. 2% milk
¼ tsp. vanilla extract
⅓ cup chopped pistachios
  Fresh mint leaves

In a bowl, whisk first 5 ingredients. Place nectarines, grapes and mint in a large bowl. Drizzle with the honey mixture; stir gently. Refrigerate, covered, 1-2 hours. For topping, mix mascarpone, confectioners' sugar, milk and vanilla. Serve the fruit salad with the topping, pistachios and fresh mint leaves.
1 serving: 254 cal., 16g fat (7g sat. fat), 35mg chol., 44mg sod., 27g carb. (22g sugars, 3g fiber), 4g pro.

Nectarine Fruit Salad
with Lime Spice Dressing

Minty
Watermelon Salad

MINTY WATERMELON SALAD

My 4-year-old twin grandchildren love to cook in the kitchen with me. Last summer, the three of us were experimenting with watermelon and cheese, and that's where this recipe began. It's amazing for picnics, at neighborhood gatherings or as a healthy snack on a hot summer day.
—Gwendolyn Vetter, Rogers, MN

PREP: 20 min. + chilling
MAKES: 8 servings

- 6 cups cubed watermelon
- ½ cup thinly sliced fennel bulb
- ⅓ cup crumbled feta cheese
- 2 Tbsp. minced fresh mint
- 2 Tbsp. thinly sliced pickled onions
- ½ tsp. pepper

In a large bowl, combine all ingredients. Refrigerate, covered, at least 1 hour.
¾ cup: 45 cal., 1g fat (1g sat. fat), 2mg chol., 65mg sod., 11g carb. (10g sugars, 1g fiber), 1g pro. **Diabetic exchanges:** ½ fruit.

Test Kitchen Tip
Feel free to replace the pickled onions with regular onions or simply leave them out altogether.

Dutch-Oven
Bread, Page 274

Page 292

Page 288

Breads, Biscuits & More

Whether you're a weekend baker or a seasoned pro, you understand how golden buttery gems dress up any meal. Turn here for dozens of freshly baked delights that can share the spotlight with the any entree.

Page 289

Page 282

DUTCH OVEN BREAD

Crackling homemade bread makes an average day extraordinary. Try this lovely crusty bread recipe as is, or stir in a few favorites such as cheese, garlic, herbs or even dried fruits.
—Catherine Ward, Mequon, WI

PREP: 15 min. + rising
BAKE: 45 min. + cooling
MAKES: 1 loaf (16 pieces)

    3   to 3½ cups (125 grams per cup)
        all-purpose flour
    1   tsp. active dry yeast
    1   tsp. salt
    1½ cups water (70° to 75°)

1. In a large bowl, whisk 3 cups flour, yeast and salt. Stir in water and enough remaining flour to form a moist, shaggy dough. Do not knead. Cover and let rise in a cool place until doubled, 7-8 hours.
2. Preheat oven to 450°; place a Dutch oven with lid onto center rack and heat for at least 30 minutes. Once Dutch oven is heated, turn dough onto a generously floured surface. Using a metal scraper or spatula, quickly shape into a round loaf. Gently place dough on top of a piece of parchment.
3. Using a sharp knife, make a slash (¼ in. deep) across top of loaf. Using the parchment, immediately lower bread into heated Dutch oven. Cover; bake for 30 minutes. Uncover and bake until the bread is deep golden brown and sounds hollow when tapped, 15-20 minutes longer, partially covering if browning too much. Remove loaf from pan and cool completely on wire rack.

1 piece: 86 cal., 0 fat (0 sat. fat), 0 chol., 148mg sod., 18g carb. (0 sugars, 1g fiber), 3g pro.

Test Kitchen Tip

This is a soft, gentle dough that should be baked immediately after shaping. Preheating the Dutch oven prior to shaping and working quickly are keys to success.

SIMPLE BISCUITS

It's super easy to whip up a batch of these buttery biscuits to serve with breakfast or dinner. The dough is very easy to work with, so there's no need to roll with a rolling pin; just pat to the right thickness.
—Taste of Home *Test Kitchen*

TAKES: 25 min. • **MAKES:** 15 biscuits

    2   cups all-purpose flour
    3   tsp. baking powder
    1   tsp. salt
    ⅓   cup cold butter, cubed
    ⅔   cup 2% milk

1. Preheat oven to 450°. In a large bowl, whisk flour, baking powder and salt. Cut in the butter until mixture resembles coarse crumbs. Add the milk; stir just until moistened.
2. Turn onto a lightly floured surface; knead gently 8-10 times. Pat the dough to ½-in. thickness. Cut with a 2½-in. biscuit cutter.
3. Place 1 in. apart on an ungreased baking sheet. Bake until golden brown, 10-15 minutes. Serve warm.

1 biscuit: 153 cal., 7g fat (4g sat. fat), 18mg chol., 437mg sod., 20g carb. (1g sugars, 1g fiber), 3g pro.

Dutch Oven Bread

Sausage Bread Dressing

SAUSAGE BREAD DRESSING

My husband and father go crazy for this dressing. To save time, chop the veggies and prepare the stuffing mix ahead of time.
—Bette Votral, Bethlehem, PA

PREP: 30 min. • **BAKE:** 40 min.
MAKES: about 12 cups

- 4 cups seasoned stuffing cubes
- 1 cup cornbread stuffing mix (about 3 oz.)
- ½ lb. bulk Italian sausage
- 1 large onion, chopped
- 3 Tbsp. butter
- 1 large tart apple, peeled and chopped
- 1⅓ cups sliced fresh shiitake mushrooms (about 4 oz.)
- 1¼ cups sliced fresh mushrooms (about 4 oz.)
- 1 celery rib, chopped
- ½ cup minced fresh parsley
- 1 Tbsp. fresh sage or 1 tsp. dried sage leaves
- ⅛ tsp. salt
- ⅛ tsp. pepper
- 1 can (14½ oz.) chicken broth
- 1 cup pecan halves

1. Preheat oven to 325°. In a large bowl, combine the stuffing cubes and the stuffing mix.
2. In a large skillet, cook sausage and onion over medium heat until sausage is no longer pink, 4-6 minutes breaking up sausage into crumbles. Remove from pan with a slotted spoon and add to stuffing mixture.
3. Add butter to same pan. Add the apple, mushrooms and celery; cook and stir over medium-high heat until mushrooms are tender. Stir in parsley, sage, salt and pepper. Stir into stuffing mixture. Stir in broth and pecans.
4. Transfer to a greased 3-qt. baking dish. Bake, covered, 30 minutes. Uncover; bake until lightly browned, 10 minutes longer.

¾ cup: 166 cal., 10g fat (2g sat. fat), 12mg chol., 455mg sod., 17g carb. (4g sugars, 2g fiber), 4g pro.

CONFETTI CORNBREAD

My grandmother Virginia always served Southwest cornbread. To honor her, I created a recipe that cuts down on the chopping but never skimps on flavor.
—Angie Price, Bradford, TN

PREP: 20 min. • **BAKE:** 50 min.
MAKES: 12 servings

- 2 **pkg. (8½ oz. each) cornbread/muffin mix**
- ¼ **tsp. cayenne pepper**
- 2 **large eggs, room temperature**
- 1 **can (14¾ oz.) cream-style corn**
- ½ **cup buttermilk**
- ¼ **cup plus 1½ tsp. canola oil, divided**
- 1 **cup shredded cheddar cheese**
- 1 **small onion, chopped**
- 1 **can (4 oz.) chopped green chiles**
- 1 **jar (2 oz.) pimiento strips, drained**
- 1 **jalapeno pepper, seeded and chopped**

1. Preheat oven to 350°. In large bowl, combine muffin mixes and cayenne pepper. In another bowl, mix eggs, corn, buttermilk and ¼ cup oil until blended. Add to dry ingredients; stir just until moistened. Fold in cheese, onion, chiles, pimiento strips and jalapeno.
2. Brush remaining oil onto bottom of a 13x9-in. baking pan; place in oven until hot, 4-5 minutes. Pour batter into hot pan. Bake until edges are golden brown and a toothpick inserted in center comes out clean, 50-60 minutes. Cool in pan on a wire rack. Serve warm.
Note: To substitute for each cup of buttermilk, use 1 Tbsp. white vinegar or lemon juice plus enough milk to measure 1 cup. Stir, then let stand 5 min. Or, use 1 cup plain yogurt or 1¾ tsp. cream of tartar plus 1 cup milk. Wear disposable gloves when cutting hot peppers; the oils can burn skin. Avoid touching your face.
1 piece: 299 cal., 14g fat (4g sat. fat), 42mg chol., 547mg sod., 36g carb. (10g sugars, 3g fiber), 7g pro.

Confetti Cornbread

Sweet Potato & Pesto
Slow-Cooker Bread

SWEET POTATO & PESTO SLOW-COOKER BREAD

I like to bake fresh bread at home, both as a way to offer my family a delicious accompaniment to their dinners and just because I enjoy the process. Baking bread in the slow cooker allows you to achieve a tender, perfectly baked loaf without turning on the oven.
—Shauna Havey, Roy, UT

PREP: 45 min. + rising
COOK: 3 hours + cooling
MAKES: 1 loaf (12 pieces)

- 1 pkg. (¼ oz.) active dry yeast
- ⅔ cup warm half-and-half cream (110° to 115°)
- 1 large egg, room temperature
- 1 cup canned sweet potato puree or canned pumpkin
- 1 tsp. sugar
- 1 tsp. kosher salt
- ¼ tsp. ground nutmeg
- 3½ to 4 cups bread flour
- 1 container (7 oz.) refrigerated prepared pesto
- ½ cup plus 2 Tbsp. grated Parmesan cheese, divided

1. Dissolve yeast in warm cream. In a large bowl, combine egg, sweet potato puree, sugar, salt, nutmeg, yeast mixture and 2 cups flour; beat on medium speed until smooth. Stir in enough remaining flour to form a soft dough (dough will be sticky).

2. Turn onto a lightly floured surface; knead dough until smooth and elastic, 6-8 minutes. Place in a greased bowl, turning once to grease the top. Cover and let rise in a warm place until doubled, about 1 hour.

3. Punch down the dough. Turn onto a lightly floured surface; roll into a 18x9-in. rectangle. Spread pesto to within 1 in. of edges; sprinkle with ½ cup Parmesan. Roll up jelly-roll style, starting with a long side; pinch seam and ends to seal.

4. Using a sharp knife, cut the roll lengthwise in half; carefully turn each half cut side up. Loosely twist strips around each other, keeping cut surfaces facing up. Shape into a coil; place on parchment. Transfer to a 6-qt. slow cooker; sprinkle with remaining 2 Tbsp. Parmesan. Let rise until doubled, about 1 hour.

5. Cook, covered, on low until bread is lightly browned, 3-3½ hours. Remove from slow cooker and cool slightly before slicing.

1 piece: 271 cal., 10g fat (3g sat. fat), 26mg chol., 464mg sod., 36g carb. (3g sugars, 2g fiber), 8g pro.

Triple Mustard & Gruyere Bread Thins

CHEESY BACON RANCH POTATO STUFFING

Every family seems to have a favorite stuffing recipe. My family and I have been making this one for many years. It's so delicious that no gravy is required!
—Sandra Dombek, Camillus, NY

PREP: 25 min. • **BAKE:** 40 min.
MAKES: 16 servings

- 3⅓ cups cubed potato dinner rolls
- ⅔ envelope ranch salad dressing mix
- 6 cups mashed potatoes (with added milk and butter)
- 2 medium celery ribs, finely chopped
- 1 cup sliced baby portobello mushrooms
- 5 bacon strips, cooked and crumbled
- 1⅓ cups shredded Monterey Jack cheese
  Chopped green onions, optional

1. Preheat the oven to 350°. On an ungreased 15x10x1-in. baking pan, bake rolls until toasted, 7-10 minutes. Meanwhile, stir dressing mix into mashed potatoes.

2. Fold in 2 cups cubed rolls, celery, mushrooms and bacon. Transfer to a greased 13x9-in. baking dish; top with the remaining cubed rolls. Place baking dish on a baking sheet. Bake, uncovered, 35 minutes. Sprinkle with cheese; bake until cheese is melted and top is golden brown, 5-10 minutes longer. If desired, top with green onions.

¾ cup: 156 cal., 7g fat (4g sat. fat), 20mg chol., 473mg sod., 17g carb. (2g sugars, 1g fiber), 5g pro.

Test Kitchen Tip

The next time you're making mashed potatoes prepare extra so you can assemble this dish. Simply freeze the additional spuds in a resealable freezer storage bag, and thaw in the fridge the day before you plan to serve this stuffing.

TRIPLE MUSTARD & GRUYERE BREAD THINS

As a bread baker, the perfect sandwich in my home is more about the bread. I'm always experimenting with new combinations, and I created this winning bread last year.
—Veronica Fay, Knoxville, TN

PREP: 1 hour • **BAKE:** 30 min.
MAKES: 1½ dozen

- 1 Tbsp. active dry yeast
- 1 cup warm water (110° to 115°)
- 1 large egg, room temperature
- ⅓ cup canola oil
- 3 Tbsp. dried minced onion
- 3 Tbsp. stone-ground mustard
- 1 Tbsp. ground mustard
- 2 tsp. onion powder
- 1½ tsp. salt
- 3½ to 4 cups bread flour
- 8 oz. smoked Gruyere cheese, shredded
- ¼ cup Dijon mustard
  Optional: 1 Tbsp. each sesame seeds, poppy seeds and mustard seeds

1. In a small bowl, dissolve yeast in warm water. In a large bowl, combine egg, oil, minced onion, stone-ground mustard, ground mustard, onion powder, salt, yeast mixture and 2 cups flour; beat on medium speed until smooth. Stir in enough remaining flour to form a soft dough (dough will be sticky). Stir in cheese.

2. Turn the dough onto a floured surface; knead until smooth and elastic, 6-8 minutes. Place in a greased bowl, turning once to grease the top. Cover and let rise in a warm place until almost doubled, about 1½ hours.

3. Punch down dough. Turn onto a lightly floured surface; divide and shape into 18 balls, about 2 oz. each. Flatten each ball to a 4-in. circle. Place 2 in. apart on greased baking sheets. Cover with kitchen towels; let rise in a warm place until slightly puffed, about 30 minutes.

4. Preheat oven to 375°. Brush rolls with Dijon mustard; if desired, sprinkle with seeds. Bake rolls until lightly browned, 15-18 minutes. Remove from pans to wire racks to cool completely.

Freeze option: Freeze cooled rolls in freezer containers. To use, thaw at room temperature or, if desired, microwave each roll on high until heated through, 10-15 seconds.

1 roll: 204 cal., 9g fat (3g sat. fat), 24mg chol., 423mg sod., 21g carb. (1g sugars, 1g fiber), 8g pro.

Cheesy Bacon Ranch
Potato Stuffing

SLOW-COOKER BACON-MUSHROOM DRESSING

My favorite stuffing uses a slow cooker, which helps when your oven's busy. It goes with everything from turkey to game hens.
—*Hope Wasylenki, Gahanna, OH*

PREP: 20 min. • **COOK:** 3 hours
MAKES: 16 servings (¾ cup each)

- 4 bacon strips, chopped
- 4 cups sliced fresh mushrooms
- 1 large onion, chopped
- 3 celery ribs, chopped
- 2 large eggs
- 1½ to 2 cups reduced-sodium chicken broth, divided
- 1 pkg. (14 oz.) seasoned stuffing cubes
- 1 pkg. (6 oz.) cornbread stuffing mix

1. In a large skillet, cook bacon over medium heat until crisp, stirring occasionally. Remove with a slotted spoon; drain on paper towels. Discard drippings, reserving 1 Tbsp. in pan.
2. Add the mushrooms, onion and celery to drippings; cook and stir over medium-high heat 5-6 minutes or until onion is tender.
3. In a bowl, whisk eggs and 1½ cups broth until blended. In a large bowl, combine stuffing cubes, stuffing mix, bacon and mushroom mixture. Stir in egg mixture and enough additional broth to reach desired moistness.
4. Transfer to a greased 6-qt. slow cooker. Cook, covered, on low until heated through and edges are lightly browned, 3-3½ hours, stirring once.
¾ cup: 172 cal., 4g fat (1g sat. fat), 26mg chol., 657mg sod., 29g carb. (3g sugars, 2g fiber), 6g pro. **Diabetic exchanges:** 2 starch, ½ fat.

Best Ever
Crescent Rolls

BEST EVER CRESCENT ROLLS

My daughter and I have cranked out dozens of these homemade crescent rolls. It's a real team effort. I cut the dough into pie-shaped wedges and she rolls them up.
—Irene Yeh, Mequon, WI

PREP: 40 min. + chilling
BAKE: 10 min./batch • **MAKES:** 32 rolls

- 3¾ to 4¼ cups all-purpose flour
- 2 pkg. (¼ oz. each) active dry yeast
- 1 tsp. salt
- 1 cup 2% milk
- ½ cup butter, cubed
- ¼ cup honey
- 3 large egg yolks, room temperature
- 2 Tbsp. butter, melted

1. Combine 1½ cups flour, yeast and salt. In a small saucepan, heat milk, cubed butter and honey to 120°-130°. Add to dry ingredients; beat on medium speed 2 minutes. Add egg yolks; beat on high 2 minutes. Stir in enough remaining flour to form a soft dough (dough will be sticky).
2. Turn dough onto a floured surface; knead until smooth and elastic, 6-8 minutes. Place in a greased bowl, turning once to grease top. Cover and let rise in a warm place until doubled, about 45 minutes.
3. Punch down dough. Cover and refrigerate overnight.
4. Turn chilled dough onto a lightly floured surface; divide in half. Roll each portion into a 14-in. circle; cut each circle into 16 wedges. Lightly brush wedges with melted butter. Roll up from wide ends, pinching pointed ends to seal. Place 2 in. apart on parchment-lined baking sheets, point side down. Cover; let rise in a warm place until doubled, about 45 minutes.
5. Preheat oven to 375°. Bake until golden brown, 9-11 minutes. Remove from pans to wire racks; serve warm.
Freeze option: Immediately after shaping, freeze rolls on parchment-lined baking sheets until firm. Transfer rolls to a freezer container; return to freezer. Freeze up to 4 weeks. To use, let rise, increasing rise time to 2½-3 hours, and bake as directed.
1 unfilled roll: 104 cal., 4g fat (3g sat. fat), 28mg chol., 107mg sod., 14g carb. (3g sugars, 1g fiber), 2g pro.
CHIVE CRESCENTS: Divide ⅔ cup minced fresh chives between 2 circles of dough.
ORANGE-PECAN CRESCENTS: Toss 1 cup finely chopped pecans with ⅓ cup sugar and 4 tsp. grated orange zest; divide mixture between 2 circles.
CRANBERRY-THYME CRESCENTS: Toss 1 cup finely chopped dried cranberries with ⅔ cup finely chopped walnuts and 2 tsp. minced fresh thyme leaves; divide mixture between 2 circles.

Test Kitchen Tip

To make filled crescent rolls, sprinkle dough with filling of choice immediately after brushing with butter; shape and bake as directed.

GOUDA & ROASTED POTATO BREAD

Our family tried roasted potato bread at a bakery on a road trip, and I came up with my own recipe when we realized we lived much too far away to have it regularly. It makes for a really amazing roast beef sandwich and is also fantastic with soups.
—Elisabeth Larsen, Pleasant Grove, UT

PREP: 45 min. + rising • **BAKE:** 40 min.
MAKES: 1 loaf (16 pieces)

- ½ lb. Yukon Gold potatoes, chopped (about ¾ cup)
- 1½ tsp. olive oil
- 1½ tsp. salt, divided
- 1 pkg. (¼ oz.) active dry yeast
- 2½ to 3 cups all-purpose flour
- 1 cup warm water (120° to 130°)
- ½ cup shredded smoked Gouda cheese

1. Arrange 1 oven rack at lowest rack setting; place second rack in middle of oven. Preheat oven to 425°. Place potatoes in a greased 15x10x1-in. baking pan. Drizzle with oil; sprinkle with ½ tsp. salt. Toss to coat. Roast potatoes until tender, 20-25 minutes, stirring occasionally.

2. In a large bowl, mix yeast, remaining 1 tsp. salt and 2 cups flour. Add warm water; beat on medium speed until smooth. Stir in enough remaining flour to form a soft dough (dough will be sticky). Turn the dough onto a floured surface; knead until smooth and elastic, 6-8 minutes. Gently knead in roasted potatoes and cheese. Place in a greased bowl, turning once to grease the top. Cover and let rise in a warm place until doubled, about 1 hour.

3. Punch down dough. Shape into a 7-in. round loaf. Place on a parchment-lined baking sheet. Cover with a kitchen towel; let rise in a warm place until dough expands to a 9-in. loaf, about 45 minutes.

4. Place an oven-safe skillet on bottom oven rack. Meanwhile, in a teakettle, bring 2 cups water to a boil. Using a sharp knife, make a slash (¼ in. deep) across top of loaf. Place bread on top rack. Pull bottom rack out by 6-8 in.; add boiling water to skillet. (Work quickly and carefully, pouring water away from you. Don't worry if some water is left in the kettle.) Carefully slide bottom rack back into place; quickly close door to trap steam in oven.

5. Bake 10 minutes. Reduce oven setting to 375°. Bake until deep golden brown, 30-35 minutes longer. Remove loaf to a wire rack to cool.

1 piece: 101 cal., 2g fat (1g sat. fat), 4mg chol., 253mg sod., 18g carb. (0 sugars, 1g fiber), 3g pro.

Gouda & Roasted Potato Bread

Cranberry Apple Stuffing

CRANBERRY APPLE STUFFING

One Thanksgiving, I lost the recipe I planned to use, so I threw this cranberry stuffing together. My cousin Sandy, a die-hard traditional stuffing fan, said this was the best stuffing she'd ever tasted! Talk about a compliment!
—Beverly A. Norris, Evanston, WY

PREP: 30 min. • **BAKE:** 30 min.
MAKES: 12 servings

¾	lb. bulk Italian sausage
2	celery ribs, finely chopped
1	small onion, finely chopped
6	garlic cloves, minced
1	can (14½ oz.) chicken broth
½	cup butter, cubed
1	pkg. (12 oz.) seasoned stuffing cubes
1½	cups chopped apples
1	cup dried cranberries
½	cup slivered almonds
1½	tsp. dried sage leaves
1½	tsp. dried thyme
⅛	tsp. pepper
	Dash salt
1	to 1½ cups apple cider or juice

1. Preheat oven to 350°. In a Dutch oven, cook sausage, celery, onion and garlic over medium heat until sausage is no longer pink; drain. Add broth, stirring to loosen browned bits from pan. Add butter; cook and stir until the butter is melted. Remove from heat.
2. Stir in the stuffing cubes, apples, cranberries, almonds, sage, thyme, pepper, salt and enough cider to reach desired moistness. Transfer to a greased 13x9-in. baking dish.
3. Cover and bake 25 minutes. Uncover; bake until lightly browned, 5-10 minutes.
¾ cup: 338 cal., 17g fat (7g sat. fat), 36mg chol., 809mg sod., 40g carb. (16g sugars, 4g fiber), 8g pro.

Make-Ahead Cornbread Dressing

MAKE-AHEAD CORNBREAD DRESSING

My family has always been big on veggies. I wanted to share a taste of my childhood with my in-laws, so I created this dish. You don't have to let it sit overnight, but it's a nice make-ahead option and the flavors blend more that way.
—Patricia Broussard, Lafayette, LA

PREP: 1½ hours + chilling • **BAKE:** 55 min.
MAKES: 14 servings (¾ cup each)

- 1   medium spaghetti squash (about 4 lbs.)
- 1   pkg. (8½ oz.) cornbread/muffin mix
- 1   medium onion, finely chopped
- 2   celery ribs, thinly sliced
- ½   cup butter, cubed
- 2   garlic cloves, minced
- ½   lb. bulk pork sausage, cooked and drained
- 1   cup frozen corn
- 2   Tbsp. poultry seasoning
- ¾   tsp. salt
- ¼   tsp. pepper
- 1   cup chopped walnuts, toasted
- 1   cup chicken broth
- ¼   cup grated Parmesan cheese

1. Cut squash lengthwise in half; remove and discard seeds. Place squash in a roasting pan, cut side down; add ½ in. of hot water. Bake, uncovered, at 375° for 45 minutes. Drain water from pan; turn squash cut side up. Bake until squash is tender, about 5 minutes longer.

2. Prepare and bake cornbread mix according to package directions, using an 8-in. square baking dish. Cool to room temperature; crumble bread. Place in an ungreased 13x9-in. baking pan. Bake at 350° until lightly browned, 8-13 minutes, stirring twice.

3. In a skillet, cook onion and celery in butter over medium heat for 4 minutes. Add garlic; cook 2 minutes longer. Stir in sausage, corn, poultry seasoning, salt and pepper; heat through.

4. When squash is cool enough to handle, use a fork to separate strands. In a large bowl, combine the sausage mixture, cornbread, squash and walnuts. Stir in broth.

5. Transfer to a greased 13x9-in. baking dish. Cover and refrigerate for 8 hours or overnight. Remove from refrigerator 30 minutes before baking. Cover and bake at 350° for 45 minutes. Uncover; sprinkle with cheese; bake until heated through, 10-15 minutes longer.

¾ cup: 295 cal., 19g fat (7g sat. fat), 42mg chol., 549mg sod., 26g carb. (5g sugars, 4g fiber), 7g pro.

HERB-HAPPY GARLIC BREAD

You'll love the fresh garlic and herbs in this recipe. The mild goat cheese that's sprinkled on top makes it extra rich and wonderful.
—Taste of Home *Test Kitchen*

TAKES: 15 min. • **MAKES:** 12 servings

- ½ cup butter, softened
- ¼ cup grated Romano cheese
- 2 Tbsp. minced fresh basil or 2 tsp. dried basil
- 1 Tbsp. minced fresh parsley
- 3 garlic cloves, minced
- 1 French bread baguette
- 4 oz. crumbled goat cheese

1. In a small bowl, mix first 5 ingredients until blended. Cut baguette crosswise in half; cut each piece lengthwise in half. Spread cut sides with butter mixture. Place on an ungreased baking sheet.
2. Bake, uncovered, at 425° until lightly toasted, 7-9 minutes. Sprinkle with the goat cheese; bake until the goat cheese is softened, 1-2 minutes longer. Cut into slices.
1 piece: 169 cal., 11g fat (7g sat. fat), 35mg chol., 307mg sod., 14g carb. (0 sugars, 1g fiber), 5g pro.

Zucchini & Cheese
Drop Biscuits

ZUCCHINI & CHEESE DROP BISCUITS

These colorful little drop biscuits are very easy to put together and yet are packed full of flavor. I serve them warm out of the oven.
—Keith Mesch, Mount Healthy, OH

PREP: 25 min. + standing • **BAKE:** 25 min.
MAKES: 1 dozen

- ¾ cup shredded zucchini
- 1¼ tsp. salt, divided
- 2½ cups all-purpose flour
- 1 Tbsp. baking powder
- ½ cup cold butter, cubed
- ½ cup shredded cheddar cheese
- ¼ cup shredded part-skim mozzarella cheese
- ¼ cup shredded Parmesan cheese
- 2 Tbsp. finely chopped oil-packed sun-dried tomatoes, patted dry
- 2 Tbsp. minced fresh basil or 2 tsp. dried basil
- 1 cup 2% milk

1. Preheat oven to 425°. Place the zucchini in a colander over a plate; sprinkle with ¼ tsp. salt and toss. Let stand 10 minutes. Rinse and drain well. Squeeze zucchini to remove excess liquid. Pat dry.
2. In a large bowl, whisk flour, baking powder and remaining salt. Cut in butter until mixture resembles coarse crumbs. Stir in zucchini, cheeses, tomatoes and basil. Add milk; stir just until moistened.
3. Drop by scant ⅓ cupfuls into a greased 13x9-in. baking pan. Bake until golden brown, 22-26 minutes. Serve warm.
1 biscuit: 205 cal., 11g fat (7g sat. fat), 29mg chol., 482mg sod., 22g carb. (2g sugars, 1g fiber), 6g pro.

WHY YOU'LL LOVE IT...

"I absolutely love these biscuits! They are delicious served with white chili. Perfection on a plate."
—DYLAN'S MAMA, TASTEOFHOME.COM

HONEY CHALLAH

I use these shiny beautiful loaves as the centerpiece of my spread. I love the taste of honey, but you can also add chocolate chips, cinnamon, orange zest or almonds. Leftover slices work well in bread pudding or for French toast.
—Jennifer Newfield, Los Angeles, CA

PREP: 45 min. + rising
BAKE: 30 min. + cooling
MAKES: 2 loaves (24 pieces each)

2	pkg. (¼ oz. each) active dry yeast
½	tsp. sugar
1½	cups warm water (110° to 115°), divided
5	large eggs, room temperature
⅔	cup plus 1 tsp. honey, divided
½	cup canola oil
2	tsp. salt
6	to 7 cups bread flour
1	cup boiling water
2	cups golden raisins
1	Tbsp. water
1	Tbsp. sesame seeds

1. In a small bowl, dissolve yeast and sugar in 1 cup warm water. Separate 2 eggs; refrigerate the whites. Place the egg yolks and eggs in a large bowl. Add ⅔ cup honey, oil, salt, yeast mixture, 3 cups flour and remaining warm water; beat on medium speed 3 minutes. Stir in enough remaining flour to form a soft dough (dough will be sticky).
2. Pour boiling water over the raisins in a small bowl; let stand 5 minutes. Drain and pat dry. Turn dough onto a floured surface; knead until smooth and elastic, 6-8 minutes. Knead in raisins. Place in a greased bowl, turning once to grease top. Cover and let rise in a warm place until almost doubled, about 1½ hours.

3. Punch down dough. Turn onto a lightly floured surface. Divide dough in half. Divide 1 portion into 6 pieces. Roll each into a 16-in. rope. Place ropes parallel on a greased baking sheet; pinch ropes together at the top.
4. To braid, take the rope on the left and carry it over the 2 ropes beside it, then slip it under the middle rope and carry it over the last 2 ropes. Lay the rope down parallel to the other ropes; it is now on the far right side. Repeat these steps until you reach the end. As the braid moves to the right, you can pick up the loaf and recenter it on your work surface as needed. Pinch ends to seal and tuck under. For a fuller loaf, using your hands, push the ends of the loaf closer together. Repeat process with remaining dough. Cover with kitchen towels; let rise in a warm place until almost doubled, about 30 minutes.
5. Preheat oven to 350°. In a small bowl, whisk the 2 chilled egg whites and honey with water; brush over loaves. Sprinkle with sesame seeds. Bake 30-35 minutes or until bread is golden brown and sounds hollow when tapped. Remove from pans to a wire rack to cool.

1 piece: 125 cal., 3g fat (0 sat. fat), 19mg chol., 107mg sod., 21g carb. (8g sugars, 1g fiber), 3g pro.

Test Kitchen Tip

If your challah is dry, it could be because you added a little too much flour. Next time, let your dough stay sticky! It may be a little harder to work with, but sticky dough means you've used just the right ratio of water, oil and flour.

Honey Challah

HERB FOCACCIA ROLLS

Yeast rolls speckled with fresh thyme and rosemary are a breeze to make without kneading and long wait times. Break out the good butter for these adorable rolls.
—Linda Schend, Kenosha, WI

PREP: 15 min. + rising • **BAKE:** 20 min.
MAKES: 1½ dozen

- 3 cups all-purpose flour
- 1 pkg. (¼ oz.) quick-rise yeast
- 2 Tbsp. minced fresh thyme, divided
- 2 Tbsp. minced fresh rosemary, divided
- 1 Tbsp. sugar
- 1½ tsp. kosher salt, divided
- 1½ cups warm water (120° to 130°)
- 6 Tbsp. extra-virgin olive oil, divided

1. Combine flour, yeast, 1 Tbsp. thyme, 1 Tbsp. rosemary, sugar and 1 tsp. salt. Add water and 2 Tbsp. oil; beat 1 minute (dough will be very sticky).
2. Divide dough among 18 greased muffin cups. Let rise in a warm place until doubled, about 30 minutes.
3. Preheat oven to 375°. In a small saucepan over medium-low heat, stir together remaining herbs, salt and olive oil just until herbs are fragrant and oil is hot, about 1½ minutes. Remove from heat; cool.
4. Gently spoon cooled herb mixture over each roll. Bake until golden brown, 20-25 minutes.
1 roll: 120 cal., 5g fat (1g sat. fat), 0 chol., 161mg sod., 17g carb. (1g sugars, 1g fiber), 2g pro.

SOUR CREAM & CHEDDAR BISCUITS

Here's my go-to recipe for biscuits. Brushing them with the garlic-butter topping before baking seals the deal!
—Amy Martin, Vancouver, WA

PREP: 25 min. • **BAKE:** 15 min.
MAKES: 1½ dozen

2½ cups all-purpose flour
3 tsp. baking powder
2 tsp. sugar
1 tsp. garlic powder
½ tsp. cream of tartar
¼ tsp. salt
¼ tsp. cayenne pepper
½ cup cold butter, cubed
1½ cups shredded cheddar cheese
¾ cup 2% milk
½ cup sour cream
TOPPING
6 Tbsp. butter, melted
1½ tsp. garlic powder
1 tsp. minced fresh parsley

1. Preheat oven to 450°. In a large bowl, whisk the first 7 ingredients. Cut in cold butter until mixture resembles coarse crumbs; stir in cheese. Add milk and sour cream; stir just until moistened.
2. Drop by ¼ cupfuls 2 in. apart onto greased baking sheets. Mix topping ingredients; brush over tops. Bake until light brown, 12-15 minutes. Serve warm.
1 biscuit: 206 cal., 14g fat (8g sat. fat), 36mg chol., 256mg sod., 15g carb. (2g sugars, 1g fiber), 5g pro.

Sour Cream & Cheddar Biscuits

Coconut
Garlic Naan

COCONUT GARLIC NAAN

One of my favorite comfort foods is naan. I love the airy, chewy inside and the crisp, salty exterior. I drew inspiration from using ingredients like whole wheat flour and coconut oil to create a healthier but even tastier snack. You'll love this nutty bread smeared with garlic confit and sea salt.
—Morgan Harrison, Astoria, NY

PREP: 2 hours + cooling
COOK: 5 min./batch • **MAKES:** 8 servings

- ¼ cup coconut oil
- 6 garlic cloves, peeled

NAAN
- 1 pkg. (¼ oz.) active dry yeast
- ½ cup warm water (110° to 115°)
- ¾ cup whole wheat flour
- ½ cup plain yogurt
- 2 Tbsp. coconut oil, divided
- 1 tsp. sugar
- 1 tsp. salt
- 1¼ to 1½ cups all-purpose flour
- 1 Tbsp. canola oil

1. For garlic confit, preheat oven to 250°. Place coconut oil and garlic in a small ovenproof bowl. Cover and bake until garlic is soft and golden, about 2 hours. Cool completely.

2. For naan, in a small bowl, dissolve yeast in warm water. In a large bowl, combine whole wheat flour, yogurt, 1 Tbsp. coconut oil, sugar, salt, yeast mixture and ½ cup flour; beat on medium speed until smooth. Stir in enough remaining flour to form a soft dough (dough will be sticky).

3. Turn dough onto a floured surface; knead until smooth and elastic, 6-8 minutes. Place in a greased bowl, turning once to grease the top. Cover and let rise in a warm place until doubled, about 1 hour.

4. Punch down the dough. Turn onto a lightly floured surface; divide into 8 pieces. Roll each piece into a ¼-in.-thick oval. In a large skillet, heat the canola oil and remaining 1 Tbsp. coconut oil over medium-high heat. Working in batches, cook naan until golden brown, 1-2 minutes. Turn; cook until golden brown, 1-2 minutes longer. Repeat with remaining dough. Serve with the garlic confit.

1 piece: 232 cal., 13g fat (10g sat. fat), 2mg chol., 304mg sod., 25g carb. (1g sugars, 2g fiber), 5g pro.

JOSH'S MARBLED RYE BREAD

This impressive marble rye bread may look like it would be difficult to make, but it's actually quite easy! The flavors of the bread are mild yet satisfying. I enjoy eating it with just a simple spread of butter or on a hearty sandwich loaded with my favorite fixings.
—Josh Rink, Milwaukee, WI

PREP: 50 min. + rising
BAKE: 45 min. + cooling
MAKES: 1 loaf (16 pieces)

- 5 cups bread flour, divided
- 2 cups plus 1 Tbsp. rye flour, divided
- ½ cup potato flour
- ⅓ cup nonfat dry milk powder
- 2 Tbsp. sugar
- 2 Tbsp. caraway seeds
- 3 tsp. instant or quick-rise yeast
- 2½ tsp. onion powder
- 2 tsp. salt
- 2¾ cups warm water (110° to 115°)
- ¼ cup vegetable oil
- 2 Tbsp. dark baking cocoa
- 1 large egg, lightly beaten with 1 Tbsp. water

1. In a large bowl, whisk together 4 cups bread flour, 2 cups rye flour, potato flour, milk powder, sugar, caraway seeds, yeast, onion powder and salt. In another bowl, whisk together warm water and oil; pour over flour mixture and stir until combined. Dough will be sticky. Turn dough onto a lightly floured surface; with floured hands, knead dough, incorporating remaining 1 cup bread flour as needed until dough becomes smooth and elastic, 8-10 minutes. Divide dough in half. Mix dark cocoa powder with remaining 1 Tbsp. rye flour; knead cocoa mixture into 1 portion of dough until fully incorporated.

2. Lightly coat 2 large bowls with oil. Place 1 portion of dough into each bowl and turn to coat. Cover and allow dough to rise until doubled in size, 1-1½ hours. Working with 1 portion of dough at a time, turn onto lightly floured surface; roll each into a 14x12-in. rectangle. Place dough with cocoa on top of remaining dough; starting with a long side, roll jelly-roll style to form a spiral, pinching seam together to seal. Place seam side down in a greased 13x4-in. Pullman loaf pan, tucking ends under to form smooth loaf. Loosely cover pan with damp cloth and allow to rise until doubled in size, 1-1½ hours; dough should rise ½-¾ in. above edge of the loaf pan.

3. Brush loaf with egg wash; using a sharp knife, cut 3-4 deep diagonal slashes on top of loaf. Cover with nonstick foil and place in preheated 400° oven; bake 15 minutes. Reduce heat to 375°; bake 20 minutes. Remove foil; bake until loaf is deep golden brown and reaches an internal temperature of 200° when measured with an instant-read thermometer, about 10 minutes longer. Remove from oven; allow bread to cool 10 minutes. Remove loaf from pan. Cool completely on wire rack.

1 piece: 273 cal., 5g fat (1g sat. fat), 12mg chol., 312mg sod., 49g carb. (3g sugars, 4g fiber), 8g pro.

Test Kitchen Tip

If you do not have a Pullman loaf pan, use two 8x4-in. loaf pans instead. After rolling dough into spiral, cut in half and place each half in greased 8x4-in. pan and bake as directed.

Josh's Marbled Rye Bread

TORTILLA DRESSING

This is not your typical stuffing. Tortillas, jalapenos, chili powder and cilantro lend to its southwestern flavor.
—Dorothy Bray, Adkins, TX

PREP: 30 min. • **BAKE:** 35 min.
MAKES: 9 cups

- 8 corn tortillas (6 in.), cut into ¼-in. strips
- ¼ cup canola oil
- 8 flour tortillas (6 in.), cut into ¼-in. strips
- 1 cup crushed cornbread stuffing
- 1 small onion, finely chopped
- ⅓ cup finely chopped sweet red pepper
- 1 jalapeno pepper, seeded and chopped
- 1 Tbsp. minced fresh cilantro
- 1 Tbsp. chili powder
- 1 tsp. minced fresh sage or ¼ tsp. dried sage leaves
- ½ tsp. ground coriander
- ½ tsp. ground cumin
- ¼ tsp. salt
- 1 large egg, lightly beaten
- 1 cup chicken broth

1. In a large skillet, saute the corn tortilla strips in oil in batches for 1 minute or until golden brown. Drain strips on paper towels.

2. In a large bowl, combine the corn tortilla strips, flour tortilla strips, stuffing, onion, red pepper, jalapeno, cilantro, chili powder, sage, coriander, cumin and salt. Stir in egg and broth.

3. Transfer mixture to a greased 13x9-in. baking dish. Cover and bake at 325° until a thermometer reads 160°, 35-45 minutes.

Note: Wear disposable gloves when cutting hot peppers; the oils can burn skin. Avoid touching your face.

¾ cup: 171 cal., 8g fat (1g sat. fat), 18mg chol., 370mg sod., 22g carb. (1g sugars, 2g fiber), 4g pro. **Diabetic exchanges:** 1½ starch, 1 fat.

HOMEMADE FRY BREAD

Crispy, doughy and totally delicious, this fry bread is fantastic with nearly any sweet or savory toppings you can think of. We love it with a little butter, a drizzle of honey and a squeeze of lemon.
—Thelma Tyler, Dragoon, AZ

PREP: 20 min. + standing • **COOK:** 15 min.
MAKES: 12 servings

- 2 cups unbleached flour
- ½ cup nonfat dry milk powder
- 3 tsp. baking powder
- ½ tsp. salt
- 4½ tsp. shortening
- ⅔ to ¾ cup water
  Oil for deep-fat frying
  Optional: Butter, honey and lemon juice

1. Combine the flour, dry milk powder, baking powder and salt; cut in the shortening until crumbly. Add water gradually, mixing to form a firm ball. Divide dough; shape into 12 balls. Let stand, covered, for 10 minutes. Roll each ball into a 6-in. circle. With a sharp knife, cut a ½-in.-diameter hole in the center of each.

2. In a large cast-iron skillet, heat oil over medium-high heat. Fry dough circles, 1 at a time, until puffed and golden, about 1 minute on each side. Drain on paper towels. If desired, serve warm with butter, honey and fresh lemon juice.

1 piece: 124 cal., 5g fat (1g sat. fat), 1mg chol., 234mg sod., 17g carb. (2g sugars, 1g fiber), 3g pro.

Homemade
Fry Bread

SAUSAGE STUFFING MUFFINS

Here's a clever new take on stuffing. You can also bake the stuffing in a greased baking dish for a more traditional presentation.
—Tricia Bibb, Hartselle, AL

PREP: 45 min. • **BAKE:** 20 min.
MAKES: 1½ dozen

- 1 lb. bulk pork sausage
- 4 celery ribs, chopped
- 2 medium onions, chopped
- ¼ cup butter, cubed
- 1 pkg. (14 oz.) crushed cornbread stuffing
- 2 medium apples, peeled and chopped
- 1 pkg. (5 oz.) dried cranberries
- 1 cup chopped pecans
- 1 tsp. salt
- 1 tsp. pepper
- 2 to 3 cups reduced-sodium chicken broth
- 2 large eggs
- 2 tsp. baking powder

1. Preheat oven to 375°. In a large skillet, cook sausage over medium heat until no longer pink; drain. Transfer to a large bowl; set aside.

2. In same skillet, saute the celery and onions in butter until tender. Transfer to bowl; add stuffing, apples, cranberries, pecans, salt and pepper. Stir in enough broth to reach desired moistness. Whisk the eggs and baking powder; add to the stuffing mixture.

3. Spoon into 18 greased muffin cups. Bake 20-25 minutes or until lightly browned. Cool 10 minutes. Run a knife around edges of muffin cups to loosen. Serve immediately.

Freeze option: Freeze cooled stuffing muffins in airtight freezer containers. To use, partially thaw in the refrigerator overnight. Place muffins on greased baking sheets, cover with foil and reheat in a preheated 375° oven until heated through, 6-10 minutes.

1 muffin: 258 cal., 14g fat (4g sat. fat), 39mg chol., 625mg sod., 30g carb. (10g sugars, 3g fiber), 6g pro.

Sesame Onion Breadsticks

SESAME ONION BREADSTICKS

My family has enjoyed these golden brown breadsticks at numerous gatherings over the years. The recipe is a snap to prepare using frozen bread dough and just five other ingredients.
—Mary Relyea, Canastota, NY

PREP: 30 min. + rising • **BAKE:** 15 min.
MAKES: 32 breadsticks

- 2 Tbsp. butter
- 1½ cups finely chopped onions (about 2 medium)
- ¼ tsp. paprika
- 1 loaf (1 lb.) frozen bread dough, thawed
- 1 large egg, lightly beaten
- 1 Tbsp. sesame seeds

1. In a large skillet, heat butter over medium heat. Add onions; cook and stir until tender. Stir in paprika; cool mixture completely.

2. On a lightly floured surface, roll dough to a 16x14-in. rectangle. Spread onion mixture down 1 half of the rectangle. Fold dough lengthwise in half over onion mixture, forming a 16x7-in. rectangle; seal edges.

3. Cut dough lengthwise into thirty-two ½-in.-thick strips. Twist each strip 2 or 3 times. Place 2 in. apart on greased baking sheets. Cover with kitchen towels; let rise in a warm place until almost doubled, about 45 minutes. Preheat oven to 375°.

4. Brush the breadsticks with beaten egg; sprinkle with sesame seeds. Bake 13-16 minutes or until golden brown. Remove from pans to wire racks to cool.

1 breadstick: 53 cal., 2g fat (1g sat. fat), 8mg chol., 88mg sod., 8g carb. (1g sugars, 1g fiber), 2g pro.

Cranberry
Cornbread
Casserole

BEST HUSH PUPPIES

Some years ago, I was a cook on a large cattle ranch. One day, I thought back to the hush puppies I'd had as a child on a southern trip, and I ended up creating my own version. They go very well as part of an old-fashioned fried chicken dinner with mashed potatoes and gravy, buttermilk biscuits, corn on the cob and watermelon pickles!
—Karyl Goodhart, Geraldine, MT

PREP: 15 min. • **COOK:** 20 min.
MAKES: 3 dozen

- 2 cups yellow cornmeal
- ½ cup all-purpose flour
- 2 Tbsp. sugar
- 2 tsp. baking powder
- 1 tsp. salt
- ½ tsp. baking soda
- 1 large egg, room temperature, lightly beaten
- ¾ cup 2% milk
- ¾ cup cream-style corn
  Oil for deep-fat frying

1. In a large bowl, whisk cornmeal, flour, sugar, baking powder, salt and baking soda. Add egg, milk and corn; stir just until combined.
2. In a deep-fat fryer, heat oil to 375°. Drop tablespoons of batter, a few at a time, into hot oil. Fry until golden brown on both sides. Drain on paper towels. Serve warm.

1 hush puppy: 66 cal., 2g fat (0 sat. fat), 6mg chol., 129mg sod., 10g carb. (1g sugars, 0 fiber), 1g pro.

WHY YOU'LL LOVE IT...

"This was a good recipe and our first time making hush puppies. We added chives to the recipe, which was a great addition."
—RACHDBO, TASTEOFHOME.COM

CRANBERRY CORNBREAD CASSEROLE

What could be better on a cold, windy day than a warm casserole and creamy sweet cornbread put together? Since it starts with a mix, this side takes no time to make. Just bake, scoop and eat. Yum!
—Valery Anderson, Sterling Heights, MI

PREP: 15 min. • **BAKE:** 20 min.
MAKES: 9 servings

- ½ cup dried cranberries
- ½ cup boiling water
- 1 pkg. (8½ oz.) cornbread/muffin mix
- 1 tsp. onion powder
- ¼ tsp. rubbed sage
- 1 large egg
- 1 can (14¾ oz.) cream-style corn
- 2 Tbsp. butter, melted
- ¼ cup chopped pecans
- ½ tsp. grated orange zest

1. Place cranberries in a small bowl; cover with boiling water. Let stand for 5 minutes; drain.

2. In a small bowl, combine the muffin mix, onion powder and sage. In another bowl, whisk the egg, corn and butter; stir into dry ingredients just until moistened. Fold in pecans, orange zest and cranberries.
3. Transfer to a greased 8-in. square baking dish. Bake uncovered at 400° for 20-25 minutes or until set.
Freeze option: Cool baked cornbread in pan; cover and freeze. To use, partially thaw in refrigerator overnight. Remove from refrigerator 30 minutes before baking. Preheat oven to 350°. Reheat the cornbread 10-12 minutes or until heated through.
1 piece: 225 cal., 9g fat (3g sat. fat), 28mg chol., 369mg sod., 35g carb. (14g sugars, 3g fiber), 4g pro. **Diabetic exchanges:** 2 starch, 1 fat.

Best Hush
Puppies

Tomato Pie,
Page 309

Page 310

Page 306

Bring-a-Dish Potluck Greats

If you need a dish to pass, you've come to the right place! Turn here for two dozen sides that will feed a crowd, travel well and steal the show at potlucks, block parties, church suppers, barbecues and other delicious happenings.

Page 305

Page 306

Fennel-Bacon Pasta Salad

FENNEL-BACON PASTA SALAD

I love when a recipe is simple to prepare but elegant enough to serve at a formal dinner. This pasta is best served warm, but you can chill it if you'd like.
—*Julian Wong, La Jolla, CA*

PREP: 15 min. • **COOK:** 20 min.
MAKES: 16 servings

- 1   pkg. (16 oz.) spiral pasta
- 6   thick-sliced bacon strips, chopped
- 3   small fennel bulbs, thinly sliced
- 1½ cups walnut halves
- 1¼ cups (5 oz.) crumbled Stilton cheese, divided
- 1   tsp. coarsely ground pepper
- ¾   tsp. salt

1. Cook pasta according to the package directions.

2. Meanwhile, in a large skillet, cook bacon over medium heat until crisp. Remove bacon with a slotted spoon; drain on paper towels. Remove bacon drippings, reserving 3 Tbsp. in pan. Saute fennel in reserved drippings for 4-6 minutes or until crisp-tender. Add walnuts; cook 3-4 minutes longer or until toasted.

3. Drain the pasta, reserving ⅓ cup pasta water. Add the pasta, bacon and ¾ cup cheese to fennel mixture; sprinkle with pepper and salt. Toss lightly until the cheese is melted, adding enough reserved pasta water to coat pasta. Serve warm with remaining cheese. Refrigerate leftovers.
¾ cup: 252 cal., 13g fat (3g sat. fat), 15mg chol., 301mg sod., 26g carb. (1g sugars, 3g fiber), 9g pro.

FREEZER SLAW

This convenient slaw recipe is from my mother. She combines all the ingredients, then stores it in the freezer for later.
—*Alice Campbell, Dickinson, ND*

PREP: 30 min. + standing
COOK: 10 min. + freezing
MAKES: 18 servings

- 2   medium heads cabbage, shredded (about 16 cups)
- 2   tsp. salt
- 2   cups sugar
- 2   cups water
- 2   cups cider vinegar
- 2   tsp. celery seed
- 2   tsp. mustard seed
- 2   medium sweet red peppers, chopped
- 2   medium carrots, shredded

1. Place cabbage in a very large bowl; toss with salt. Let stand 1 hour.
2. Meanwhile, in a large saucepan, combine sugar, water, vinegar, celery seed and mustard seed. Bring to a boil, stirring to dissolve sugar. Cook 1 minute. Remove from heat; cool slightly.
3. Drain excess liquid from cabbage, if necessary. Add red peppers and carrots to cabbage. Add dressing; toss to coat. Cool completely. Transfer to freezer containers. Freeze, covered, up to 3 months.
4. To serve, thaw coleslaw overnight in refrigerator. Stir before serving.
¾ cup: 126 cal., 0 fat (0 sat. fat), 0 chol., 287mg sod., 30g carb. (26g sugars, 3g fiber), 2g pro.

WHY YOU'LL LOVE IT...

"Made this recipe a couple of weeks ago, froze it and enjoyed it this past weekend when I had company. It was a hit! Very tasty. All the flavors blended perfectly. Thank you for a real keeper!"
—KRISTINECHAYES, TASTEOFHOME.COM

Cheesy Corn Spoon Bread

CHEESY CORN SPOON BREAD

Homey and comforting, this custard-like side dish is a much-requested recipe at potlucks and holiday dinners. The jalapeno adds just the right bite. Second helpings of this tasty casserole are common—leftovers aren't.
—Katherine Franklin, Carbondale, IL

PREP: 15 min. • **BAKE:** 35 min.
MAKES: 15 servings

- ¼ cup butter, cubed
- 1 medium onion, chopped
- 2 large eggs
- 2 cups sour cream
- 1 can (15¼ oz.) whole kernel corn, drained
- 1 can (14¾ oz.) cream-style corn
- ¼ tsp. salt
- ¼ tsp. pepper
- 1 pkg. (8½ oz.) cornbread/muffin mix
- 2 medium jalapeno peppers, divided
- 2 cups shredded cheddar cheese, divided

1. Preheat oven to 375°. In a large skillet, heat butter over medium-high heat. Add onion; saute until tender. Set aside.

2. Beat eggs; add the sour cream, both cans of corn, salt and pepper. Stir in the cornbread mix just until blended. Mince 1 jalapeno pepper; fold into the corn mixture with the sauteed onion and 1½ cups cheese.

3. Transfer to a greased shallow 3-qt. baking dish. Sprinkle with remaining cheese. Bake, uncovered, until a toothpick inserted in center comes out clean, 35-40 minutes; cool slightly. Slice remaining jalapeno; sprinkle over dish.

Note: Wear disposable gloves when cutting hot peppers; the oils can burn skin. Avoid touching your face.

1 serving: 266 cal., 17g fat (9g sat. fat), 56mg chol., 470mg sod., 21g carb. (7g sugars, 2g fiber), 8g pro.

5i

POTATO PUMPKIN MASH

I swirl fresh pumpkin into potatoes for a little extra holiday color. No more plain white potatoes for us! If you'd like, you can use butternut squash instead. Either way it's super pretty.
—Michelle Medley, Dallas, TX

PREP: 20 min. • **COOK:** 25 min.
MAKES: 8 servings

- 8   cups cubed peeled pie pumpkin (about 2 lbs.)
- 8   medium Yukon Gold potatoes, peeled and cubed (about 2 lbs.)
- ½ to ¾ cup 2% milk, divided
- 8   Tbsp. butter, softened, divided
- 1   tsp. salt, divided
- 1   Tbsp. olive oil
- ¼   tsp. coarsely ground pepper

1. Place pumpkin in a large saucepan; add water to cover. Bring to a boil. Reduce heat; cook, uncovered, for 20-25 minutes or until tender.
2. Meanwhile, place potatoes in another saucepan; add water to cover. Bring to a boil. Reduce heat; cook, uncovered, for 10-15 minutes or until tender.
3. Drain potatoes; return to pan. Mash potatoes, adding ¼ cup milk, 4 Tbsp. butter and ½ tsp. salt. Add additional milk if needed to reach desired consistency. Transfer to a serving bowl; keep warm.
4. Drain pumpkin; return to pan. Mash pumpkin, gradually adding the remaining butter and salt and enough remaining milk to reach desired consistency; spoon evenly over potatoes. Cut through mashed vegetables with a spoon or knife to swirl. Drizzle with olive oil; sprinkle with pepper. Serve immediately.
¾ cup: 214 cal., 13g fat (8g sat. fat), 31mg chol., 384mg sod., 23g carb. (3g sugars, 2g fiber), 3g pro.

Potato
Pumpkin
Mash

CRUNCHY COOL COLESLAW

*This recipe is my version of the peanut slaw
I love at Lucille's Smokehouse Bar-B-Que,
a popular restaurant chain in California.
I think it's a pretty close match!*
—Elaine Hoffmann, Santa Ana, CA

TAKES: 30 min. • **MAKES:** 16 servings

- 2 pkg. (16 oz. each) coleslaw mix
- 2 medium Honeycrisp apples, julienned
- 1 large carrot, shredded
- ¾ cup chopped red onion
- ½ cup chopped green pepper
- ½ cup cider vinegar
- ⅓ cup canola oil
- 1½ tsp. sugar
- ½ tsp. celery seed
- ½ tsp. salt
- ½ cup coarsely chopped dry-roasted peanuts or cashews

1. In a large bowl, combine the first
5 ingredients. In a small bowl, whisk
vinegar, oil, sugar, celery seed and salt.
2. Just before serving, pour dressing
over salad; toss to coat. Sprinkle with
the peanuts.
1 cup: 100 cal., 7g fat (1g sat. fat),
0 chol., 128mg sod., 9g carb. (5g sugars,
2g fiber), 2g pro. **Diabetic exchanges:**
1½ fat, 1 vegetable.

Makeover Spinach &
Artichoke Casserole

MAKEOVER SPINACH & ARTICHOKE CASSEROLE

*Spinach never tasted better than it does in
this creamy, colorful dish that I've lightened
up a bit with reduced-fat ingredients.*
—Judy Armstrong, Prairieville, LA

PREP: 35 min. • **BAKE:** 30 min.
MAKES: 12 servings

- 5 celery ribs, finely chopped
- 2 medium sweet red peppers, chopped
- 2 medium onions, finely chopped
- 2 Tbsp. butter
- 1 Tbsp. canola oil
- 6 garlic cloves, minced
- 3 Tbsp. all-purpose flour
- 1 cup half-and-half cream
- 1 cup fat-free milk
- 3 cups shredded reduced-fat Mexican cheese blend
- 4 pkg. (10 oz. each) frozen chopped spinach, thawed and squeezed dry
- 2 cans (14 oz. each) water-packed artichoke hearts, rinsed, drained and quartered
- 1 tsp. salt
- 1 tsp. cayenne pepper
- 1 tsp. pepper
- ½ tsp. crushed red pepper flakes
- 1 cup grated Parmesan cheese

1. Preheat oven to 350°. In a Dutch oven,
saute the celery, red peppers and onions
in butter and oil until tender. Add garlic;
cook 1 minute longer. Stir in flour until
blended; gradually add cream and milk.
Bring to a boil; cook and stir 2 minutes
or until thickened. Stir in shredded
cheese until melted.
2. Add the spinach, artichokes, salt,
cayenne, pepper and pepper flakes.
Transfer to a 13x9-in. baking dish
coated with cooking spray. Sprinkle
with the Parmesan cheese.
3. Bake, uncovered, 30-35 minutes or
until bubbly.
1 cup: 245 cal., 13g fat (7g sat. fat), 41mg
chol., 781mg sod., 17g carb. (4g sugars,
4g fiber), 17g pro.

Winter Squash,
Sausage & Feta Bake

MAKE-AHEAD HEARTY SIX-LAYER SALAD

I reach for this all-time favorite recipe whenever I need a dish to pass. It is easy, can be assembled ahead and looks marvelous.
—Noreen Meyer, Madison, WI

PREP: 20 min. + chilling
MAKES: 12 servings

- 1½ cups uncooked small pasta shells
- 1 Tbsp. canola oil
- 3 cups shredded lettuce
- 3 hard-boiled large eggs, sliced
- ¼ tsp. salt
- ⅛ tsp. pepper
- 2 cups shredded cooked chicken breast
- 1 pkg. (10 oz.) frozen peas, thawed

DRESSING
- 1 cup mayonnaise
- ¼ cup sour cream
- 2 green onions, chopped
- 2 tsp. Dijon mustard

TOPPINGS
- 1 cup shredded Colby or Monterey Jack cheese
- 2 Tbsp. minced fresh parsley

1. Cook pasta according to package directions; drain and rinse with cold water. Drizzle with oil and toss to coat.
2. Place the lettuce in a 2½-qt. glass serving bowl; top with pasta and eggs. Sprinkle with salt and pepper. Layer with chicken and peas. In a small bowl, mix dressing ingredients until blended; spread over top. Refrigerate, covered, for several hours or overnight.
3. Just before serving, sprinkle with cheese and parsley.
¾ cup: 310 cal., 22g fat (5g sat. fat), 84mg chol., 287mg sod., 13g carb. (2g sugars, 2g fiber), 14g pro.

WHY YOU'LL LOVE IT...

"This is a terrific salad, easy to make, light, and tasty for summer, but I will be making it year-round."
—JUDYDEGRAAF, TASTEOFHOME.COM

WINTER SQUASH, SAUSAGE & FETA BAKE

I can't resist butternut squash because of its bright color and fall flavor. I make this casserole for potlucks—it's a guaranteed hit.
—Craig Simpson, Savannah, GA

PREP: 30 min. • **BAKE:** 45 min.
MAKES: 20 servings

- 1 lb. bulk Italian sausage
- 2 large onions, chopped
- ½ tsp. crushed red pepper flakes, divided
- ¼ cup olive oil
- 2 tsp. minced fresh rosemary
- 1½ tsp. salt
- 1 tsp. Worcestershire sauce
- 1 tsp. pepper
- 1 medium butternut squash (about 4 lbs.), peeled and cut into 1-in. cubes
- 1 medium acorn squash, peeled and cut into 1-in. cubes
- 2 cups crumbled feta cheese
- 2 small sweet red peppers, chopped

1. Preheat oven to 375°. In a skillet, cook the sausage, onions and ¼ tsp. pepper flakes over medium heat 8-10 minutes or until sausage is no longer pink and onions are tender, breaking up sausage into crumbles; drain.
2. In a large bowl, combine oil, rosemary, salt, Worcestershire sauce, pepper and remaining pepper flakes. Add butternut and acorn squash, cheese, red peppers and sausage mixture; toss to coat.
3. Transfer to an ungreased shallow roasting pan. Cover; bake 35 minutes. Uncover; bake until squash is tender, 10-15 minutes longer.
¾ cup: 160 cal., 10g fat (4g sat. fat), 22mg chol., 481mg sod., 10g carb. (3g sugars, 3g fiber), 7g pro.

Make-Ahead
Hearty Six-Layer Salad

BAKED CORN PUDDING

Here's a comforting side dish that turns even ordinary meals into something to celebrate. A favorite with our entire family, it spoons up as sweet and creamy as custard. Our guests love it just as much as we do.
—Peggy West, Georgetown, DE

PREP: 10 min. • **BAKE:** 45 min.
MAKES: 10 servings

- ½ cup sugar
- 3 Tbsp. all-purpose flour
- 3 large eggs
- 1 cup whole milk
- ¼ cup butter, melted
- ½ tsp. salt
- ½ tsp. pepper
- 1 can (15¼ oz.) whole kernel corn, drained
- 1 can (14¾ oz.) cream-style corn

1. In a large bowl, combine sugar and flour. Whisk in the eggs, milk, butter, salt and pepper. Stir in the corn and cream-style corn.

2. Pour into a greased 1½-qt. baking dish. Bake, uncovered, at 350° for 45-50 minutes or until a knife inserted in the center comes out clean.

½ cup: 186 cal., 7g fat (4g sat. fat), 79mg chol., 432mg sod., 26g carb. (14g sugars, 1g fiber), 4g pro.

Test Kitchen Tip
Feel free to cut the sugar in half without sacrificing much of the flavor in this recipe.

Baked Corn
Pudding

Sweet & Spicy
Baked Beans

SWEET & SPICY BAKED BEANS

This recipe is a hit with friends and family.
It's sweet, simple and delicious, and
someone always asks for the recipe.
—*Elliot Wesen, Arlington, TX*

PREP: 15 min. • **BAKE:** 50 min.
MAKES: 14 servings

2   **cans (28 oz. each) baked beans**
1   **can (20 oz.) unsweetened**
    crushed pineapple, drained
1   **cup spicy barbecue sauce**
½   **cup molasses**
2   **Tbsp. prepared mustard**
½   **tsp. pepper**
¼   **tsp. salt**
1   **can (6 oz.) french-fried onions,**
    crushed, divided
5   **bacon strips, cooked and crumbled,**
    divided

1. In a large bowl, combine the first
7 ingredients. Stir in half the onions
and bacon. Transfer to a greased
13x9-in. baking dish.
2. Cover and bake at 350° for
45 minutes. Sprinkle with the
remaining onions and bacon. Bake,
uncovered, 5-10 minutes longer
or until bubbly.

¾ cup: 285 cal., 9g fat (3g sat. fat), 10mg
chol., 860mg sod., 46g carb. (14g sugars,
7g fiber), 7g pro.

Lattice
Corn Pie

SAVORY ZUCCHINI BREAD PUDDING

I have been serving this dish for years and always receive compliments on it. If you don't have day-old bread in your pantry, simply slice fresh bread and bake it at 300° for 10 minutes before cubing it.
—Mary Ann Dell, Phoenixville, PA

PREP: 25 min. • **BAKE:** 40 min.
MAKES: 12 servings

- 1 small onion, chopped
- 1 celery rib, chopped
- 3 Tbsp. butter
- 1 cup all-purpose flour
- 2 Tbsp. sugar
- 1 tsp. baking powder
- 1 tsp. salt
- 1 tsp. ground cinnamon
- 1 tsp. poultry seasoning
- ½ cup canned pumpkin
- 2 large eggs
- ⅓ cup 2% milk
- ¼ cup butter, melted
- 4 cups cubed day-old bread
- 3 medium zucchini, chopped
- ½ cup shredded cheddar cheese

1. In a small skillet, saute onion and celery in butter until tender; set aside.
2. In a large bowl, combine the flour, sugar, baking powder, salt, cinnamon and poultry seasoning. In a small bowl, whisk the pumpkin, eggs, milk and butter; stir into dry ingredients just until moistened. Fold in bread cubes, zucchini, cheese and onion mixture.
3. Transfer to a greased 13x9-in. baking dish. Cover and bake at 325° for 30 minutes. Uncover; bake until lightly browned, 10-15 minutes longer.
¾ cup: 182 cal., 10g fat (6g sat. fat), 58mg chol., 408mg sod., 20g carb. (5g sugars, 2g fiber), 5g pro.

LATTICE CORN PIE

This unique side dish is full of old-fashioned goodness, with tender diced potatoes and a fresh, sweet corn flavor. Once you've tasted this delicious pie, you'll never want to serve corn any other way!
—Kathy Spang, Manheim, PA

PREP: 25 min. • **BAKE:** 35 min.
MAKES: 8 servings

- 1 cup diced peeled potatoes
- ⅓ cup 2% milk
- 2 large eggs, room temperature
- 2 cups fresh or frozen corn, thawed
- 1 tsp. sugar
- ½ tsp. salt
- 2 sheets refrigerated pie crust

1. Preheat oven to 375°. Place the potatoes in a small saucepan and cover with water. Bring to a boil. Reduce heat; cover and cook until tender, 6-8 minutes. Drain; set aside.
2. In a blender, combine the milk, eggs, corn, sugar and salt; cover and process until blended.
3. Unroll 1 sheet crust into a 9-in. pie plate. Trim crust to ½ in. beyond rim of plate; flute edge. Spoon potatoes into crust; top with corn mixture (crust will be full). Roll out remaining crust; make a lattice top with crust. Seal and flute edges.
4. Bake until crust is golden brown and filling is bubbly, 35-40 minutes.
1 piece: 308 cal., 16g fat (7g sat. fat), 57mg chol., 373mg sod., 37g carb. (5g sugars, 1g fiber), 5g pro.

Savory Zucchini
Bread Pudding

CHESTNUT STUFFING

It wouldn't be Thanksgiving without my family's favorite stuffing. If you can't find jarred chestnuts at your grocery store, check gourmet cooking shops or order online.
—Lee Bremson, Kansas City, MO

PREP: 40 min. • **BAKE:** 35 min.
MAKES: 21 servings

- 1 large onion, chopped
- ½ cup chopped fennel bulb
- 1½ cups butter, cubed, divided
- 2 garlic cloves, minced
- 2 cups peeled cooked chestnuts, coarsely chopped
- 1 large pear, chopped
- 1 cup chicken broth
- ½ cup mixed dried fruit, coarsely chopped
- 2 tsp. poultry seasoning
- 2 tsp. minced fresh rosemary
- 2 tsp. minced fresh thyme
- ½ tsp. salt
- ½ tsp. pepper
- 2 loaves day-old white bread (1 lb. each), cubed
- 3 large eggs
- ¼ cup 2% milk

1. Preheat oven to 350°. In a large skillet, saute onion and fennel in ½ cup butter until tender. Stir in garlic; cook 2 minutes longer. Stir in chestnuts, pear, broth, dried fruit, seasonings and remaining butter; cook until butter is melted. Bring to a boil. Reduce heat; simmer, uncovered, 3-4 minutes or until dried fruit is softened.
2. Place in a large bowl. Stir in bread cubes. Whisk eggs and milk; drizzle over stuffing and toss to coat.
3. Transfer to a greased 13x9-in. and a greased 8-in. square baking dish. Bake, covered, 25 minutes. Uncover; bake 10-15 minutes longer or until lightly browned.
¾ cup: 290 cal., 16g fat (9g sat. fat), 65mg chol., 503mg sod., 33g carb. (5g sugars, 3g fiber), 5g pro.

CREAMY SKILLET NOODLES WITH PEAS

I've made this creamy noodle side for years. Since kids and adults go for it, I keep the ingredients on hand at all times.
—Anita Groff, Perkiomenville, PA

TAKES: 25 min. • **MAKES:** 6 servings

- ¼ cup butter, cubed
- 2 Tbsp. canola oil
- 5 cups uncooked fine egg noodles
- 2½ cups frozen peas (about 10 oz.)
- 2½ cups chicken broth
- 1 cup half-and-half cream
- ½ tsp. salt
- ¼ tsp. pepper

In a large skillet, heat butter and oil over medium heat. Add noodles; cook and stir 2-3 minutes or until lightly browned. Stir in peas, broth, cream, salt and pepper. Bring to a boil. Reduce heat; simmer, covered, 10-12 minutes or until noodles are tender, stirring occasionally.
¾ cup: 329 cal., 31g fat (8g sat. fat), 76mg chol., 757mg sod., 31g carb. (6g sugars, 4g fiber), 9g pro.

Test Kitchen Tip
It's a snap to double this recipe for a crowd. The noodles are fabulous served hot or cold.

Creamy Skillet Noodles with Peas

Tomato Pie

SWEET ONION CORN BAKE

This tasty corn casserole gets plenty of flavor from sweet onions, cream-style corn and cheddar cheese, plus a little zip from hot pepper sauce. It's a popular addition to our church potlucks.
—Jeannette Travis, Fort Worth, TX

PREP: 15 min. • **BAKE:** 45 min. + standing
MAKES: 15 servings

- 2 large sweet onions, thinly sliced
- ½ cup butter, cubed
- 1 cup sour cream
- ½ cup whole milk
- ½ tsp. dill weed
- ¼ tsp. salt
- 2 cups shredded cheddar cheese, divided
- 1 large egg, lightly beaten
- 1 can (14¾ oz.) cream-style corn
- 1 pkg. (8½ oz.) cornbread/muffin mix
- 4 drops hot pepper sauce

1. In a large skillet, saute onions in butter until tender. In a small bowl, combine the sour cream, milk, dill and salt until blended; stir in 1 cup cheese. Stir into the onion mixture; remove from heat and set aside.

2. In a large bowl, combine egg, corn, cornbread mix and hot pepper sauce. Pour into a greased 13x9-in. baking dish. Spoon onion mixture over top. Sprinkle with remaining cheese.

3. Bake, uncovered, at 350° until a thermometer reaches 160°, 45-50 minutes. Let stand for at least 10 minutes before cutting.

1 piece: 241 cal., 15g fat (10g sat. fat), 62mg chol., 421mg sod., 20g carb. (7g sugars, 1g fiber), 6g pro.

TOMATO PIE

Make sure your tomatoes are firm and not too ripe. Ripe tomatoes will add too much moisture to the pie.
—Lois Morgan, Edisto Beach, SC

PREP: 50 min. + chilling • **BAKE:** 30 min.
MAKES: 8 servings

- 1 cup plus 2 Tbsp. all-purpose flour
- ¼ tsp. salt
- ½ cup cold butter, cubed
- 2 to 3 Tbsp. ice water

FILLING

- ¾ cup mayonnaise
- ½ cup shredded cheddar cheese
- ⅓ cup thinly sliced green onions
- 1 Tbsp. minced fresh oregano
- ½ tsp. ground coriander
- ¼ tsp. salt
- ¼ tsp. pepper
- 6 medium tomatoes (1¾ lbs.), cut into ¼-in. slices
- 4 bacon strips, cooked and crumbled

1. In a large bowl, mix flour and salt; cut in butter until crumbly. Gradually add ice water, tossing with a fork until dough holds together when pressed. Shape into a disk; cover and refrigerate 30 minutes or overnight.

2. Preheat oven to 350°. On a lightly floured surface, roll dough to a ⅛-in.-thick circle; transfer to a 9-in. pie plate. Trim crust to ½ in. beyond rim of plate; flute edge. Line unpricked crust with a double thickness of foil. Fill with pie weights, dried beans or uncooked rice.

3. Bake until bottom is lightly browned, 20-25 minutes. Remove the foil and weights; bake 5-10 minutes longer or until light brown. Cool on a wire rack.

4. In a small bowl, combine mayonnaise, cheese, green onions and seasonings. Arrange a third of the tomatoes in crust; spread with a third of the mayonnaise mixture. Repeat layers twice. Bake 25 minutes. Top with the bacon; bake until the filling is bubbly, 5-10 minutes longer. Let stand at least 10 minutes before cutting.

1 piece: 396 cal., 32g fat (12g sat. fat), 49mg chol., 466mg sod., 22g carb. (5g sugars, 3g fiber), 7g pro.

Corn Stuffing Balls

FAST MARINATED VEGETABLES

I was known as only an average cook before I made this lip-smacking salad.
—E. Anderson, Stockton, CA

PREP: 40 min. + marinating
MAKES: 15 servings

- 4 cups fresh broccoli florets
- 4 cups fresh cauliflowerets
- 5 medium carrots, cut into 2-in. thin strips
- 1 cup olive oil
- ⅔ cup white wine vinegar
- ⅓ cup sherry or chicken broth
- 4 tsp. Dijon mustard
- 3 garlic cloves, minced
- 2 tsp. salt
- ½ tsp. pepper
- 2 cups grape tomatoes
- 1 can (15 oz.) whole baby corn, drained and cut widthwise into quarters
- 1 can (6 oz.) pitted ripe olives, drained and halved

1. Place the broccoli, cauliflower and carrots in a large steamer basket; place in a large saucepan over 1 in. water. Bring to a boil; cover and steam for 4-6 minutes or until crisp-tender. Place basket in ice water for 1-2 minutes or until vegetables are cooled; drain well.
2. In a large bowl, whisk the oil, vinegar, sherry or broth, mustard, garlic, salt and pepper. Add the vegetables and the tomatoes, corn and olives. Stir to coat; cover and refrigerate for at least 8 hours or overnight.
3. Remove from refrigerator 30 minutes before serving. Stir to coat. Serve with a slotted spoon.
¾ cup: 180 cal., 16g fat (2g sat. fat), 0 chol., 526mg sod., 8g carb. (3g sugars, 3g fiber), 2g pro.

CORN STUFFING BALLS

My mom had many winning recipes, and this was one of our family's favorites. I can still picture these corn stuffing balls encircling the large meat platter piled high with one of her scrumptious entrees.
—Audrey Groe, Lake Mills, IA

PREP: 20 min. • **BAKE:** 30 min.
MAKES: 12 servings

- 6 cups herb-seasoned stuffing croutons
- 1 cup chopped celery
- ½ cup chopped onion
- ¾ cup butter, divided
- 1 can (14¾ oz.) cream-style corn
- 1 cup water
- 1½ tsp. poultry seasoning
- ¾ tsp. salt
- ¼ tsp. pepper
- 3 large eggs yolks, beaten

Place croutons in a large bowl and set aside. In a skillet, saute celery and onion in ½ cup butter. Add the corn, water, poultry seasoning, salt and pepper; bring to a boil. Remove from the heat; cool for 5 minutes. Pour over croutons. Add egg yolks and mix gently. Shape ½ cupfuls into balls; flatten slightly. Place in a greased 15x10x1-in. baking pan. Melt remaining butter; drizzle over stuffing balls. Bake, uncovered, at 375° for 30 minutes or until lightly browned.
1 serving: 365 cal., 16g fat (7g sat. fat), 84mg chol., 1233mg sod., 47g carb. (4g sugars, 3g fiber), 10g pro.

**Deluxe German
Potato Salad**

DELUXE GERMAN POTATO SALAD

I make this for all occasions because it goes well with any kind of meat. When I take the warm salad to bring-a-dish events, there are rarely leftovers!
—Betty Perkins, Hot Springs, AR

TAKES: 30 min. • **MAKES:** 16 servings

- ½ lb. sliced bacon, diced
- 1 cup thinly sliced celery
- 1 cup chopped onion
- 1 cup sugar
- 2 Tbsp. all-purpose flour
- 1 tsp. salt
- ¾ tsp. ground mustard
- 1 cup cider vinegar
- ½ cup water
- 5 lbs. unpeeled small red potatoes, cooked and sliced
- 2 medium carrots, shredded
- 2 Tbsp. minced fresh parsley
  Additional salt, optional

1. In a large skillet, cook the bacon over medium heat until crisp. Remove bacon to paper towels. Drain skillet, reserving ¼ cup drippings. Saute celery and onion in drippings until tender.
2. In a large bowl, combine the sugar, flour, salt, mustard, vinegar and water until smooth. Add to the skillet. Bring to a boil. Cook and stir for 1-2 minutes until mixture is thickened.
3. In a large serving bowl, combine potatoes, carrots and parsley. Drizzle with sauce and stir to coat. Season with additional salt if desired. Crumble bacon; sprinkle on salad. Serve warm. Refrigerate leftovers.
1 cup: 192 cal., 3g fat (1g sat. fat), 4mg chol., 241mg sod., 39g carb. (16g sugars, 3g fiber), 5g pro.

WHY YOU'LL LOVE IT...

"My boys go crazy over this. The best German potato salad ever. I have been making it for years."
—KSHEA, TASTEOFHOME.COM

Smoky Macaroni
& Cheese

SMOKY MACARONI & CHEESE

I found this recipe and kept working with the ingredients until I discovered the perfect combo. You can bake it in the oven, too.
—Stacey Dull, Gettysburg, OH

PREP: 40 min. • **GRILL:** 20 min. + standing
MAKES: 2 casseroles (8 servings each)

- 6 cups small pasta shells
- 12 oz. Velveeta, cut into small cubes
- 2 cups shredded smoked cheddar cheese, divided
- 1 cup shredded cheddar cheese
- 1 cup 2% milk
- 4 large eggs, lightly beaten
- ¾ cup heavy whipping cream
- ⅔ cup half-and-half cream
- ½ cup shredded provolone cheese
- ½ cup shredded Colby-Monterey Jack cheese
- ½ cup shredded pepper jack cheese
- 1 tsp. salt
- ½ tsp. pepper
- ½ tsp. smoked paprika
- ½ tsp. liquid smoke, optional
  Dash cayenne pepper, optional
- 8 bacon strips, cooked and crumbled, optional

1. Preheat grill or smoker to 350°. Cook pasta according to package directions for al dente. Drain and transfer to a large bowl. Stir in Velveeta, 1 cup smoked cheddar, cheddar cheese, milk, eggs, heavy cream, half-and-half, provolone, Colby-Monterey Jack, pepper jack, salt, pepper, paprika and, if desired, liquid smoke and cayenne pepper.
2. Transfer to 2 greased 13x9-in. baking pans; sprinkle with remaining 1 cup smoked cheddar cheese. Place on grill or smoker rack. Grill or smoke, covered, until a thermometer reads at least 160°, 20-25 minutes, rotating pans partway through cooking. Do not overcook. Let stand 10 minutes before serving; if desired, sprinkle with bacon.
1 cup: 403 cal., 23g fat (13g sat. fat), 117mg chol., 670mg sod., 30g carb. (4g sugars, 1g fiber), 18g pro.

Summer Squash
& Zucchini Salad

SUMMER SQUASH & ZUCCHINI SALAD

I came up with this colorful, tasty slaw years ago for a recipe contest and was delighted when I won honorable mention! The recipe easily doubles and is the perfect dish to take to potlucks or family gatherings.
—Paula Wharton, El Paso, TX

PREP: 25 min. + chilling
MAKES: 12 servings

- 4 medium zucchini
- 2 yellow summer squash
- 1 medium sweet red pepper
- 1 medium red onion
- 1 cup fresh sugar snap peas, trimmed and halved
- ⅓ cup olive oil
- ¼ cup balsamic vinegar
- 2 Tbsp. reduced-fat mayonnaise
- 4 tsp. fresh sage or
  1 tsp. dried sage leaves
- 2 tsp. honey
- 1 tsp. garlic powder
- 1 tsp. celery seed
- 1 tsp. dill weed
- ½ tsp. salt
- ½ tsp. pepper

Thinly slice zucchini, squash, red pepper and onion; place in a large bowl. Add snap peas. In a small bowl, whisk remaining ingredients until blended. Pour over vegetables; toss to coat. Refrigerate, covered, at least 3 hours.
¾ cup: 101 cal., 7g fat (1g sat. fat), 1mg chol., 124mg sod., 8g carb. (6g sugars, 2g fiber), 2g pro. **Diabetic exchanges:** 1½ fat, 1 vegetable.

SOUTHERN CORNBREAD SALAD

To feed a crowd, I make this eye-popping cornbread salad. It's beautiful in a trifle bowl and instant sunshine by the spoonful.
—Debbie Johnson, Centertown, MO

PREP: 30 min. + chilling
MAKES: 16 servings

- 1 pkg. (8½ oz.) cornbread/muffin mix
- 1 cup sour cream
- 1 cup mayonnaise
- 1 envelope ranch salad dressing mix
- 3 large tomatoes, seeded and chopped
- ½ cup chopped sweet red pepper
- ½ cup chopped green pepper
- 1 cup thinly sliced green onions, divided
- 2 cans (15 oz. each) pinto beans, rinsed and drained
- 2 cups shredded cheddar cheese
- 10 bacon strips, cooked and crumbled
- 3½ cups frozen corn, thawed

1. Prepare and bake cornbread mix according to package directions, using an 8-in. square baking dish. Crumble when cool.
2. Mix sour cream, mayonnaise and salad dressing mix until blended. In a separate bowl, combine tomatoes, peppers and ½ cup green onions.
3. In a 3-qt. glass bowl, layer half of each: cornbread, beans, tomato mixture, cheese, bacon, corn and dressing. Repeat layers. Top with remaining green onions. Refrigerate 3 hours.

¾ cup: 367 cal., 23g fat (7g sat. fat), 46mg chol., 607mg sod., 29g carb. (7g sugars, 4g fiber), 11g pro.

CRUNCHY VEGETABLE BAKE

While traveling in Kentucky a few years ago, my husband and I enjoyed an excellent mixed vegetable dish at a restaurant—and the owners were kind enough to share the recipe. It makes four casseroles, so it's terrific for a church supper or other large group.
—Jean Voan, Shepherd, TX

PREP: 20 min. • **BAKE:** 40 min.
MAKES: 80 servings

- 4 celery ribs, chopped
- 2 large onions, chopped
- ¼ cup canola oil
- 4 cans (10¾ oz. each) condensed cream of chicken soup, undiluted
- 4½ cups sour cream
- 4 to 6 tsp. salt
- ½ to 1 tsp. pepper
- 8 pkg. (16 oz. each) frozen cut green beans, thawed
- 8 pkg. (16 oz. each) frozen corn, thawed
- 8 cans (8 oz. each) sliced water chestnuts, drained
- 1 pkg. (8 oz.) butter-flavored crackers, crushed
- 1 cup sliced almonds
- ½ cup butter, melted

1. In a large skillet, saute celery and onions in oil until tender. Remove from the heat. Stir in the soup, sour cream, salt and pepper. Stir in the beans, corn and water chestnuts. Transfer to 4 greased 13x9-in. baking dishes.
2. In a large bowl, combine the cracker crumbs, almonds and butter. Sprinkle over mixture in each baking dish. Bake, uncovered, at 350° for 40-45 minutes or until golden brown.

¾ cup: 78 cal., 6g fat (3g sat. fat), 12mg chol., 201mg sod., 5g carb. (1g sugars, 1g fiber), 1g pro.

Southern Cornbread Salad

Smoky
Baked
Beans

SMOKY BAKED BEANS

They'll be standing in line for this saucy bean recipe, full of campfire flavor. A variation on colorful calico beans, it'll make a delightful side dish with many of your favorite entrees.
—Lynne German, Buford, GA

PREP: 25 min. • **COOK:** 7 hours
MAKES: 16 servings

1 lb. bulk spicy pork sausage
1 medium onion, chopped
2 15-oz. cans pork and beans
1 can (16 oz.) kidney beans, rinsed and drained
1 can (16 oz.) butter beans, rinsed and drained
1 can (15½ oz.) navy beans, rinsed and drained
1 can (15 oz.) black beans, rinsed and drained
1 can (10 oz.) diced tomatoes and green chiles, drained
½ cup hickory smoke-flavored barbecue sauce
½ cup ketchup
½ cup packed brown sugar
1 tsp. ground mustard
1 tsp. steak seasoning
1 tsp. liquid smoke, optional

1. In a large skillet, cook sausage and onion over medium heat until meat is no longer pink, breaking it into crumbles; drain.
2. In a 5-qt. slow cooker, combine the beans, tomatoes and sausage mixture. In a small bowl, combine the barbecue sauce, ketchup, brown sugar, mustard, steak seasoning and liquid smoke if desired. Stir into bean mixture.
3. Cover and cook on low for 7-8 hours or until heated through.
¾ cup: 244 cal., 6g fat (2g sat. fat), 10mg chol., 896mg sod., 39g carb. (15g sugars, 8g fiber), 11g pro.

Recipe Index

Cutting Techniques

MINCING AND CHOPPING

Holding the handle of a chef's knife with one hand, rest the fingers of your other hand on the top of the blade near the tip. Using the handle to guide and apply pressure, move knife in an arc across the food with a rocking motion until pieces of food are the desired size. Mincing results in pieces that are no larger than ⅛ in. and chopping produces ¼- to ½-in. pieces.

DICING AND CUBING

Using a utility knife, trim each side of the fruit, vegetable or other food, squaring it off. Cut lengthwise into evenly spaced strips. The narrower the strips, the smaller the pieces will be. Stack the strips and cut lengthwise into uniformly sized strips. Arrange the square-shaped strips into a pile and cut widthwise into uniform pieces.

MAKING BIAS OR DIAGONAL CUTS

Holding a chef's knife at an angle to the length of the food, slice as thick or thin as desired. This technique is often used in stir-fry recipes.

MAKING JULIENNE STRIPS

Using a utility knife, cut a thin strip from one side of vegetable. Turn so flat side is down. Cut into 2-in. lengths, then cut each piece lengthwise into thin strips. Stack the strips and cut lengthwise into thinner strips.

CUTTING WEDGES

Using a chef's knife or serrated knife cut the produce in half from stem end to blossom end. Lay halves cut side down on a cutting board. Set knife at the center of one the halves and cut in half vertically, then cut each quarter in half vertically. Repeat with the other half.

ZESTING

Pull a citrus zester across limes, lemons or oranges being careful not to remove the bitter white pith. The small holes in the zester will yield thin, narrow strips of zest. Use full strips to garnish or, if recipe instructs, chop into fine pieces and use as directed.

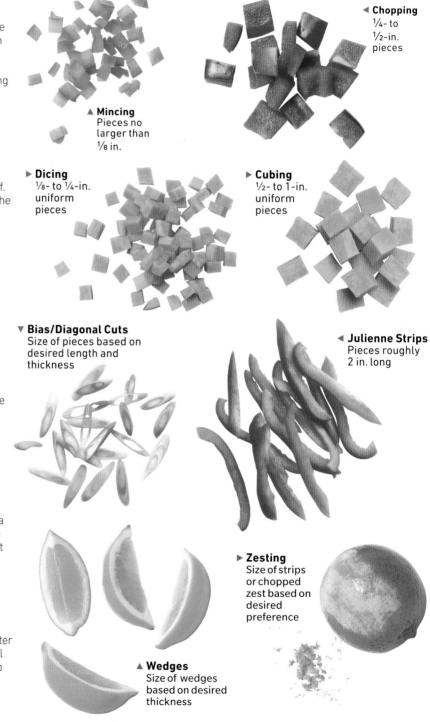

◀ **Chopping**
¼- to ½-in. pieces

▲ **Mincing**
Pieces no larger than ⅛ in.

▶ **Dicing**
⅛- to ¼-in. uniform pieces

▶ **Cubing**
½- to 1-in. uniform pieces

▼ **Bias/Diagonal Cuts**
Size of pieces based on desired length and thickness

◀ **Julienne Strips**
Pieces roughly 2 in. long

▶ **Zesting**
Size of strips or chopped zest based on desired preference

▲ **Wedges**
Size of wedges based on desired thickness